Houghton Mifflin Science
DiscoveryWorks

HOUGHTON MIFFLIN

Boston • Atlanta • Dallas • Denver • Geneva, Illinois • Palo Alto • Princeton

Authors

William Badders
Elementary Science Teacher
Cleveland Public Schools
Cleveland, OH

Lowell J. Bethel
Professor of Science Education
The University of Texas at Austin
Austin, TX

Victoria Fu
Professor of Child Development
and Early Childhood Education
Virginia Polytechnic Institute and
State University
Blacksburg, VA

Donald Peck
Director (retired)
The Center for Elementary Science
Fairleigh Dickinson University
Madison, NJ

Carolyn Sumners
Director of Astronomy and Physical Sciences
Houston Museum of Natural Science
Houston, TX

Catherine Valentino
Author-in-Residence, Houghton Mifflin
West Kingston, RI

Acknowledgements appear on page H38, which constitutes an extension of this copyright page.

Copyright © 2000 by Houghton Mifflin Company. All rights reserved.

No part of this work may be reproduced or transmitted in any form or by any means, electronic or mechanical, including photocopying or recording, or by any information storage or retrieval system without the prior written permission of Houghton Mifflin Company unless such copying is expressly permitted by federal copyright law. Address inquiries to School Permissions, 222 Berkeley Street, Boston, MA 02116.

Printed in the U. S. A.

ISBN 0-618-00632-X

3 4 5 6 7 8 9 10 RRD 08 07 06 05 04 03 02 01 00

CONTENTS

THINK LIKE A SCIENTIST

How to Think Like a Scientist S2
Practice Thinking Like a Scientist S4
Using Science Process Skills S10
Reading to Learn S12
Safety S14

UNIT A — Life Cycles

THINK LIKE A SCIENTIST
HITCHING A RIDE A2

CHAPTER 1 — Life Cycles of Animals A4

Investigation 1 **What Is a Life Cycle?** A6
Activity: The Changes Chart A6
Resource: City Life A8
Resource: What's Wrong With This Picture? . . A10

Investigation 2 **What Is the First Stage in an Animal's Life Cycle?** A12
Activity: Be "Eggs-act"! A12
Resource: "Eggs-traordinary" Eggs! A14
Resource: Hatching Chicks A17
Resource: The Baby Book A18

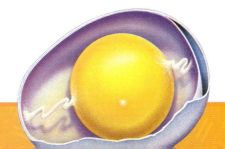

Investigation 3 **How Do Some Animals Grow and Change?** **A20**
Activity: Look at What You've Become A20
Resource: Going Around in Cycles A22

Investigation 4 **How Do Adult Animals Care for Their Young?** **A26**
Activity: The Animal-Sitter's Guide A26
Resource: Out of Sight, Out of Mind A28
Resource: A Whale of a Baby A30

Reflect and Evaluate **A33**

Chapter 2 Life Cycles of Plants — A34

Investigation 1 **What Is the First Stage in the Life Cycle of a Flowering Plant?** **A36**
Activity: The Inside Story A36
Resource: It's "A-maize-ing" A38
Resource: Plant Tricks A39

Investigation 2 How Do Flowering Plants Make Seeds?.. A42
Activity: It's a Flower! It's a Factory!........ A42
Resource: The Fantastic Flower........... A44

Investigation 3 How Do Plants With Cones Make and Protect Seeds?.......... A48
Activity: Cone Sweet Home............. A48
Resource: Evergreens................ A50

Investigation 4 How Do Plants Change During Their Life Cycles?.......... A54
Activity: Sizing Up Tree Growth.......... A54
Activity: A Change of Plants........... A56
Resource: Where Are You Growing?....... A58

Reflect and Evaluate A61

Using Reading Skills A62

Using Math Skills A63

Unit Wrap-up! A64

Sun, Moon, and Earth

THINK LIKE A SCIENTIST
EARTHRISE B2

CHAPTER 1
Comparing Sun, Moon, and Earth — B4

Investigation 1 **What Is the Moon Like?** **B6**
- **Activity:** Big Earth, Small Moon B6
- **Activity:** Making Moon Craters B8
- **Resource:** A Place Without Air B10
- **Resource:** Learning About Space B14

Investigation 2 **What Is Being on the Moon Like?** **B18**
- **Activity:** Lunar Olympics B18
- **Activity:** A Moon Outing B20
- **Resource:** Spacesuits B21
- **Resource:** Getting Around on the Moon B22

Investigation 3 **What Is the Sun Like?** **B24**
- **Activity:** Big Star, Small Earth B24
- **Activity:** Making Sunspots B26
- **Resource:** Sun Power B27
- **Resource:** Solar Storms B29

Reflect and Evaluate **B31**

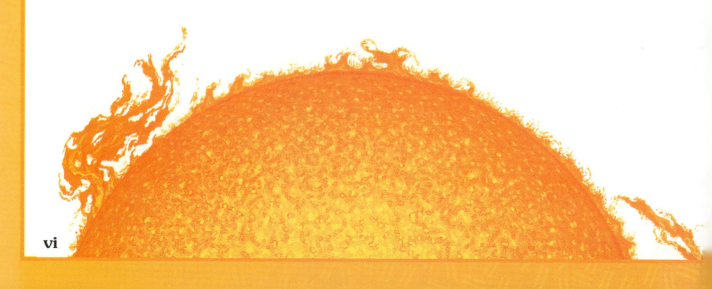

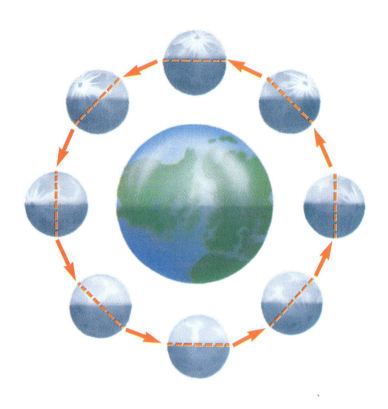

 Motions of Earth and the Moon   **B32**

Investigation 1   **How Does Earth Move Each Day?** **B34**
- **Activity:** A Shadow Stick Sundial B34
- **Activity:** Making a Star Clock. B36
- **Resource:** The Rotating Earth B38

Investigation 2   **How Does Earth Move Throughout the Year?**. **B42**
- **Activity:** Sun Paths. B42
- **Activity:** Constellations Through the Year B44
- **Resource:** Earth Moves Around the Sun B46
- **Resource:** Earth and Sun—Ideas Through Time B48

Investigation 3   **How Does the Moon Move?**. **B50**
- **Activity:** Moon Phases B50
- **Resource:** Your Changing View of the Moon. . B52
- **Resource:** The Moon: Fact and Fiction B55

Reflect and Evaluate **B57**

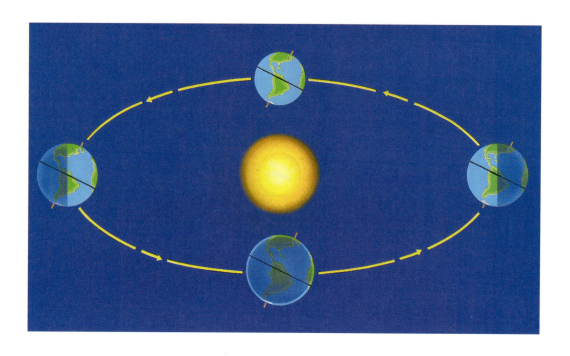

 Chapter 3 **Effects of Earth and Moon Motions** **B58**

Investigation 1 **What Causes Seasons?** **B60**
    Activity: Lines of Sunlight B60
    Activity: Earth Tilts! B62
    Resource: The Reason for Seasons B64
    Resource: The First Calendar Makers B67
    Resource: Near the Equator, Near the Pole ... B70

Investigation 2 **What Are Eclipses?** **B72**
    Activity: Homemade Eclipses B72
    Resource: How an Eclipse Occurs B74

Reflect and Evaluate **B77**

Using Reading Skills **B78**

Using Math Skills **B79**

Unit Wrap-up! **B80**

Unit C: Matter, Energy, and Forces

THINK LIKE A SCIENTIST
SLIDERS **C2**

Chapter 1: All About Matter — **C4**

Investigation 1 — **What Is Matter?** **C6**
- **Activity:** Grouping Things C6
- **Activity:** Measuring Things C8
- **Resource:** What's the Matter? C10
- **Resource:** Properties of Matter C12

Investigation 2 — **How Can Matter Be Changed?** **C16**
- **Activity:** States of Matter C16
- **Activity:** Change Without Change C18
- **Resource:** The Nature of Matter C19
- **Resource:** Changes in Matter C22

Reflect and Evaluate **C25**

Chapter 2 — Energy and Change ... C26

Investigation 1 — **What Is Energy?** ... **C28**
- **Activity:** Mystery Can ... C28
- **Resource:** Do You Have the Energy? ... C30
- **Resource:** Energy You Can See ... C34
- **Resource:** Using Solar Energy ... C36
- **Resource:** Energy Changes Form ... C37

Investigation 2 — **What Is Heat, and How Can It Move?** ... **C40**
- **Activity:** Bottle Thermometer ... C40
- **Activity:** Side by Side ... C42
- **Activity:** Heat Takes a Trip ... C43
- **Resource:** Heat Waves ... C44
- **Resource:** Heat on the Move ... C47
- **Resource:** Keeping Warm! ... C50

Investigation 3 — **How Can Heat Change Materials?** ... **C52**
- **Activity:** Cool Fingers ... C52
- **Activity:** Wet or Dry ... C53
- **Resource:** Adding and Subtracting Heat ... C54

Reflect and Evaluate ... **C57**

Chapter 3

Force, Motion, and Machines — **C58**

Investigation 1 **What Is a Force?** **C60**
- **Activity:** Roll On! C60
- **Activity:** Gravity Roll. C62
- **Resource:** Force, Energy, and Friction C64
- **Resource:** The Greatest Invention C66

Investigation 2 **How Do Machines Make Work Easier?** ... **C68**
- **Activity:** The Ups and Downs of a Seesaw.... C68
- **Activity:** Ramps and Rocks C70
- **Resource:** Machines—Force Changers C72
- **Resource:** More About Machines.......... C74

Reflect and Evaluate **C77**

Using Reading Skills **C78**

Using Math Skills **C79**

Unit Wrap-up! **C80**

UNIT D — Earth's Resources

THINK LIKE A SCIENTIST
FLOATING BERRIES **D2**

CHAPTER 1 — Air as a Natural Resource D4

Investigation 1
What Are Natural Resources? **D6**
- **Activity:** Be Resourceful D6
- **Activity:** Working Air D7
- **Resource:** Earth Matters D8
- **Resource:** Here Today, Gone Tomorrow? D10

Investigation 2
How Is Air Used? **D12**
- **Activity:** Greenhouse Gas D12
- **Resource:** It's Got Atmosphere D14
- **Resource:** A Fresh, Clean Start D17

Reflect and Evaluate **D19**

CHAPTER 2 — Water on Earth D20

Investigation 1
Where Is Water Found on Earth, and Why Is Water Important? **D22**
- **Activity:** The Water Planet D22
- **Activity:** Water Ups and Downs D24
- **Resource:** A Watery World D25
- **Resource:** Nature Recycles D28
- **Resource:** The Salty Problem D32

Investigation 2 — **How Can Sources of Fresh Water Be Protected?** **D34**
    Activity: Let's Clear This Up D34
    Activity: Testing Clear Water D36
    Resource: Wee Beasties D37
    Resource: Industrial-Revolution Pollution D40
    Resource: Water Worries D42

Reflect and Evaluate **D45**

Chapter 3 — Land as a Natural Resource   D46

Investigation 1 — **How Do the Forces of Nature Change Earth's Surface?** **D48**
    Activity: Hard Rock D48
    Activity: A Force of Nature D49
    Resource: Wearing Down and Building Up . . . D50

Investigation 2 — **Why Are Rocks and Soil Important?** **D54**
    Activity: Soak It Up D54
    Resource: On Rocky Ground D56
    Resource: Save It From a Rainy Day D59

Reflect and Evaluate **D61**

Using Reading Skills **D62**

Using Math Skills **D63**

Unit Wrap-up! **D64**

UNIT E: Roles of Living Things

THINK LIKE A SCIENTIST
FIND THAT INSECT E2

CHAPTER 1: Relationships Among Living Things — E4

Investigation 1 **What Do Living Things Need?** E6
- **Activity:** Needs of Plants E6
- **Activity:** A Pill Bug's Home E8
- **Resource:** A Perfect Place to Live E10

Investigation 2 **How Do Living Things Get the Food They Need?** E14
- **Activity:** Meat and Potatoes E14
- **Activity:** A Menu for Molds E15
- **Resource:** What's for Dinner? E16
- **Resource:** Saber Teeth! E20

Investigation 3 **What Are Food Chains and Food Webs?** . E22
- **Activity:** Making a Food-Chain Mobile E22
- **Activity:** More Links in the Food Chain E24
- **Resource:** Who Eats Whom? E26
- **Resource:** Cane Toads in Leaping Numbers .. E30
- **Resource:** Deadly Links E32

Reflect and Evaluate E35

Chapter 2: Adaptations of Living Things — E36

Investigation 1 How Are Living Things Adapted for Getting Food? **E38**
Activity: The Right Beak for the Job E38
Resource: Catching Lunch E40
Resource: A Quick Tongue E44

Investigation 2 How Are Living Things Adapted for Protection? **E46**
Activity: Blending In E46
Resource: Hiding Out and Other Defenses . . . E48
Resource: Medicines From Nature E54

Reflect and Evaluate **E57**

Chapter 3: Living Things in the Environment — E58

Investigation 1 How Can Living Things Change the Environment? **E60**
Activity: My Neighborhood Keeps Changing! . . E60
Resource: Busy Beaver Construction Co. E62
Resource: People Change the Environment . . . E64
Resource: Bringing Back the Buffaloes E66

Investigation 2 **How Are Living Things Adapted to Their Environments?** **E68**
Activity: Keeping Heat In E68
Resource: Beating the Heat E70
Resource: When the Going Gets Tough...... E74

Reflect and Evaluate **E77**

Using Reading Skills **E78**

Using Math Skills **E79**

Unit Wrap-up! **E80**

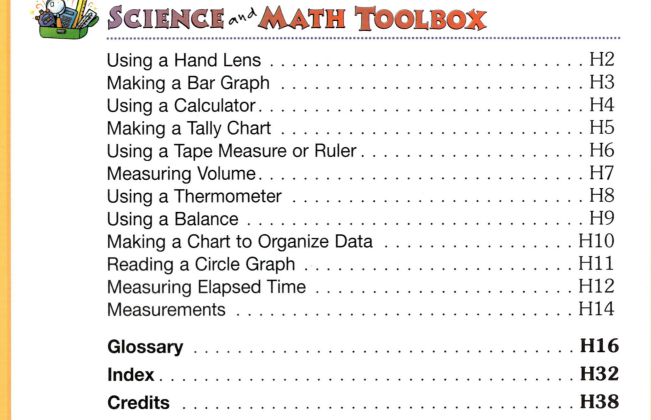

Science and Math Toolbox

Using a Hand Lens H2
Making a Bar Graph H3
Using a Calculator H4
Making a Tally Chart H5
Using a Tape Measure or Ruler H6
Measuring Volume H7
Using a Thermometer H8
Using a Balance H9
Making a Chart to Organize Data H10
Reading a Circle Graph H11
Measuring Elapsed Time H12
Measurements H14

Glossary **H16**

Index **H32**

Credits **H38**

Extra Practice **R1**

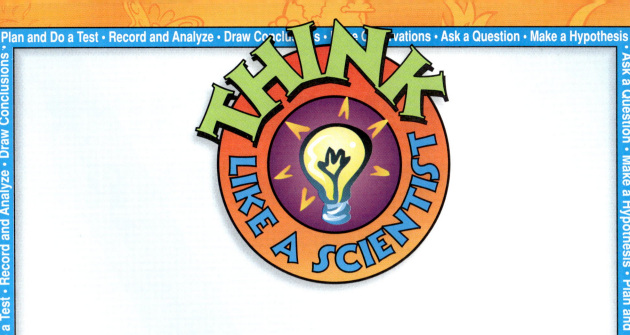

How to Think Like a Scientist S2

Practice Thinking Like a Scientist

Bubble Shapes

Make Observations S4

Ask a Question S5

Make a Hypothesis S6

Plan and Do a Test S7

Record and Analyze S8

Draw Conclusions S9

Using Science Process Skills S10

Reading to Learn S12

SAFETY S14

HOW TO THINK LIKE A SCIENTIST

Make Observations

To think like a scientist, learn as much as you can by observing things around you. Everything you hear, smell, taste, touch, and see is a clue about how the world works. As you test your ideas, you'll continue to make careful observations.

Make Observations

Ask a Question

Look for patterns. You'll get ideas. For example, you can smell certain odors, such as that of vanilla flavoring, from a distance. Ask questions such as this.

How does the odor travel from the open container to my nose?

Make a Hypothesis

If you have an idea about why something happens, make an educated guess, or hypothesis, that you can test. For example, suppose that you have a hypothesis about how odors travel. You think that odors travel by invisible particles that move through the air.

Make Observations

Plan and Do a Test

Plan how to test your hypothesis. Your plan would need to consider some of these problems.

How will you determine if the odor takes longer to travel a greater distance?

How will you measure the time between opening a bottle of vanilla and detecting the odor?

Then test your hypothesis.

Record and Analyze

When you test your idea, you need to observe carefully and record, or write down, everything that happens. When you finish collecting data, you may need to do some calculations with it. For example, you may need to compare the distance between you and the container of vanilla with the time it takes for the odor to reach you.

Draw Conclusions

Whatever happens in a test, think about all the reasons for your results. Sometimes this thinking leads to a new hypothesis. If it takes longer for odors to travel a greater distance, think about what else the data shows. Would all odors travel at the same speed?

Make Observations

Make Observations

Now read "Bubble Shapes" to see scientific thinking in action.

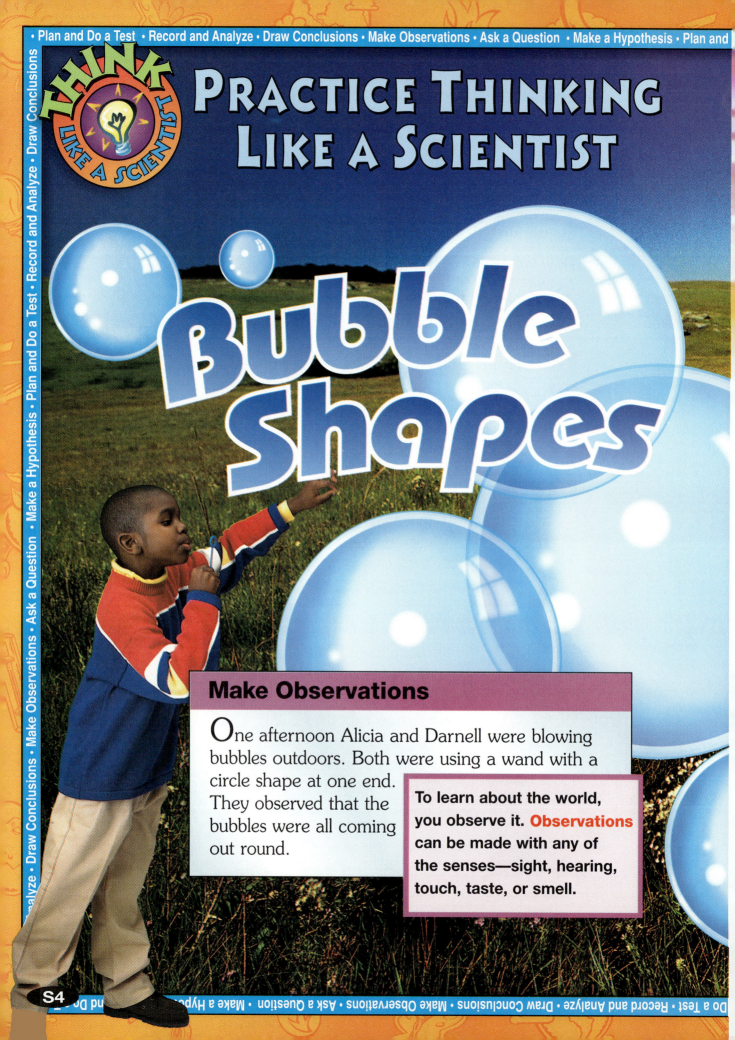

THINK LIKE A SCIENTIST

PRACTICE THINKING LIKE A SCIENTIST

Bubble Shapes

Make Observations

One afternoon Alicia and Darnell were blowing bubbles outdoors. Both were using a wand with a circle shape at one end. They observed that the bubbles were all coming out round.

To learn about the world, you observe it. **Observations** can be made with any of the senses—sight, hearing, touch, taste, or smell.

Ask a Question

Alicia wondered whether the bubbles were all round because the wand shape was round. Both children thought about the shapes of bubbles. All the bubbles they had ever seen were round. But all had been blown though a wand with a circle shape. Alicia and Darnell had questions about the shapes of bubbles.

Do bubbles take the shape of the object that they are blown through?

Will a square shape make a square bubble?

Will an oval shape make an oval bubble?

They decided to try to answer the first question. They thought they would find the answers to all the questions by answering just that one.

Scientific investigations usually begin with ideas that you're not sure about. Such ideas can help you ask a question that you really want to answer.

Make a Hypothesis

Alicia and Darnell had an idea that blowing a bubble through a square wand would make a square bubble. They thought that an oval bubble would come from an oval-shaped wand. They both thought the shape of a wand would make a bubble of that same shape. So they made that their hypothesis.

Darnell wanted to know if the bubbles would come out square if the wand shape was square. Alicia was eager to learn if a wand with an oval shape would make an oval-shaped bubble.

When you use what you've observed to suggest a possible answer to your question, you're making a hypothesis. Make sure that your hypothesis is an idea that you can test. If you can't test your hypothesis, try changing it.

Plan and Do a Test

Later that day Alicia and Darnell planned how they would test their hypothesis. They decided to make different shaped wands for blowing bubbles. They used a length of straight wire to make a square-shaped wand. With a second length of wire they made an oval-shaped wand. They already had the bubble mixture, so they began their test.

One way to try out your hypothesis is to use a **test** called a **controlled experiment**. The setups in this kind of experiment are identical in all ways except one. The one difference is the **variable**. In Alicia and Darnell's experiment the variable is the shape of the bubble wand.

Record and Analyze

Alicia blew through the oval-shaped wand six times and through the square-shaped wand six times. Each time she blew counted as one trial. Darnell recorded the shape of the bubbles from each trial on a chart like the one shown.

Next, Darnell took a turn and repeated exactly what Alicia had done. Then, to check their results, they each took another turn. They noticed that as a bubble formed, it had the shape of the wand it was made from. But as soon as the bubble left the wand, the bubble became round.

When you do an experiment, you make observations so that you can obtain information called **data**. You need to write down, or **record**, this data and then organize it. Graphs and tables are ways to organize data. **Analyze** the information that you collect by looking for patterns. To see if your results are reliable, **repeat the experiment** several times.

Shapes of Wands and Bubbles – Alicia

Trial	Bubble Shape from Oval Wand	Bubble Shape from Square Wand
1	round	round
2		
3		
4		
5		
6		

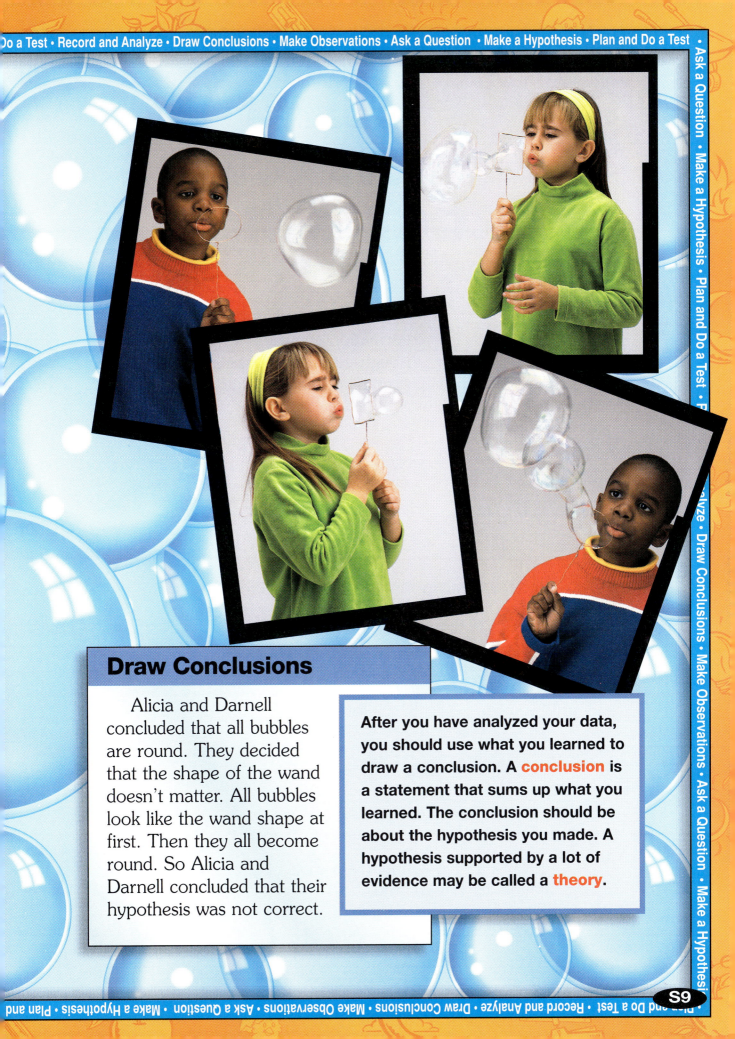

Draw Conclusions

Alicia and Darnell concluded that all bubbles are round. They decided that the shape of the wand doesn't matter. All bubbles look like the wand shape at first. Then they all become round. So Alicia and Darnell concluded that their hypothesis was not correct.

After you have analyzed your data, you should use what you learned to draw a conclusion. A **conclusion** is a statement that sums up what you learned. The conclusion should be about the hypothesis you made. A hypothesis supported by a lot of evidence may be called a **theory**.

Using Science Process Skills

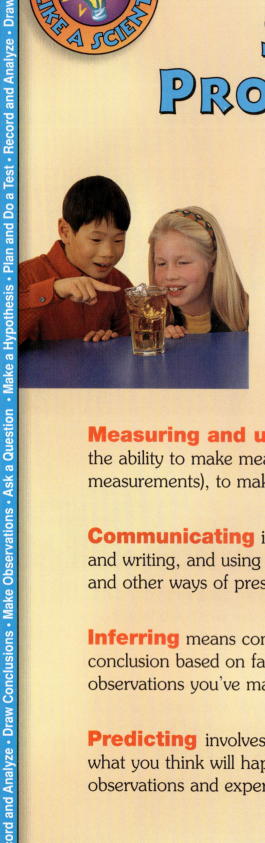

Observing involves gathering information about the environment through your five senses—seeing, hearing, smelling, touching, and tasting.

Classifying is grouping objects or events according to common properties or characteristics. Often you can classify in more than one way.

Measuring and using numbers involves the ability to make measurements (including time measurements), to make estimates, and to record data.

Communicating involves using words, both speaking and writing, and using actions, graphs, tables, diagrams, and other ways of presenting information.

Inferring means coming to a conclusion based on facts and observations you've made.

Predicting involves stating in advance what you think will happen based on observations and experiences.

Collecting, recording, and interpreting data all involve gathering and understanding information. This skill includes organizing data in tables, graphs, and in other ways. Interpretation includes finding patterns and relationships that lead to new questions and new ideas.

Identifying and controlling variables involves determining the effect of a changing factor, called the variable, in an experiment. To do this, you keep all other factors constant, or unchanging.

Defining operationally means to describe an object, an event, or an idea based on personal observations. An operational definition of a plant might be that it is a green living thing that is attached to soil and that does not move around.

Making a hypothesis is suggesting a possible answer to a question or making an educated guess about why something happens. Your hypothesis should be based on observations and experiences.

Experimenting is testing your hypothesis to collect evidence that supports the hypothesis or shows that it is false.

Making and using models includes designing and making physical models of processes and objects, or making mental models to represent objects and ideas.

READING TO LEARN

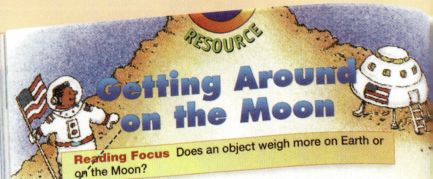

Before You Read

1. **Scan** each page.
   - titles
   - subheads
   - highlighted words
   - photos and illustrations
   - captions

2. **Identify** the main topic.

3. **Ask** yourself what you know about the topic.

4. **Predict** what you will learn by turning subheads into questions.

Scientists use scientific methods when they do experiments. They also use special methods when they read to learn. You can read like a scientist, too. Just follow the steps below.

While You Read

1. **Look** for words that signal cause and effect and sequence.

2. **Make** inferences and draw conclusions.

3. **Ask** questions when you don't understand and then reread.

Astronaut Buzz Aldrin jumps down from his ship in the Moon's low gravity. ▼

▲ Astronaut Aldrin carries out experiments on the Moon.

Moonwalkers

In 1969 two Americans, Neil Armstrong and Edwin "Buzz" Aldrin, became the first people to walk on the Moon. To learn about the Moon, they took photos, collected rocks and soil, and performed experiments. They had to go through a lot of training to learn how to do these jobs in only one sixth of the gravity they were used to on Earth.

The astronauts' visit to the Moon wasn't all work. They had a lot of fun hopping around like kangaroos in the Moon's low gravity. They had to be careful how they moved, though. What goes up must come down, even on the Moon! ■

INVESTIGATION 2 WRAP-UP

REVIEW

1. Describe the conditions on the Moon that require astronauts to wear spacesuits.

2. What holds the Moon in place near Earth?

CRITICAL THINKING

3. Explain why an astronaut on the moon can easily carry a much heavier load than on Earth.

4. At first, when astronauts came back from walking on the Moon, they had difficulty walking on Earth. Explain why this happened.

B23

After You Read

1. **Say** or **write** what you've learned.

2. **Draw**, **chart**, or **map** what you've learned.

3. **Share** what you've learned.

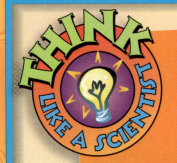

SAFETY

The best way to be safe in the classroom and outdoors is to use common sense. Prepare for each activity before you start it. Get help from your teacher when there is a problem. Always pay attention.

Stay Safe From Stains
- Wear protective clothing or an old shirt when you work with messy materials.
- If anything spills, wipe it up or ask your teacher to help you clean it up.

Stay Safe From Flames
- Keep your clothes away from open flames. If you have long or baggy sleeves, roll them up.
- Don't let your hair get close to a flame. If you have long hair, tie it back.

Make Wise Choices About Materials
- Use only the amount of material you need.
- Recycle materials so they can be reused.
- Take care when using valuable tools so they can be used again.

Stay Safe From Injuries
- Protect your eyes by wearing safety goggles when you are told that you need them.
- Keep your hands dry around electricity. Water is a good conductor of electricity, so you can get a shock more easily if your hands are wet.
- Be careful with sharp objects. If you have to press on them, keep the sharp side away from you.
- Cover any cuts you have that are exposed. If you spill something on a cut, be sure to wash it off immediately.
- Don't eat or drink anything unless your teacher tells you that it's okay.

Stay Safe During Cleanup
- Wash up after you finish working.
- Dispose of things in the way that your teacher tells you to.

HAIR Keep it out of the way of a flame.

EYES Wear safety goggles when you are told to.

MOUTH Don't eat or drink ANYTHING unless your teacher tells you it's okay.

CLOTHES Keep long sleeves rolled up. Protect yourself from stains. Stay away from open flames.

HANDS Keep your hands dry around electricity. Cover any cuts. Wear gloves when told to. Wash up after you finish.

DON'T MAKE A MESS If you spill something, clean it up right away. When finished with an activity, clean up your work area. Dispose of things in the way your teacher tells you to.

MOST IMPORTANTLY

If you ever hurt yourself, or one of your group members gets hurt, tell your teacher right away.

Life Cycles

Theme: Models

THINK LIKE A SCIENTIST
HITCHING A RIDE A2

CHAPTER 1 — Life Cycles of Animals A4
Investigation 1	What Is a Life Cycle? A6
Investigation 2	What Is the First Stage in an Animal's Life Cycle? A12
Investigation 3	How Do Some Animals Grow and Change? A20
Investigation 4	How Do Adult Animals Care for Their Young? A26

CHAPTER 2 — Life Cycles of Plants A34
Investigation 1	What Is the First Stage in the Life Cycle of a Flowering Plant? A36
Investigation 2	How Do Flowering Plants Make Seeds? A42
Investigation 3	How Do Plants With Cones Make and Protect Seeds? A48
Investigation 4	How Do Plants Change During Their Life Cycles? A54

Using Reading Skills A62
Using Math Skills A63
Unit Wrap-up! A64

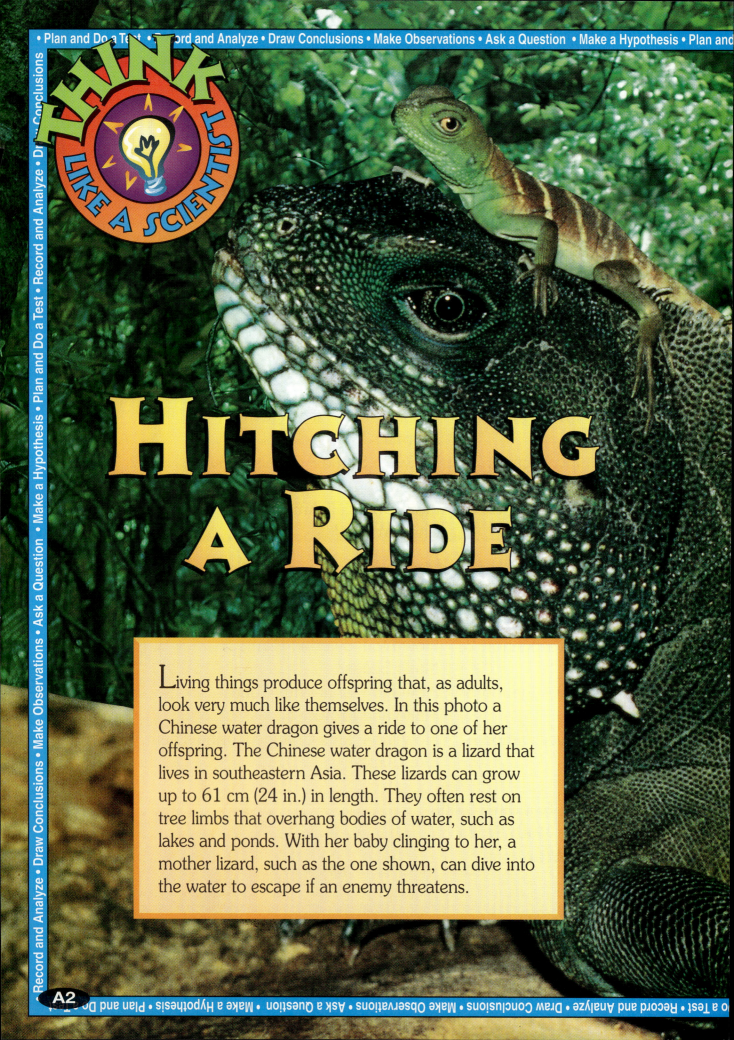

THINK LIKE A SCIENTIST

Hitching a Ride

Living things produce offspring that, as adults, look very much like themselves. In this photo a Chinese water dragon gives a ride to one of her offspring. The Chinese water dragon is a lizard that lives in southeastern Asia. These lizards can grow up to 61 cm (24 in.) in length. They often rest on tree limbs that overhang bodies of water, such as lakes and ponds. With her baby clinging to her, a mother lizard, such as the one shown, can dive into the water to escape if an enemy threatens.

THINK LIKE A SCIENTIST

Questioning In this unit you'll study how animals and plants grow, change, and produce young. You'll investigate questions such as these.
- What Is a Life Cycle?
- How Do Flowering Plants Make Seeds?

Observing, Testing, Hypothesizing In the Activity "Look at What You've Become," you'll make a model home for mealworms. Then you'll observe how the mealworms grow and change. You'll also hypothesize why some mealworms grow faster than others.

Researching In the Resource "Going Around in Cycles," you'll find out about the life cycles of two other insects—the butterfly and the grasshopper.

Drawing Conclusions After you've completed your investigations, you'll draw conclusions about what you've learned—and get new ideas.

CHAPTER 1
LIFE CYCLES OF ANIMALS

Think about some animals that you know. What were they like when they were young? How did they change as they grew older? Do you think all members of the animal kingdom grow and change throughout their lives?

People Using Science

Biologist Would you like to be alone in a small plane with a large bear? Jay Hammond, a biologist and bush pilot, was flying high above the Alaskan wilderness. Suddenly his passenger, a 275-kg (600-lb) bear, started to awaken. The bear had been drugged to keep it calm during the flight.

Minutes later, Hammond landed and unloaded the bear on the shore of a lonely lake. Now wide awake, the animal ran off to find a new home. Here the bear will mate, raise cubs, and spend the rest of its life. Like all animals, it will grow and change.

How are animals alike in the ways they change? How are they different? To find out, read this chapter!

Coming Up

INVESTIGATION 1
WHAT IS A LIFE CYCLE?
............A6

INVESTIGATION 2
WHAT IS THE FIRST STAGE IN AN ANIMAL'S LIFE CYCLE?
...........A12

INVESTIGATION 3
HOW DO SOME ANIMALS GROW AND CHANGE?
............A20

INVESTIGATION 4
HOW DO ADULT ANIMALS CARE FOR THEIR YOUNG?
............A26

◀ Biologist Jay Hammond flew a bear to its new home.

INVESTIGATION 1

WHAT IS A LIFE CYCLE?

Arrange these words in order—*teenager, child, adult, baby.* How did you do it? Each word names a stage in the life cycle of a human. All living things go through stages, or life cycles. In this investigation, you'll find out about the life cycles of some plants and animals.

Activity

The Changes Chart

How have you changed since you were a baby? How do other living things change during their life cycles? Find out.

MATERIALS
- strip of white paper
- pictures of plants and animals
- books about plants and animals
- *Science Notebook*

Procedure

1. With your group, brainstorm a list of living things that you've observed near your home or school. **Record** your list in your *Science Notebook*.

2. Make a Changes Chart. Fold a strip of paper lengthwise into four equal sections.

 To fold a piece of paper into four equal sections, fold it in half. Then fold it in half again.

3. Look at the list of living things you made in step 1. Choose one of the living things from your list.

A6

4. In the left-hand section of the chart, **draw** a picture or **write** a description of how you think the plant or animal you chose looked when it was very young. For help, look at pictures in books. **Predict** how the plant or animal will change as it gets older.

5. In each of the other three sections of the chart, **draw** or **write** your ideas about how the animal will change. Do not name the animal.

6. Exchange Changes Charts with another group. Study the other group's chart. Name the plant or animal that this chart is about. Ask the other group if you guessed correctly.

Analyze and Conclude

1. Make a plan to test your predictions from steps 4 and 5.

2. Show your teacher your plan. Then carry it out. How do the predictions you recorded on your Changes Chart **compare** with what you found out?

INVESTIGATE FURTHER!

EXPERIMENT

Fold a paper strip into eight sections. In the sections write these ages: 1, 3, 5, 7, 9, 15, 25, 55. In the sections, write how you have changed. For the ages you have not reached, predict how you'll change.

Step 4

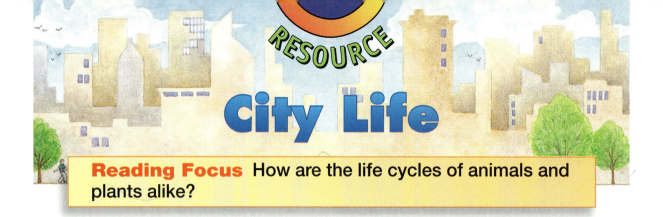

City Life

Reading Focus How are the life cycles of animals and plants alike?

A city is full of life. People, ants, spiders, birds, squirrels, roses, and earthworms are only a few of the things that live in a city. You might have to look closely to see some forms of city life. But if you observe the living things in a city over time, you'll notice that they change.

A chart showing how an animal changes is made in the activity on pages A6 and A7. All living things go through certain changes. These changes include growth, development, reproduction, and death. Growth refers to changes in size—that is, plants and animals becoming larger. Development refers to changes in plants and animals as they mature, or become adults. Reproduction is the process by which plants and animals produce offspring, or young of their kind. Death marks the end of each plant's or animal's lifetime.

Animals go through ordered life stages, as you can see in the pictures of the dogs below. After several

Life Cycle of a Dog

PUPPIES Puppies are born and then grow.

ADULT Puppies develop into mature, or adult, dogs that reproduce, or have puppies.

▲ Living things in the spring

years, an adult dog dies. But because it has reproduced, that kind of dog continues.

Plants go through life stages, too. A milkweed plant grows, blooms, and produces seeds. Some seeds fall to the ground. From these seeds new plants grow. The mature plant dies. But because it has reproduced, that kind of plant continues to exist.

Look at the two pictures above and below. What living things can you find? Compare the pictures. What changes have taken place in the living things over time?

The ordered stages that occur in a plant's or animal's lifetime are called a **life cycle**. A life cycle is like a circle. It has no end. One life cycle leads to another.

Living things in the summer ▼

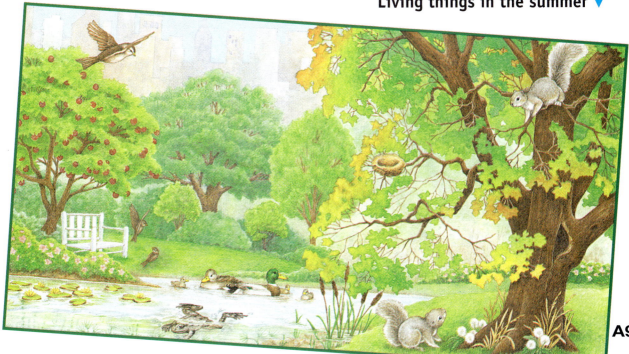

What's Wrong With This Picture?

Reading Focus When ducks mate, why do they produce ducklings and not chicks?

If you heard that a duck had hatched out of a chicken egg, you probably wouldn't believe it. Animals produce young just like themselves. Chickens mate and produce chicks. Ducks mate and produce ducklings.

Chicks belong to one species (spē'shēz) and ducks belong to another species. A **species** is a group of living things that can produce living things of the same kind. Now do you know what's wrong with this picture?

Passed On or Learned?

Animals of the same species pass on certain traits to their offspring. A trait is a characteristic. It describes something. The offspring receive, or inherit, traits from their parents.

You and your classmates belong to the human species. Though each of you is special, you all have many of the same human traits.

Some things are not passed from parents to offspring. These things are learned. For example, having feet is a human trait that is passed from parents to children. But using your feet to kick a soccer ball is a skill you learn. Chicks hatch knowing how to peck for food. But suppose a chick pecks at a caterpillar that tastes bitter. The chick then learns to avoid that kind of food.

How Long Do Animals Live?

By producing young, each species can continue beyond the life span of each parent. An animal's life span is the time between its birth, or hatching, and its death.

Look at the table below. As you can see, each species' life span is different from another's. A spider's life span is only one to twenty years. Yet box turtles have been known to live as long as 123 years. About how long does an elephant live?

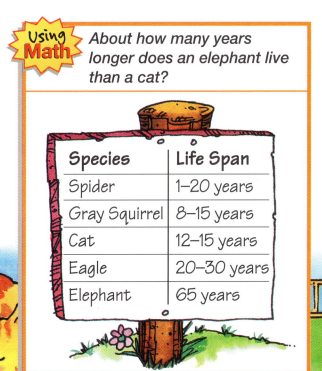

Using Math: *About how many years longer does an elephant live than a cat?*

Species	Life Span
Spider	1–20 years
Gray Squirrel	8–15 years
Cat	12–15 years
Eagle	20–30 years
Elephant	65 years

INVESTIGATION 1 WRAP-UP

REVIEW
1. What is a species?
2. What is a life cycle?

CRITICAL THINKING
3. What must happen so that the life cycle of a species does not end?
4. Explain the differences between inherited traits and those that are learned. Give two examples of each.

What Is the First Stage in an Animal's Life Cycle?

A newborn kitten and a newborn puppy look *so* tiny. But each developed from something much tinier. What is that something? Find out and become an "eggs-pert" as you explore the first stage in an animal's life cycle.

Activity

Be "Eggs-act"!

To a scientist, observing something means much more than just looking. In this activity you must be "eggs-act" as you explore the first stage in a chicken's life cycle.

MATERIALS
- goggles
- plastic gloves
- uncooked egg
- small dish
- hand lens
- paper towel
- *Science Notebook*

SAFETY
Wear goggles and gloves during this activity. Clean up any spills immediately.

Procedure

1. Think of an uncooked egg cracked into a dish. **Make a drawing** in your *Science Notebook* to show the inside parts of the egg that you remember. If you can, label each part. Mark the drawing *A*.

2. Get an uncooked egg from your teacher. With your group, use a hand lens to **observe** the outside of the egg. **Draw** what you see.

See **Science and Math Toolbox** page H2 if you need to review **Using a Hand Lens**.

A12

3. Crack the egg into a dish. Use the hand lens to **observe** the egg and the inside of the shell. **Draw** all the parts that you see. Mark this drawing *B*.

4. Compare drawing *A* with drawing *B*. What new parts did you discover?

Step 3

Analyze and Conclude

1. Based on the drawings your class did, do you think that all chicken eggs have the same parts? A chicken is a kind of bird. Do you think that all bird eggs have the same parts? How could you find out?

2. Each part you observed has a different job. Find the white spot on the yellow part of the egg. This spot could have developed into a new chick. **Infer** how the eggshell helps the developing chick.

INVESTIGATE FURTHER!

EXPERIMENT

Make a plan to study the eggs of another animal—for example, a fish. How are these eggs different from chicken eggs? How are they the same?

"Eggs-traordinary" Eggs!

Reading Focus How do the parts of an egg help an embryo grow?

Do you think eggs "eggs-ist" only to boil, poach, scramble, or fry? Actually, the job of an egg is to help produce offspring, or young. An **egg** is the first stage in the life cycle of almost all animals.

Some animals, such as baby horses, develop from eggs inside their mothers' bodies. Other animals, such as chickens, develop from eggs outside their mothers' bodies.

Eggs are "eggs-traordinary" in many ways. Even the tiniest egg contains everything needed for developing a new animal. Study the parts of the egg shown.

"Eggs-actly" How Would You Describe an Egg?

Eggs come in many shapes, colors, textures, and sizes. Chicken eggs, observed in the activity on pages A12 and A13, are round on one end and pointed on the other. Owl eggs are round. Plover eggs are

Using Math These bird eggs are shown actual size. Estimate which two are about the same size.

◀ Caspian tern
American robin ▼
◀ Blue jay
House wren ▶

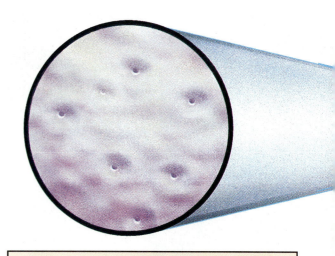

PORES A close-up look at tiny openings, called pores, in the shell of a chicken egg. Pores let water and oxygen enter the egg and carbon dioxide leave.

pear-shaped. Tortoise eggs are shaped like globes and sand grouse eggs like tubes.

Eggs can be brightly colored, dull, plain, or very fancy. From green and blue to black and red, eggs can be freckled, speckled, spotted, or dotted.

There are many kinds of egg coverings, too. Bird eggs have hard, chalky shells. Fish and frog eggs have a soft outer covering. They don't dry out, because they're laid in water. Slug and snail eggs have shiny, round shells.

Inside a Bird Egg

TWISTED STRANDS Twisted strands of the shell lining keep the embryo upright as the mother turns her egg. Turning the eggs warms them evenly.

SHELL The egg is covered by a shell. The shell protects everything inside the egg. A material called calcium makes the shell hard and helps to form the embryo's bones.

EMBRYO The white spot is where the embryo begins to grow. The **embryo** (em'brē-ō) is the developing chick. By the twenty-first day, the chick will start to hatch.

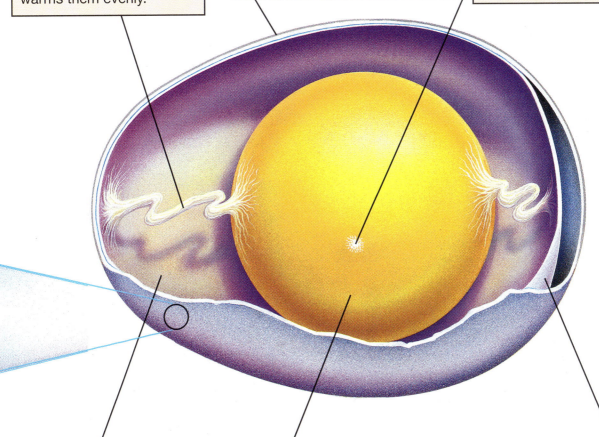

EGG WHITE The egg white cushions the embryo and provides it with water.

YOLK The yolk is the stored food for the embryo.

SHELL LININGS Just inside the shell are the shell linings. At the rounded end of the egg is an air space, which allows the embryo to get oxygen.

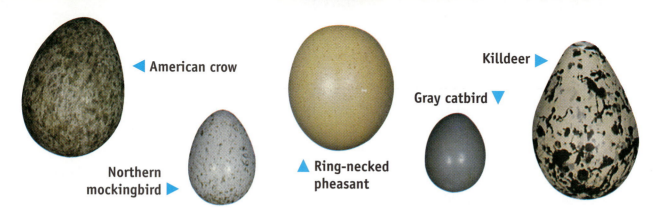

◀ American crow

Northern mockingbird ▶

▲ Ring-necked pheasant

Gray catbird ▼

Killdeer ▶

Ostrich eggs are the largest in the world. Each ostrich egg is about 16 cm (6 in.) long and has a mass of about $1\frac{1}{2}$ kg (3 lb). Compare the size of the ostrich egg with the size of the hummingbird egg in the picture below.

▲ A tiny hummingbird egg compared with an ostrich egg

"Eggs-actly" How Many?

The number of eggs that an animal lays varies with the species. The hornbill lays only 1 egg a year, but an oyster lays 500 million eggs a year. Chickens lay almost 1 egg a day, or up to 350 eggs a year. Each time an ocean sunfish produces eggs, it makes about 300 million.

Not every egg produces young. The eggs you eat do not contain embryos. For a chick or another animal to begin growing inside an egg, the mother must first mate with the father. Then—just think—the egg can grow into all the parts of an animal's body. An egg really is "eggs-traordinary"!

INVESTIGATE FURTHER!

EXPERIMENT

You can't easily see pores in a shell, but you can prove they are there. Place an egg in a clear container. A brown egg is best to use. Cover the egg with water. Don't touch or move the egg for 20 minutes. Use a hand lens to observe the shell. How has the shell changed? What do you think caused the change?

Hatching Chicks

Reading Focus What is an incubator and what is its function?

An incubator (in'kyōō-bāt ər) is a device that provides enough warmth, water, and fresh air to help keep something alive. An incubator in a hospital may help a tiny baby grow stronger. Other incubators are found on large chicken farms. These incubators are used to hatch eggs. Incubators for eggs, like the one shown here, come in two parts—the setter and the hatcher. Read the captions to find out the difference.

The trays in the setter move to turn the eggs many times each day. Eggs are warmed to a temperature of 37°C (99°F).

Large fans keep the air moving around the eggs.

① SETTER Chicken eggs are placed on trays and loaded into a setter. Some setters are as large as rooms and can hold thousands of eggs at one time. The eggs stay in the setter for 18 days.

② HATCHER On the nineteenth day, the eggs are put into metal or plastic baskets and moved to the hatcher. After 2 or 3 days in the hatcher, baby chicks hatch out of the eggs.

The Baby Book

Reading Focus What are two animals that are born live and two animals that hatch?

Almost all animals come from eggs. Some animal babies develop from eggs inside their mothers' bodies. Those babies are born live. Other offspring develop from eggs outside their mothers' bodies. Those babies hatch. Whether born live or hatched, each baby develops from a single egg.

Here are some baby animals from around the world. Look at the pictures and read about them. Which were born live? Which were hatched?

Baby African elephants grow inside their mothers' bodies for nearly two years. When a baby elephant, called a calf, is finally born, it weighs as much as a fully grown man. ▼

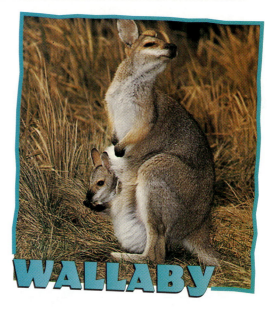

WALLABY

▲ Wallabies, from Australia, belong to the kangaroo family. A baby wallaby is called a joey. It is born live. Then it wriggles into its mother's pouch, where it drinks its mother's milk until it is about eight months old.

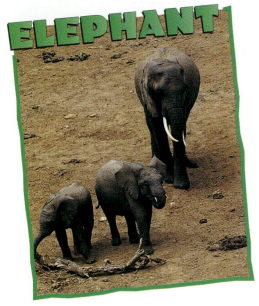

ELEPHANT

This mother crocodile from Egypt carries her hatched babies into the water to protect them from enemies. She will crack the eggs that are slow to hatch inside her mouth and let the babies wiggle into the water. ▼

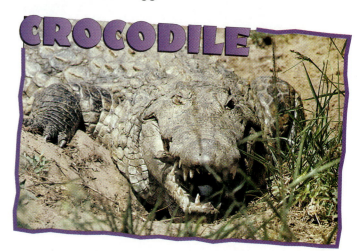

CROCODILE

◀ This bear cub had a mass of less than $\frac{1}{2}$ kg (1 lb) when it was born live. The rings of fur around its eyes make it look as if it's wearing spectacles, or eyeglasses. The spectacled bear is the only kind of bear that lives in South America.

▲ These baby snowy owls hatched in a nest on the ground. Their home in the far north is a cold place called the tundra (tun′drə). Both parents care for their chicks. All the chicks are born with white fluff, which later turns gray. The gray color helps to hide the young owls from enemies.

▲ Gentoo penguins live in the Antarctic. The penguin parents take turns sitting on the nest. Both parents feed and care for the chicks that hatch. When the young penguins are about nine weeks old, they swim out to sea and live on their own.

INVESTIGATION 2 WRAP-UP

REVIEW

1. What is the first life-cycle stage in animals that hatch and in animals that are born live?

2. Draw and label the parts of a bird egg that help an embryo grow.

CRITICAL THINKING

3. On page A15 you read about the parts of an egg. Explain what would happen to the developing chick if each part didn't work.

4. What may happen to a chick embryo if the shell has a small crack in it? Explain.

How Do Some Animals Grow and Change?

Have you ever worn a costume and found that no one knew you? As some animals go through their life cycles, they change so much that you may not know what animals they are. Find out about one animal as it grows and changes.

Activity

Look at What You've Become

Imagine how you will change as you grow up. Do all animals change in the same ways you do? The animals in this activity are masters at some amazing changes. Find out what they are.

MATERIALS
- goggles
- plastic gloves
- 5 mealworms
- dry cereal without a sugar coating
- thin slices of apple and potato
- dish with a cover
- hand lens
- metric ruler
- *Science Notebook*

SAFETY
Wear goggles and gloves when handling the mealworms. Wash your hands when you have finished.

Procedure

1. Look at the list of materials with your group. **Predict** what a mealworm needs in order to survive. Explain which material meets which need. **Infer** which material might provide a mealworm with water.

2. Use the materials to make a home for the mealworms. In your *Science Notebook*, **describe** the home you made. Place the mealworms in the home.

3. Every two days, clean the home and give the mealworms fresh food.

Step 4

4. **Observe** the mealworms with a hand lens each day for three weeks. Use a ruler to **measure** changes in size. **Make a chart** to **record** any changes you observe.

5. **Make a bar graph** of your data. **Compare** your graph with the graphs of other students in your class. Continue to **observe** your mealworms as they become adults.

 See **SCIENCE and MATH TOOLBOX** page H3 if you need to review **Making a Bar Graph.**

Analyze and Conclude

1. How did the mealworms change?

2. The adult stage of this insect is called a beetle. How many different stages did you observe in the life cycle of the mealworm beetle? **Draw** each stage.

3. **Hypothesize** why some mealworms grew faster than others.

INVESTIGATE FURTHER!

Use the **Best of the Net—Science CD-ROM**, Life Sciences, *Sockeye Salmon*, to find out about the unusual life cycle of a sockeye salmon. And find out the names of three other types of Pacific salmon.

A21

Going Around in Cycles

Reading Focus What are the differences between complete and incomplete metamorphosis?

▲ People grow and change. How has this person changed?

Your life cycle is special. You are first a baby, then a child, then a teenager, and then an adult. Suppose you saw a baby picture of an adult. You'd probably be able to say who the baby in the picture grew up to be. But if you saw an insect such as a butterfly in an early stage, you might not know what the animal was.

A Four-Stage Cycle

There are four stages in the life cycles of most species of insects, including butterflies, moths, flies, and beetles. The stages in order are (1) egg, (2) larva, (3) pupa, and (4) adult. Each stage looks very different from the stage before it and the stage after it.

Life Cycle of a Butterfly
Complete Metamorphosis

LARVA A larva, called a caterpillar, hatches from the egg. It sheds its outer covering several times as it grows.

PUPA In the pupa stage, the caterpillar makes a covering called a chrysalis (kris′ə lis).

ADULT After developing fully, an adult butterfly comes out of the chrysalis.

EGG The female adult mates, lays eggs, and the cycle starts over again.

A four-stage life cycle is called **complete metamorphosis** (met ə-môr′fə sis). The first stage is the egg. The second stage, called the **larva** (lär′və), is a wormlike stage that doesn't look at all like the adult. The larval stage of certain insects has a special name. Look at the pictures. What is the butterfly larva called?

The larva eats and grows and then makes a covering for itself. At that time, the insect is in the third stage, called the **pupa** (pyo͞o′pə). Inside the pupa, the adult insect develops. When it is fully developed, the adult insect comes out. The **adult** is the last stage of a life cycle. The adult female insect then mates and lays eggs, and the pattern continues.

Internet Field Trip
Visit **www.eduplace.com** to find out more about the life cycles of butterflies.

The beetle also goes through complete metamorphosis in its life cycle. The activity on pages A20 and A21 used mealworms, the larvas of beetles. The larva of the mealworm beetle is called a grub.

Now you can see that an insect in some stages doesn't look at all like the adult. A caterpillar certainly doesn't look like a butterfly. And a mealworm doesn't look like a beetle.

A Three-Stage Cycle

There are three stages in the life cycles of some insects. The names of the stages in order are (1) egg, (2) nymph, and (3) adult. A three-stage life cycle is called **incomplete metamorphosis**.

As with all animals, the first stage in the life cycle is the egg. The animal in the second stage, called a **nymph**, looks almost like a small adult. As the nymph eats and grows larger, it sheds its outer covering several times and then develops into an adult.

Then the female adult lays eggs that can go through the same cycle. Look at the pictures of the life cycle of a grasshopper. In what ways is the nymph like the adult grasshopper? How is it different?

A cricket goes through incomplete metamorphosis. A fly goes through complete metamorphosis. What life-cycle stages would take place in each of these insects?

Science in Literature

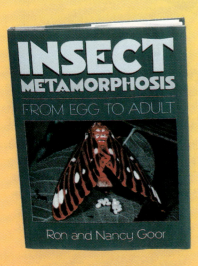

Insect Metamorphosis From Egg to Adult
by Ron and Nancy Goor
Atheneum, 1990

Insect Invasion

"In 1987, an enormous brood of millions of cicadas hatched out. If you took a walk late at night, you would see hundreds of cicadas crawling across streets. They covered every upright surface—even blades of grass. Their mating song was deafening. Such a gigantic brood of cicadas will appear again in 2004."

A cicada is a flying insect that takes 17 years to undergo metamorphosis! You can read more about this insect's invasion in the book *Insect Metamorphosis: From Egg to Adult* by Ron and Nancy Goor.

Life Cycle of a Grasshopper
Incomplete Metamorphosis

NYMPH A nymph hatches from an egg. The nymph looks almost like the adult, but it is smaller and has no wings. As the nymph grows, it sheds its outer covering several times.

ADULT After 40 to 60 days, the nymph has developed into an adult. Most adult grasshoppers have wings. The adult female mates and lays eggs, and the cycle continues.

EGG The female adult lays eggs in a hole that she digs in the ground.

Using Math About how many months does it take for a nymph to develop into an adult?

INVESTIGATION 3 WRAP-UP

REVIEW

1. What are the four stages in the life cycles of most species of insects?

2. What life-cycle stage is a caterpillar?

CRITICAL THINKING

3. A scientist identifies a wormlike animal as the larva of an insect. What do you think are the stages in the life cycle of this insect?

4. How are complete and incomplete metamorphoses the same? different?

INVESTIGATION 4

How Do Adult Animals Care for Their Young?

Have you ever had a sitter? Hiring a sitter is one way adult humans might care for their children. In this investigation you'll learn how animals differ in the ways they care for their young.

Activity

The Animal-Sitter's Guide

What's a sitter's job? Suppose an animal such as a baby whale or a young giraffe had a human sitter. What do you think that sitter would need to know to care for the young animals? In this activity you'll find out.

MATERIALS
- animal-sitting assignment cards in a box
- construction paper
- colored markers
- discarded magazines
- reference books
- *Science Notebook*

Procedure

1. Take a card from your group's animal-sitting assignment box. Look at the name of the animal on the card and **record** the name in your *Science Notebook*. Find out about the baby animal's needs and how the parents care for the baby. **Record** what you find out. **Infer** the care the baby animal should receive.

Step 1

A26

2. On a sheet of construction paper, write a list of instructions for an Animal-Sitter's Guide for the class. Give information that would answer questions such as these: What kind of food does the baby animal need? When does it sleep? Does it make unusual noises? What might threaten or harm the baby animal?

Step 2

3. Include a drawing or picture of your animal.

4. Put your instructions in the class Animal-Sitter's Guide, where others can refer to them.

Analyze and Conclude

1. What would be the hardest part of taking care of the animal you wrote about? Explain your answer.

2. **Compare** the care needed by your animal with the care needed by other baby animals in the Guide. Which animal would be the hardest to sit for? Which would be the easiest? Explain your answers.

UNIT PROJECT LINK

For this Unit Project you will make an Animal-Sitter's Guide and a Plant-Sitter's Guide. Predict which pets are hardest to care for. With your group, interview owners of different kinds of pets. Record the information in a special pet section of your Animal-Sitter's Guide.

 Technology Link

For more help with your Unit Project, go to **www.eduplace.com**.

A27

Out of Sight, Out of Mind

Reading Focus What are some adaptations that help sea turtles survive?

It's easy to forget about something that you can't see. "Out of sight, out of mind" is a short way to say this. This saying describes how some animals behave toward their eggs. For example, a cowbird lays her eggs, one at a time, in the nests of other, smaller birds. Then she flies away, never to see her eggs again. The "foster parent" birds care for their own offspring as well as for the young cowbirds. You can see that for the mother cowbird, her eggs are "out of sight, out of mind."

Survival Kit

How do animals that hatch from out-of-sight, out-of-mind eggs survive? One thing that helps cowbirds survive is that the adult females lay their eggs in the nests of smaller birds. Because the young cowbirds are larger than the other young birds, they get more food.

The behavior of the female cowbird is an adaptation. An **adaptation** (ad əp tā'shən) is a behavior or part of a living thing that helps the living thing survive.

1 A female sea turtle swims to shore.

2 The female lays her eggs.

Many Eggs—Few Survive

Frogs and most fish lay many eggs but don't protect them. Laying many eggs is another animal adaptation.

A frog lays thousands of jelly-covered eggs. Many frog eggs become food for other animals. The frog eggs that do survive develop into tadpoles. Some tadpoles become food for snakes. Although a frog lays thousands of eggs, few eggs survive to develop into adult frogs. Laying many eggs, then, is an adaptation that helps frogs survive as a species.

Some animals hide their eggs before leaving them. Hiding eggs is also an adaptation. It is a way that animals help their offspring survive.

A female sea turtle crawls out of the sea at night. Using her flippers as shovels, she digs a nest in the sand. She lays at least a hundred eggs in the nest. The sea turtle's flippers, used as shovels, are also adaptations. They are a part of a living thing that helps it to survive.

After the sea turtle lays the eggs in the nest, she covers them with sand. Then she crawls back into the sea and never sees her young.

Although the female sea turtle has laid many eggs, probably only one baby turtle out of a hundred will survive. Other animals, such as raccoons, steal eggs from turtle nests. When the surviving eggs do hatch, the baby turtles crawl toward the sea. But sea birds swoop down upon them for food. And many of those that reach the water become food for sea animals. You can see how laying many eggs is an adaptation that helps sea turtles survive as a species.

❸ The baby turtles hatch.

❹ The baby turtles crawl to the sea.

A Whale of a Baby

Reading Focus What are some ways that a female whale cares for her young?

Did you know that the world's biggest baby is about 8 m (26 ft) long and has a mass of about 1,800 kg (2 T)? It's longer than a station wagon and weighs as much as a small truck. This baby is a blue whale calf. The blue whale calf's mother is much bigger than her baby. She's about 30 m (100 ft) long and has a mass of over 90,000 kg (100 T). That's as long as two big tractor-trailers and heavier than the largest dinosaur. A land animal's legs couldn't support that mass. But ocean water can.

A Whale of a Birth

A whale develops inside a mother whale and then is born live. Whales are born underwater in early winter, almost a year after the mother and father mate. A mother whale is called a cow. The baby is a calf. Normally, the calf slithers out of the cow, tail first.

The mother watches the newborn calf float to the surface. There the calf takes its first deep breath and sends up a fountain of mist from the blowhole on top of its head.

A mother humpback whale with her calf ▼

From the time it is born, the calf can swim. For several weeks the calf swims close to its mother. She gently strokes the calf with her flipper. A mother whale never leaves her baby unattended. She watches as it takes in fresh air before diving and as it blows out its warm breath when surfacing.

To feed, the calf dives underwater, where its mother squirts rich, warm milk into its mouth. A blue whale calf drinks about 500 L (132 gal) of milk every day and gains about 90 kg (200 lb) a day.

A Whale of a Journey

One kind of whale is called a humpback. During the winter, the mother whales never eat. They live off their stored fat. But in the spring, thousands of humpbacks head for the colder waters of the Arctic, where there is food. For protection

▲ A closeup look at baleen

the whales swim in small groups called pods. On this long journey north, the mother whale watches out for dangers. Killer whales can hurt and even kill a baby humpback whale. A whale can get caught in nets dragged by fishing boats. Then it can't swim to the surface to breathe. A mother whale will protect her baby even if it means that she is putting herself in danger.

A Whale of a Summer

By summer, humpback whales arrive at the Arctic. The waters there are their feeding grounds. Since the mother whale hasn't eaten for six months, she's hungry. She will eat a year's worth of food—probably a ton a day—in the next six months.

Humpback whales don't have teeth. Instead, they have baleen, or flat bony plates that hang down from the roof of the mouth like the teeth of a comb.

Humpback whales feeding (*left and below*).

Using Math: A baby humpback whale is about 1,800 kg at birth. If it doubles its weight in one year, about how much does a one-year-old calf weigh?

The mother whale gulps big mouthfuls of sea water. She closes her mouth part way and then squirts the water out. She swallows the food that is trapped by the baleen. A whale's mouth can hold a ton of food.

All summer, as the mother whale eats and her calf drinks milk, they build up layers of fat. They play together. They slap the water with their tails. They roll over. Sometimes the little whale breaches—it hurls itself out of the water, twists high in the air, and lands with a splash!

A Whale of a Whale

In the fall the whales travel south toward warmer waters. There the calf's mother may mate again.

The young humpback whale has grown strong. It can find its own food. Now only a year old, it has doubled its birth size. It is truly a whale of a whale. ■

INVESTIGATION 4 WRAP-UP

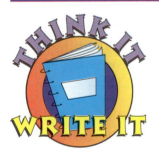

REVIEW

1. What are adaptations? Give an example.

2. Choose an animal that you learned about in this investigation. Describe the care that the animal gets as it grows and develops.

CRITICAL THINKING

3. Explain why laying many eggs is an adaptation for the survival of a species.

4. Compare the needs of a baby whale with those of a human baby.

CHAPTER 1 REVIEW: REFLECT & EVALUATE

Word Power

Write the letter of the term that best matches the definition. *Not all terms will be used.*

1. First stage in the life cycle of almost all animals
2. Developing chick
3. Ordered stages in a plant's or animal's lifetime
4. Last stage of complete and incomplete metamorphosis
5. Behaviors that help a living thing survive
6. Group of living things that can produce living things of the same kind

a. adaptations
b. adult
c. egg
d. embryo
e. larva
f. life cycle
g. pupa
h. species

Check What You Know

Write the term in each pair that best completes each sentence.

1. The wormlike second stage of complete metamorphosis is the (nymph, larva).
2. The pecking behavior of a chick is (learned, inherited).
3. A four-stage life cycle in insects is called (complete metamorphosis, incomplete metamorphosis).

Problem Solving

1. A female sea turtle may lay a hundred eggs at one time. A female elephant gives birth to only one baby elephant at a time. How does each mother differ in the way she cares for her offspring?
2. How might your life be different today if you skipped the development that occurs between the ages of two and four?

A mealworm is the larva stage of a beetle. Draw what you think the stages in the life cycle of the beetle would look like. Label each stage.

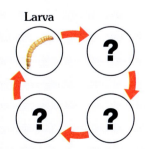

CHAPTER 2
LIFE CYCLES OF PLANTS

Many members of the plant kingdom grow from seeds. Have you ever planted a seed and watched it grow into a plant? What happened to the plant as time passed?

Connecting to Science
ARTS

Nature Poem Gwendolyn Brooks, an African American poet, tells in this poem about a child who plants a seed.

Tommy
I put a seed into the ground
And said, "I'll watch it grow."
I watered it and cared for it
As well as I could know.
One day I walked in my back yard
And oh, what did I see!
My seed had popped itself right out
Without consulting me.
—Gwendolyn Brooks

In this chapter you'll learn how plants grow and change. And you'll discover other things plants do "without consulting you."

Coming Up

 **What Is the First Stage in the Life Cycle of a Flowering Plant?** A36

 **How Do Flowering Plants Make Seeds?** A42

 **How Do Plants With Cones Make and Protect Seeds?** A48

 **How Do Plants Change During Their Life Cycles?** A54

◀ Planting flowers

A35

INVESTIGATION 1

WHAT IS THE FIRST STAGE IN THE LIFE CYCLE OF A FLOWERING PLANT?

What a survival story! In Egypt, seeds buried for over 1,000 years were able to start a new life cycle. You'll dig up more about seeds in Investigation 1.

Activity

The Inside Story

Seeds come in many sizes. But even the smallest seed can begin a new plant life cycle. Find out what's inside a seed.

Procedure

1. Use a toothpick to pry open the halves of one lima bean seed that was soaked overnight. With your group, **observe** the parts of the seed. Place the two halves so that their inside surfaces are facing up. **Draw** the two halves in your *Science Notebook*. **Draw** arrows that point to each part. Number the arrows.

MATERIALS
- goggles
- plastic gloves
- soaked lima bean seeds
- toothpicks
- water
- paper towels
- 2 sealable plastic bags
- stapler
- metric ruler
- tape
- hand lens
- Science Notebook

SAFETY
Wear goggles during this activity. Clean up any spills immediately.

Step 1

A36

2. Place a piece of wet paper towel in a plastic bag. Staple the bag about 2 cm from the bottom. Pry open a second bean seed and separate the two halves. Place all four seed halves in the bag.

 See **SCIENCE and MATH TOOLBOX** page H6 if you need to review **Using a Tape Measure or Ruler.**

Step 3

3. Prepare a second plastic bag like the first one. Add four whole bean seeds to the bag. Seal both bags and tape them to a wall or bulletin board. **Record** the date.

4. Use a hand lens to **observe** the whole seeds and seed halves each day. Add water as needed to keep the seeds moist. **Record** any changes. After three days, remove one of the whole seeds from its bag. Separate the halves. **Record** what you see. Every three days, remove another whole seed and separate its halves. **Record** all observations.

Analyze and Conclude

1. What changes occurred in the whole seeds? What changes occurred in the seed halves? **Hypothesize** about what might account for the differences.

2. How many different seed parts did you find? **Describe** each part. Beside each description, write the number that matches the number of the same part on your drawing.

3. Based on your observations, **infer** which seed part provides food for the young plant that grows from the seed. Explain your inference.

Step 4

A37

It's "A-maize-ing"

Reading Focus When was maize first planted in Mexico?

Corn is one of the most important foods in the world. People and many kinds of farm animals eat corn. Corn, also called maize, can be used to make food products, such as cooking oil and bread. The time line shows how important corn has been.

Because the action in World War I has destroyed much of the farmland in Europe, the United States sends ships loaded with food to Europe. Corn and wheat from America save thousands of people from starving.

1920

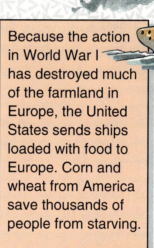

1999
There are 3,500 uses for corn products, including fuels, plastics, inks, vitamins, and cleaners.

Farmers grow different kinds of maize and invent better ways to store crops for winter.

800

Maize is planted and harvested in Mexico. Seeds are gathered from wild plants.

2700 B.C.

1620
The Pilgrims land at what is now Plymouth, Massachusetts. Native Americans show the Pilgrims how to plant, grow, and use corn. The Pilgrims have a day of thanks, which we celebrate today as Thanksgiving.

A.D. 200
Maize, along with beans and squash, becomes a main part of people's diets in the Americas. Ways are found to increase the food production.

A38

Plant Tricks

Reading Focus What are some ways that plants scatter their seeds?

Seeds can do stupendous tricks! Have you ever blown on the fluffy round head of a dandelion? Each little parachute that floats away is a seed that can produce a plant.

The Many Kinds of Seeds

The first stage in the life cycle of a flowering plant is a seed. Seeds are as different as the plants that grow from them. Seeds come in many sizes. A carrot seed is tiny. A coconut is a large seed. Seeds come in many shapes—round, pointed, oval, flat, and thin. They come in many patterns and colors—solid, speckled, white, brown, black, yellow, and red.

Whatever its size, shape, or color, a seed has three parts—a seed coat, stored food, and an embryo. Find out about these parts as you study the drawings below.

Seed Adaptations

Seeds are survivors. Plants have grown from lotus seeds that are centuries old. And seeds perform all kinds of tricks. Seeds can burst open, pop out, explode, fly, float, hitchhike, and parachute. These tricks help a seed get away from its parent plant. The new plant that develops from the seed may then get the things it needs to grow.

PARTS OF A SEED

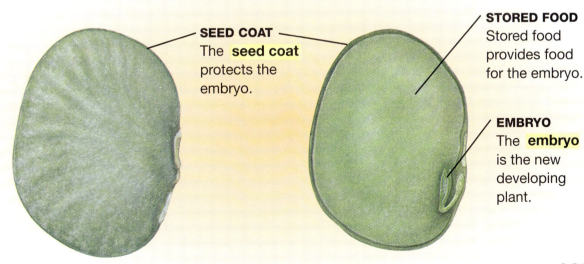

SEED COAT The seed coat protects the embryo.

STORED FOOD Stored food provides food for the embryo.

EMBRYO The embryo is the new developing plant.

Wind scatters some seeds. As the tumbleweed plant is blown along the ground, its seeds scatter. Wind also blows seeds away from the parent plant. Some seeds have a shape that helps them travel in the wind. Because of its shape, the milkweed seed travels easily in the wind.

Animals also scatter seeds. As animals roam, their fur can pick up and carry sticky seeds. Animals, such as mice, carry seeds away and bury them. Birds carry seeds on their feathers and in their beaks. People sometimes carry seeds on their clothing.

▲ Seed in a bird's beak

What Seeds Need

A seed needs warmth, air, and moisture to **germinate** (jur′mə-nāt), or sprout. In the activity on pages A36 and A37, a wet paper towel in the bags provided moisture for the seeds. When a seed is in the ground, a tiny hole in the seed coat allows moisture to enter the seed. In addition to warmth and water, a seed needs oxygen from the air before it can germinate.

▲ What adaptation does a milkweed seed have for scattering?

Water also scatters seeds. Lotus seeds fall into water and float away. Some settle in the muddy bottoms of rivers and lakes and grow into new plants. Some seeds, such as coconuts, even float across oceans.

▼ Sticktight seeds in a squirrel's fur

With the proper conditions, a seedling develops. A **seedling** is a new plant that develops from an embryo. The growing plant has adaptations that help it get what it needs to grow. Some plants have long taproots that can reach far underground for water. Other plants have fuzzy stems and leaves that capture and hold in moisture.

▼ **A bean seedling**

Seed Plants Not From Seeds

All seed plants produce and can grow from seeds. However, some can also grow from trailing plant stems called runners or from underground plant parts called tubers (tōō′bərz). A strawberry plant produces runners. A potato is an example of a tuber. Plants, such as tulips, can grow from bulbs. Some plants can even grow from a piece of stem or leaf. But all seed plants produce seeds.

Runners, tubers, bulbs, and cuttings don't produce seedlings—only seeds produce seedlings. Seedlings develop into plants that produce food. This food is used by the plants and by animals that eat the plants. ■

Internet Field Trip
Visit **www.eduplace.com** to see amazing images of how seeds travel through air, in the sea, and on animals.

INVESTIGATION 1 WRAP-UP

REVIEW

1. What is the first stage in the life cycle of a flowering plant?

2. List three adaptations of seeds that help scatter them.

CRITICAL THINKING

3. In Chapter 1 you found out about the stages in the life cycles of animals. How is the seed stage in the life cycle of a flowering plant like the egg stage in an animal's life cycle?

4. Suppose you planted seeds but they did not grow. Explain what seeds need to germinate. Tell what may have gone wrong with the seeds you planted.

How Do Flowering Plants Make Seeds?

Have you ever picked or chosen a flower for a friend? What helped you decide which one to take? Was it the scent, the color, or the interesting shapes of its parts? In this investigation you'll find out how each of these is important for flowers to make seeds.

Activity

It's a Flower! It's a Factory!

Have you ever heard about a factory that blooms? A flowering plant is a factory. What does this factory make? In this activity you'll find out about one of its products.

MATERIALS
- goggles
- disposable gloves
- flower
- sheet of plain white paper
- hand lens
- cotton swab
- *Science Notebook*

SAFETY
Wear goggles and gloves during this activity. Do not smell the flowers. You may inhale pollen grains, which cause allergic reactions in many people.

Procedure

1. Examine a flower carefully. **Make a drawing** of it in your *Science Notebook*. **Draw** an arrow to each part of the flower. Label any part that you know.

2. Carefully pull the petals apart so that you can see the center of the flower. **Make a drawing** of what you see. Write questions about what you **observe**.

Step 2

3. With your group, **compare** the parts of your flower with the photo shown. Label the parts on both of your drawings. What questions do you have about the parts of a flower?

4. Gently shake your flower over a sheet of plain white paper. The small powdery objects that fall from the flower are grains of **pollen** (päl′ən). Use a hand lens to **observe** the grains. **Describe** how they look. **Record** your observations.

Step 3

 See **SCIENCE and MATH TOOLBOX** page H2 if you need to review **Using a Hand Lens.**

Analyze and Conclude

1. The **pistil** (pis′til) is the part of the flower where seeds form. Why do you think its location in the center is important?

2. The **stamen** (stā′mən) is the part of the flower that contains pollen. For seeds to form in most plants, pollen must travel from a stamen of one plant to the pistil of another. Use a cotton swab to move pollen from a stamen to the pistil. **Hypothesize** how insects and birds might move pollen. **Talk with your group**. Explain your ideas and **record** your hypothesis.

3. A flower's petals attract insects, which feed on a sweet liquid in the plant. What is it about petals that might attract insects?

Step 4

A43

The Fantastic Flower

Reading Focus How does a flower produce a seed?

Many seed plants produce flowers. Flowers grow in many colors and sizes. Many people enjoy the beauty and smell of flowers so much that they give flowers as gifts on special occasions.

Plant Parenthood

Flowers might be called the parents of plants. A flower is part of an adult flowering plant. Seeds are formed in flowers. It is through the seed that the life cycle of the parent plant can continue.

Each flower has three parts that help a flower carry out its parent role. Their names are pistil, stamen, and petals. Look at the picture as you read about each part.

PARTS OF A FLOWER

PISTIL The pistil is the part of a flower where seeds develop and grow.

PETALS Petals are the brightly colored parts of a flower. Petals attract the insects and birds that pollinate flowers.

STAMEN The stamen produces pollen, a powdery material that is needed to make seeds form. Pollen must land on a pistil to make seeds form. This process is called pollination (päl ə nā′shən).

Seed Protection

Do you like to eat fruit? Did you know fruits come from flowers? A **fruit** is the part of a flower that forms around a seed. Pea pods, tomatoes, and apples are all fruits that we eat. A fruit protects the seed or seeds inside of it.

A fruit also provides a way for the seeds to be scattered. For example, birds like to eat cherries. Inside each cherry is a single seed, which is protected by a hard shell. When a bird swallows a cherry, it digests the soft part of the fruit. But the seed passes unchanged through and out of the bird's body. If the seed falls on the ground, it can grow into a new cherry tree.

Birds also like to eat blackberries, but they do not like blackberry seeds.

▲ Fruits protect seeds.

The birds push the seeds aside and wipe them off their beaks. The tiny seeds fall to the ground, where they can grow into new blackberry bushes.

Plant Helpers

Insects help in the pollination of flowering plants. For example, bees are attracted to the bright colors of a flower's petals and to a sweet-tasting nectar (nek′tər) inside the flower.

Pollen grains, observed in the activity on pages A42 and A43, have a sticky coating. When an insect comes to feed on the nectar in a flower, pollen grains cling to the insect's body. They then carry the pollen to the pistil of the same flower or to the pistil of another flower.

▼ A tomato is a fruit.

A45

Not all flowers are pollinated by insects. Sometimes pollen is carried by wind and water. Birds and other animals, attracted by a flower's color and scent, can also carry pollen from one flower to another.

The hummingbird hovers over a flower and pushes its long beak deep into the flower to get the nectar. Pollen from the flower sticks to the bird, which then carries the pollen to the next flower.

Bats help pollinate flowering trees. Bats drink the nectar and eat the pollen. They transfer the pollen stuck on their tongues and noses from flower to flower.

▼ **Parent plant**

Flower Child

Plants produce seeds that develop into new offspring. The offspring will inherit many of the same traits as the parent plants. For example, the seeds of a tall pea plant will likely grow into another tall pea plant. Flower color and seed color are examples of other traits that are passed from parents to offspring. Look at the parent plant and its offspring shown below. What traits did the offspring inherit from its parent?

Plant Cycles

The life cycles of flowering plants vary greatly in length. The life cycles of some trees, for example, may be hundreds or even thousands of years long! Many of the flowering plants you know have yearly life cycles. Such plants are called annuals because they live for only one year or one season. Study the life cycle of a flowering plant shown on the next page.

▼ **Offspring plant**

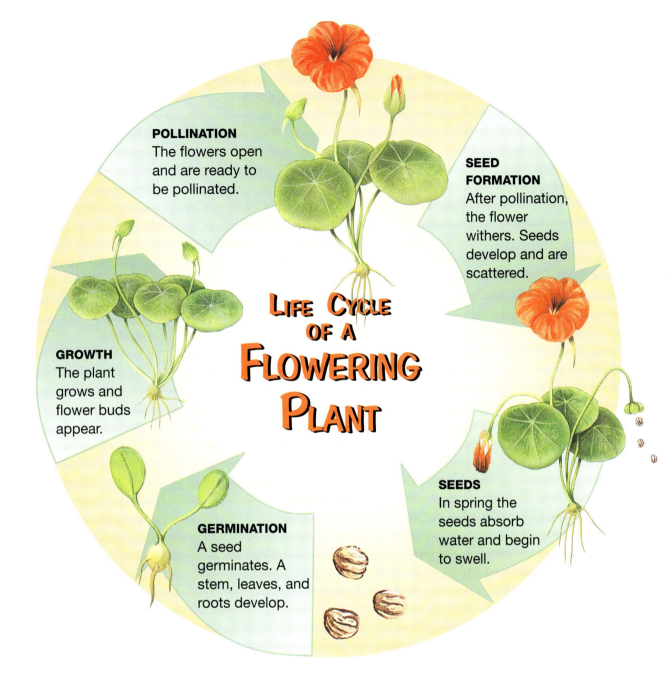

INVESTIGATION 2 WRAP-UP

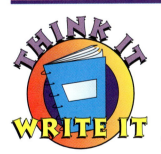

REVIEW

1. Describe the three main parts of a flower. Tell how each part helps seeds form.

2. Explain the difference between pollination and germination.

CRITICAL THINKING

3. You are having lima beans and tomatoes at dinner tonight. What plant parts are you eating? How are they different? How are they alike?

4. Write a short story about what would happen if something stopped the pollination of flowers.

A47

INVESTIGATION 3

How Do Plants With Cones Make and Protect Seeds?

Have you ever seen pine cones used to decorate something? For a pine tree, cones are more than just decoration. In this investigation you'll find out just what cones do for a plant.

Activity

Cone Sweet Home

Think of some ways your home protects you. In this activity you'll find out how cones provide protection for seeds.

MATERIALS
- many assorted cones
- hand lens
- *Science Notebook*

SAFETY
Wash your hands after handling the cones.

Procedure

1. A cone is a plant part that grows on a tree called a conifer (kän′ə fər). **Examine** some cones. **Record** questions you have about plants that make cones. **Record** your observations in your *Science Notebook*.

2. With your partner, **classify** the cones. Each group of cones should share at least one trait. Remember, a trait is a characteristic. Use traits such as size, color, and shape.

3. Look at the pictures of conifers on the next page. What kinds of conifers did your cones come from?

▲ Cedar cone

Pine cone ▲
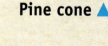

Spruce cone ▶
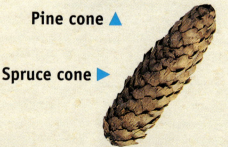

A48

4. A cone is made of woody parts called scales. Carefully pull off several scales from each cone. A conifer seed grows on the scale where the scale joins the cone. With a hand lens, **observe** the scales to find a seed. **Make a drawing** of what you observe on the scales.

Step 4

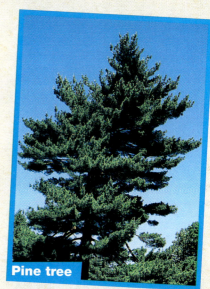

Pine tree

Spruce tree

5. Look at the picture of the cone scale at the right. **Compare** the picture with your drawing.

Cedar tree

Analyze and Conclude

1. Some cones can open and close. Cones close in damp weather. How might this action help cones? Cones open and release seeds in dry weather. **Talk with your group** and **infer** what one job of a cone is.

2. How are the cone of a conifer and the fruit of a flowering plant alike?

A49

Evergreens

Reading Focus How do conifers reproduce?

Many trees shed their leaves in the fall as part of their life cycles. But other trees have leaves (or needles) all year long. Such trees are called evergreens because they're always green. Actually, evergreens do shed their leaves, but most grow new ones at the same time. That's why they're always green.

Pine, spruce, fir, hemlock, and cedar trees are all evergreens. These evergreen trees have something else in common—they all bear cones. But not all evergreens produce cones. Those that do are called conifers. The word *conifer* means "cone-bearing." A **cone** is the part of the conifer that produces pollen or seeds.

There are two kinds of conifer cones. Pollen cones make and release pollen, much as the stamen of a flower does. Seed cones receive

DIFFERENT KINDS OF EVERGREENS

◀ Eastern hemlock

◀ Douglas fir

fish scales   roof shingles   cone scales

the pollen and use it to make seeds. Each cone is a woody stalk covered with stiff **scales**, which protect the seeds under them. The activity on pages A48 and A49 shows that the scales overlap, like the scales on a fish or the shingles on a roof.

The Life Cycle of a Conifer

What happens to the seeds of cone-bearing evergreens? Some are eaten or carried away by animals. Those seeds that are lucky enough to land on good, rich soil and receive enough warmth, moisture, and sunlight can grow into trees.

One good place for a seed to fall is on a rotting log. The log is rich in things that plants need to grow. So the log nurses the tiny seed as it sprouts and develops into a seedling. A log that feeds a seedling is called a nurse log.

As a seedling's roots grow down and its branches grow out, it develops into a young conifer. The young conifer grows taller and taller and produces cones. At the proper time, the seed cones open and their seeds fall to the ground. And the life cycle of the conifer continues.

◀ White pine

◀ Blue spruce

Conifers, Water, and Fire

If you're like most people, you probably think that fire is always harmful to a tree's life cycle. You might also think that moisture is always helpful. Read on—you might be surprised at what you find out.

Everyone knows that plants need water. But sometimes, a conifer can get too much of a good thing. When the air is dry, the scales in the cones open, allowing air to enter. When there is a lot of moisture in the air, the scales close up tightly, because seeds need to be kept dry. Moisture can cause the seeds in a tightly closed cone to rot. So moisture is not always helpful.

Are forest fires always harmful? It's true that when fire hits the leafy top of a tree, the tree almost always dies. Shrubs and bushes also die. But the forest itself is not necessarily dead. In fact, some cones, such as those of the lodgepole and jack pines, actually *need* heat as hot as a

A forest fire ▲   **Soon after the fire** ▲

fire just to open. These cones remain closed until they reach a temperature as high as about 50°C (122°F). The high temperature melts the sticky pitch inside the cone, and the cone opens. Then the seeds can be scattered. Soon, some of the seeds germinate, and seedlings appear. Fire may sometimes be harmful to plants but not to cones that contain the seeds for new conifers. ■

Within a year, regrowth begins. ▶

INVESTIGATION 3 WRAP-UP

REVIEW
1. Why are evergreens always green?
2. How do conifers make and protect seeds?

CRITICAL THINKING
3. What part of a cone do you think is most like the fruit of a flowering plant? Explain your answer.
4. Explain how a forest fire can be part of the life cycle of a conifer.

How Do Plants Change During Their Life Cycles?

You already know some changes that plants make during their life cycles. In this investigation you'll find out how some plants change as they grow and how they respond to changes around them.

Activity

Sizing Up Tree Growth

MATERIALS
- metric tape measure
- *Science Notebook*

As you grow, the bones in your legs and arms get longer. What parts of a tree get longer when it grows? Find out.

Procedure

1. Look at the tree in the pictures. How did the tree change?

2. Compare the two trunks. **Record** your observations in your *Science Notebook*.

3. Compare the height of the lowest branch in each picture. **Compare** the length of the branches in each picture. **Record** your observations.

▲ Young tree

▲ Full-grown tree

4. A tree trunk grows about $2\frac{1}{2}$ cm bigger around each year. **Measure** the distance around the trunk of a tree at a height of about 120 cm off the ground. **Record** your measurement. **Estimate** the age of the tree.

 See **SCIENCE and MATH TOOLBOX** page H6 if you need to review **Using a Tape Measure or Ruler**.

5. Find out how branches grow. The place on a branch where growth is occurring is usually a different color from the rest of the branch. **Observe** some branches on two different kinds of trees. Look for color differences. Where do they occur? Remember to look at the branches, not the leaves. **Record** what you observe.

Step 4

Analyze and Conclude

1. Based on your observations, **infer** where growth occurs on a branch. What happens to the branches of a tree as the tree ages?

2. How do the trunks of most trees change as the trees age?

INVESTIGATE FURTHER!

RESEARCH

How can you tell when a tree is sick or dying? Call a tree service and find out, or research diseases of trees in an encyclopedia or a book about plants. What changes caused by disease would you look for? What might cause the death of a tree? Share your findings with your class.

Activity

A Change of Plants

Do you squint when you walk into bright light? Find out how plants respond to changes in their environment.

MATERIALS
- goggles
- 3 seedlings, each growing in a paper cup
- shoebox with a lid that has a hole in it
- plastic wrap
- tape
- *Science Notebook*

SAFETY
Wear your goggles. Wash your hands after handling seedlings.

Procedure

1. Put one seedling into a shoebox. Make sure the soil is damp. Be sure the seedling is away from the hole in the lid and that it doesn't touch the top of the box. Put the lid on the box.

Step 1

2. Use a pencil to make a small hole in a sheet of plastic wrap. The stem of a seedling should just fit through the hole. Gently pull the seedling in the second cup through the hole. Tape the plastic wrap tightly to the cup, as shown.

3. Gently turn the cup upside down. Tape the cup to the bottom of a shelf or a desktop so that the seedling hangs upside down, as shown.

4. Place the third seedling on a flat surface where it can receive light.

5. **Talk with your group** and **predict** how each seedling will look in three days. **Record** your predictions in your *Science Notebook*.

6. After three days, **observe** the seedlings. **Record** any changes you observe. To check your results, **compare** them with those of your classmates.

Analyze and Conclude

1. **Compare** your observations with your predictions. What do you think caused any changes you observed?

2. If a plant does not adjust to changes, **infer** what might happen to it.

UNIT PROJECT LINK

Sometime you might be asked to plant-sit for a friend's plants. Ask people you know if they have had any problems in caring for their plants. Find out how the problems were solved. Record the problems and solutions in a Plant-Sitter's Guide.

Technology Link
For more help with your Unit Project, go to www.eduplace.com.

Where Are You Growing?

Reading Focus How do plants adapt to different conditions?

As children get older, they get bigger. As a plant goes through its life cycle, it gets bigger, too. The stem gets taller. The roots get longer. The roots and shoots grow more branches. All plants grow in these ways.

As shown in the activity on pages A54 and A55, plants also grow in another way. Their stems get bigger around. Imagine hugging a tree. You can reach around the trunk of a young tree. But you may not be able to do this after the tree has been growing for many years.

Responding to Light

If a bright light is shined in your eyes, you'll squint. Plants respond to light, too. Have you ever seen a photograph of a field of sunflowers? You may have noticed that all the flowers are turned the same way.

Plants respond to light by growing toward it. The seedlings grew toward the light in the activity on pages A56 and A57. If a plant is placed where it gets light on only one side, the stem of the plant will bend in the direction the light is coming from.

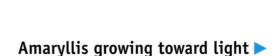

Amaryllis growing toward light ▶

Responding to Water

Plants take in water through their roots. Plant roots respond to water by growing in the direction where the water is found. For example, a willow tree is growing close to a riverbank. The tree roots that are nearer the river grow faster and in the direction of the river. The tree roots that are farther from the river are in drier soil. These roots grow very slowly.

A cactus has adaptations that help it survive in the dry desert. It has wide, shallow roots that allow it to take in rainwater quickly. A cactus also has a thick waxy stem and thin needle-like leaves. Both of these adaptations keep the plant from losing water.

Responding to a Pull

Roots and stems respond to the force of gravity, which pulls you toward Earth. Roots grow in the direction of the pull of gravity. So roots grow down. Stems grow in the direction opposite to the pull of gravity. So stems grow up. Even if you plant seeds upside down, the stems will grow up and the roots will grow down.

▲ How is a cactus adapted to the desert?

Science in Literature

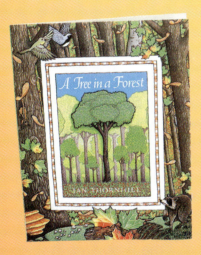

A Tree in a Forest
by Jan Thornhill
Simon & Schuster, 1991

FOREST FIRE!

"At last huge storm clouds darken the sky. Thunder grumbles through the forest. But before the rain begins to fall, a brilliant bolt of lightning slashes into a dead tree. Orange flames sweep down its trunk until they lick the dry forest floor. In an instant the flames are darting along the ground, burning up everything in their path."

To find out what happens next, read *A Tree in a Forest* by Jan Thornhill. You will learn how a 212-year-old maple tree grew and changed over its lifetime. Enjoy this amazing story about plants and animals who live together in the forest.

Plant Protection

Besides responding to light, water, and gravity, plants also respond to living things in their environment. Many plants have special adaptations that help protect them from living things that can harm them.

Quills and thorns are adaptations. Think of porcupines. They protect

▲ **Sharp thorns of musk thistle**

themselves with quills. Some plants protect themselves with thorns. Thorns seem to say, "Stay away!"

Some plants, such as poison ivy, produce chemicals that protect them. Poison ivy can cause an itchy rash on someone who handles the plant. Mature milkweed plants are harmful for cattle and sheep to eat.

Protecting the life cycle of a plant protects the species. Species that can't protect themselves may die out. ∎

▲ **Poison ivy leaves grow in threes.**

INVESTIGATION 4 WRAP-UP

REVIEW

1. Describe two ways that plants respond to gravity.

2. Give two examples of adaptations that help protect a plant.

CRITICAL THINKING

3. Scientists have put experiments on the space shuttle to see how plants grow in a weightless environment. How would roots and stems be affected? Predict some of the problems in growing seeds in space.

4. Explain one change in a plant's environment that can cause a growth change in the plant.

CHAPTER 2 REVIEW: REFLECT & EVALUATE

Word Power

Write the letter of the term that best matches the definition. *Not all terms will be used.*

1. Part of the flower that produces pollen
2. New plant that develops from an embryo
3. Woody parts of a cone
4. Part of a flower that forms around a seed
5. Part of the flower where seeds develop and grow
6. Powdery substance formed in the stamen

a. fruit
b. germinate
c. pistil
d. pollen
e. scales
f. seed coat
g. seedling
h. stamen

Check What You Know

Write the term in each pair that best completes each sentence.

1. The new developing plant is the (fruit, embryo).
2. The stamen is the part of the flower that produces (seeds, pollen).
3. A fruit is likely to contain (seeds, pollen).
4. The word *conifer* means ("evergreen," "cone-bearing").

Problem Solving

1. In the park, you notice squirrels collecting acorns, children picking flowers, and a bird building its nest. Explain which activities might help plant pollination.

2. If the conifers in a forest did not produce cones one year, how would their life cycle be affected?

On a separate sheet of paper, make a larger copy of this drawing of a flower. Color the flower parts with these colors: pistil—orange, stamen—blue, and petals—red. Label the parts.

Using Reading Skills

Finding the Main Idea

One goal in reading science is to find the important ideas and the facts that support those ideas. To find the main idea, follow clues such as the topic sentence, title, headings, or words in bold print. A topic sentence is often the first sentence of a paragraph.

Look for these clues to find the main idea.
- Topic sentence
- Title, headings
- Words in bold print

Read the paragraph below. Then complete the exercises that follow.

The Baby Book

Almost all animals come from eggs. Some animal babies develop from eggs inside their mothers' bodies. Those babies are born live. Other offspring develop from eggs outside their mothers' bodies. Those babies hatch. Whether born live or hatched, each baby develops from a single egg.

1. Write the letter of the sentence that states the main idea of the paragraph.

    a. Some animal babies develop from eggs inside their mothers' bodies.

    b. All eggs hatch outside the mother's body.

    c. Other offspring develop from eggs outside their mothers' bodies.

    d. Almost all animals come from eggs.

2. What is the important clue that helped you find the main idea?

Using Math Skills

Analyze Data

The average heights of some different types of trees are shown in this table.

Average Heights of Some Trees in the United States

Type of Tree	Height (m)
Ash	30
Birch	25
Fir	75
Oak	50
Redwood	132
Walnut	20

Use the data in the table to complete these exercises.

1. What is the difference between the average height of the tallest tree and that of the shortest tree?

2. Which tree has an average height that is three times that of the birch tree?

3. When a fir tree is 10 years old, it is about 1 m tall. Compare your height with that of a 10-year-old fir.

4. How much greater is the average height of a redwood tree than that of an oak tree?

5. Which tree has an average height that is one half the average height of the oak tree?

6. The average height of which tree is 10 m less than the average height of an ash tree?

7. What is the average height of a redwood tree rounded to the nearest hundred? to the nearest ten?

8. Write the average heights of the trees in order from least to greatest.

9. Make a bar graph of the data in the table.

A63

UNIT A WRAP-UP!

On your own, use scientific methods to investigate a question about life cycles, growth, or change.

THINK LIKE A SCIENTIST

Ask a Question

Pose a question about living things that you would like to investigate. For example, ask, "How does the color of light affect the growth of seedlings?"

Make a Hypothesis

Suggest a hypothesis that is a possible answer to the question. One hypothesis is that seedlings will grow faster under colored light than under white light.

Plan and Do a Test

Plan a controlled experiment to compare the effects of white light and blue light on seedling growth. You could start with seedlings, two lamps, and a blue filter. Develop a procedure that uses these materials to test the hypothesis. With permission, carry out your experiment. Follow the safety guidelines on pages S14–S15.

Record and Analyze

Observe carefully and record your data accurately. Make repeated observations.

Draw Conclusions

Look for evidence to support the hypothesis or to show that it is false. Draw conclusions about the hypothesis. Repeat the experiment to verify the results.

WRITING IN SCIENCE
Note Taking

As you read in science, taking notes can help you recall important ideas. Do research to find out more about the growth of seedlings. Follow these guidelines for note taking.

- Write statements in your own words.
- Use short phrases.
- State the most important facts and ideas.
- List supporting details.

Sun, Moon, and Earth

Theme: Scale

THINK LIKE A SCIENTIST
EARTHRISE B2

CHAPTER 1 Comparing Sun, Moon, and Earth B4
Investigation 1   What Is the Moon Like? B6
Investigation 2   What Is Being on the Moon Like? B18
Investigation 3   What Is the Sun Like? B24

CHAPTER 2 Motions of Earth and the Moon B32
Investigation 1   How Does Earth Move Each Day? B34
Investigation 2   How Does Earth Move
                        Throughout the Year? B42
Investigation 3   How Does the Moon Move? B50

CHAPTER 3 Effects of Earth and Moon Motions B58
Investigation 1   What Causes Seasons? B60
Investigation 2   What Are Eclipses? B72

Using Reading Skills B78
Using Math Skills B79
Unit Wrap-up! B80

Earthrise

You've probably seen a sunrise or a moonrise. That's when you first see the Sun or Moon come up over the horizon. If you circled the Moon in a spacecraft, you could watch an earthrise! Astronauts who've seen an earthrise said it was amazing to view such a large Earth rising over the Moon. And like the Moon, Earth goes through phases as shown in this photo.

THINK LIKE A SCIENTIST

Questioning In this unit you'll study how the Moon, the Sun, and Earth interact with each other. You'll investigate questions such as these.

- What Is Being on the Moon Like?
- What Causes Seasons?

Observing, Testing, Hypothesizing In the Activity "Lunar Olympics," you'll find out how high you can jump. You'll also hypothesize about what playing different sports would be like on the Moon.

Researching In the Resource "Getting Around on the Moon," you'll find out why you would weigh less on the Moon, and what the astronauts did when they visited the Moon.

Drawing Conclusions After you've completed your investigations, you'll draw conclusions about what you've learned—and get new ideas.

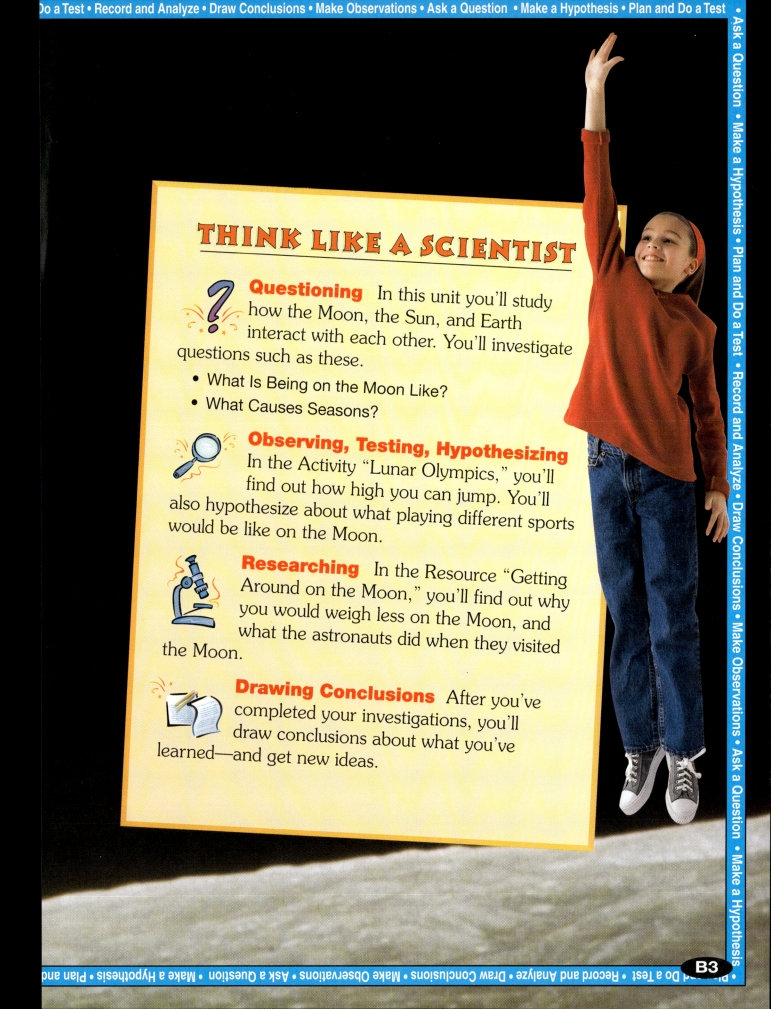

CHAPTER 1

COMPARING SUN, MOON, AND EARTH

Some scientists pick up rocks and study them. Other scientists collect and study plants and animals. But how do scientists learn about faraway objects, like the Moon and the Sun?

PEOPLE USING SCIENCE

Planetary Geologist When Adriana Ocampo was a young girl, she dreamed of building cities on other worlds. She made spacecraft out of kitchen appliances. She pretended that her dolls were astronauts.

Today, Adriana Ocampo is a planetary geologist (plan′i ter ē jē äl′ə jist). This means that she studies the soil, rocks, and features of objects in space. Planetary geologists want to know what kinds of rocks are on the Moon and the planets. Ocampo is also interested in rocks from space, called meteors (mēt′ē ərz), that sometimes strike Earth.

Be a scientist! What questions do you have about the Sun, the Moon, and our own planet Earth? Read Chapter 1 and look for answers.

GALILEO – MISSION TO JUPITER

Coming Up

INVESTIGATION 1
WHAT IS THE MOON LIKE?
.... B6

INVESTIGATION 2
WHAT IS BEING ON THE MOON LIKE?
.... B18

INVESTIGATION 3
WHAT IS THE SUN LIKE?
.... B24

◀ Adriana Ocampo, planetary geologist

INVESTIGATION 1

WHAT IS THE MOON LIKE?

What do you see when you look at the Moon? Do you imagine pictures of people or animals on its surface? In this investigation you'll learn what the Moon is *really* like.

Activity

Big Earth, Small Moon

How big is the Moon compared to Earth? This activity will help you find out.

MATERIALS
- globe
- round objects of different sizes
- string, scissors, tape
- metric tape measure
- tracing paper
- paper models of Earth and the Moon
- *Science Notebook*

Step 2

Procedure

1. Place a globe and other round objects on a table. Suppose Earth were the size of the globe. **Predict** which object would be the right size to represent the Moon. **Record** your prediction in your *Science Notebook*.

2. Your teacher will help you tape a piece of string around the middle of the globe. Have a group member cut the string so that it's the right length to wrap around the globe exactly once.

 The length of the string represents the distance around the middle of the globe.

3. Make a chart like the one shown. Then **measure** and **record** the length of the string.

Round Object	Distance Around the Object

 See **SCIENCE and MATH TOOLBOX** page H10 if you need to review **Making a Chart to Organize Data.**

4. Repeat step 2 for each round object. **Measure** and **record** the length of each string.

5. Use the pictures on this page to trace and cut out a paper model of Earth and several paper models of the Moon. Place your Moon models side by side across the middle of the Earth model. **Record** how many Moons it takes to go across Earth.

Analyze and Conclude

1. Using the models you cut out as a guide, **estimate** how much bigger across Earth is than the Moon.

2. Look at your chart of string lengths for the different objects. **Identify** the object whose string is the right length for the Moon. How did you decide which object to choose? Is it the one you predicted?

Earth

Moon

INVESTIGATE FURTHER!

EXPERIMENT

How far is the Moon from Earth? Place the globe on the floor. Place a Moon model as far away from the globe as you think it should be. To check your estimate, use the string that marks the distance around the globe. Measure nine and a half times that distance from the globe. Place the Moon model at that point.

Activity

Making Moon Craters

The Moon's surface is covered with round pits called craters. In this activity you'll discover how craters are made.

MATERIALS
- goggles
- newspaper
- sand
- baking pan
- small marble
- meterstick
- large marble
- Science Notebook

SAFETY

Wear goggles during this activity.

Procedure

1. Cover your work area with newspaper.

2. Place a 2-cm-thick layer of sand in a baking pan.

 See **SCIENCE and MATH TOOLBOX** page H6 if you need to review **Using a Tape Measure or Ruler.**

3. **Make a chart** in your *Science Notebook* like the one shown.

Height of Drop	Width of Crater

4. Drop a small marble straight down onto the sand from a height of 25 cm. **Observe** what happens.

Step 4

5. **Measure** the width of the crater you produced. **Record** the height of the drop and the width of the crater in your chart. Then carefully remove the marble.

6. Repeat steps 4 and 5, but drop the marble from each of the following heights: 50 cm, 75 cm, and 1 m. **Record** all results. **Compare** your results with those of other groups.

Step 5

7. Imagine dropping a large marble from the same height as a small marble. **Predict** how the craters will compare. Then use a large marble and a small marble to **test** your prediction. **Record** the results.

Analyze and Conclude

1. **Compare** the width of the craters when marbles of the same size were dropped from the same height. Were the craters always about the same size?

2. What can you **infer** about the relationship between the height from which a marble is dropped and the width of the crater it produces?

3. Look at the pictures of the Moon shown on pages B10 and B11. What can you **infer** about the size and speed of the objects that have struck the Moon in the past?

4. When you compared your results with those of other groups, was the data the same? What might have caused the results to differ?

UNIT PROJECT LINK

For this Unit Project you will build a model of a future base on the Moon. Using a map of the Moon, pick a place for your Moon base. Make a model of the area around your base. Include craters and mountains. Then add buildings to your Moon base.

For more help with your Unit Project, go to **www.eduplace.com**.

B9

A Place Without Air

Reading Focus How are the surface and atmosphere of the Moon different from the surface and atmosphere of Earth?

 The Moon is about 3,476 km (2,160 mi) across. Compare that with the distance across the mainland United States, which measures about 4,517 km (2,807 mi).

In the past, people observed the light and dark areas on the Moon. Some thought that the Moon looked like a ball of green cheese. You know better than to think the Moon is *really* made of cheese. What *is* the Moon made of?

A Mighty Big Rock

The Moon is a ball of gray rock covered with powdery gray soil. At about 3,476 km (2,160 mi) across, the Moon is a mighty big rock, but it is much smaller than Earth. In the activity on pages B6 and B7, a globe and different round objects are used to compare the sizes of the Moon and Earth. Earth is about four times larger than the Moon. That means if the Moon were the size of a tennis ball, Earth would be the size of a basketball.

B10

▲ Craters on the Moon

▲ This meteorite that fell to Earth is on display in Africa.

Mountains, Valleys, and Plains

Like the surface of Earth, the surface of the Moon rises and falls in mountains and valleys. The Moon's surface also has flat plains. In photos of the Moon, you can tell the mountains from the plains by differences in their brightness. Find the brightest regions in the photo on page B10. These are the hills and mountains. Find the dark areas. These are the low, flat plains.

Scientists looked through the first telescopes (tel′ə skōps) about 400 years ago. They observed the Moon's dark regions and thought they saw seas. We now know that these areas are plains, not seas. They were formed not by water but by hot, melted rock. The rock turned cold and solid long ago. Yet our ancestors' names for the dark areas remain in use today. The very first people who walked on the Moon landed on a plain. It's called the Sea of Tranquillity (tran kwil′ə tē).

How Craters Form

The activity on pages B8 and B9 shows how craters can be made by dropping marbles into sand. A **crater** is a pit shaped like a bowl. There are craters on Earth, but not as many as there are on the Moon.

Craters on the Moon formed when chunks of rock or metal fell from space and crashed on the Moon's surface. Once such pieces of space material land, they are called **meteorites** (mēt′ē ər īts). Rarely do meteorites make it to Earth. They usually burn up before reaching Earth's surface, causing "shooting stars" in the night sky.

Internet Field Trip
Visit **www.eduplace.com** to learn more about meteorites.

▲ Earth has an atmosphere.

These objects from space come in many shapes and sizes. One grain of sand is larger than the smallest meteorite. A really big meteorite can be larger than a house, but meteorites this size are very rare.

Like the meteorites that made them, some Moon craters probably can only be seen with a microscope. Others are more than 1,000 km (620 mi) across. A car traveling at highway speed would take about 11 hours to cross one of these huge craters.

It Gets Cold Without a Blanket!

Earth is surrounded by a blanket of air called the **atmosphere** (at′məs fir). This layer of gases protects living things on Earth from the Sun's most harmful rays. It also traps heat from the Sun and keeps Earth from getting too cold at night.

Earth's atmosphere allows plants and animals to live. It gives us clouds and weather. It allows us to hear sound. It makes Earth's sky look blue. It even protects us from falling meteorites.

Earth

▲ The Moon has no atmosphere.

The Moon has no atmosphere. That's why scientists have found no signs of life there. There is no air to breathe on the Moon. There is no weather. Without air, sound can't travel. So, astronauts on the Moon must use two-way radios.

Because the Moon does not have an atmosphere to protect it, the daytime temperature on the Moon's surface can rise to 104°C (220°F). Then, when the Sun goes down, the temperature drops far below freezing, as low as −173°C (−279°F). Because there's no air, the sky always looks dark from the surface of the Moon. Even in the daytime you can see stars. ■

▲ The Moon is about 384,000 km (239,000 mi) away from Earth. That means you'd have to line up about 30 Earths to reach the Moon.

Learning About Space

Reading Focus What are some ways that people can study objects in space?

Suppose you want to learn about the South Pole. One good way would be for you to visit. You'd need to bring along all your food for the trip, plus special clothing and shelter for the harsh climate. You'd need to arrange transportation and bring equipment to communicate with the outside world.

Whew! If all this work is needed to study a faraway place on Earth, how do people ever learn about the Moon and the Sun?

Astronomers and Their Tools

An **astronomer** (ə strän′ə mər) is a scientist who studies objects in space. One good thing about an astronomer's work is that it can be done without leaving Earth.

To learn about objects in space, astronomers use tools such as telescopes, cameras, computers, sound recorders, and space probes. Astronomers also study information gathered by human missions into space, including to the Moon.

A simple telescope ▼

▲ The Hubble Space Telescope

Look at the photograph of the Moon on page B10. That picture was taken through a **telescope**, a device that makes faraway objects look larger and brighter. You can see the Moon without a telescope. But even a pair of binoculars (bi näk′yə lərz), a device that looks like two small telescopes side by side, will give you a much clearer picture than you'd get with your unaided eyes.

A telescope works like a pair of eyeglasses. Both telescopes and eyeglasses use lenses, curved pieces of glass that can make objects look larger than they really are. If you wear eyeglasses, you look through lenses every day. Some kinds of telescopes use curved mirrors that make objects look larger. You may have seen a mirror like this in a fun house at an amusement park.

When people use telescopes to look into space, they must look through the atmosphere. Dust and clouds in the atmosphere often make the images hard to see. So the Hubble Space Telescope was placed into orbit above the dust and clouds. The Hubble Space Telescope is powerful. You could see the light from a firefly over 9,000 km (5,400 mi) away, using this telescope—that is, if there were fireflies in space!

INVESTIGATE FURTHER!

RESEARCH

The Hubble Space Telescope orbits Earth as do other artificial satellites. Communications satellites are used for telephones and television. Do research to compare the costs and services provided by satellite TV and cable TV. Which service would you choose? Explain your answer.

An astronaut visits a space probe that landed on the Moon. ▶

Probing Deeper

A space probe is a machine that travels through space to study what is there. Because it can get closer to the Moon and even land on it, a space probe gives a better view of the Moon than a telescope does. Like a robot, a space probe does tasks that people order it to do. Some probes take photos. Others dig into the Moon's surface to study soil.

Astronomers have also learned a lot about the Moon from human space missions. Later you'll read about the mission in which people first walked on the lunar surface. (The term *lunar* is used when referring to things about the Moon. This word comes from the Latin name for the Moon, which is *luna*.)

Science in Literature

Out of This World!

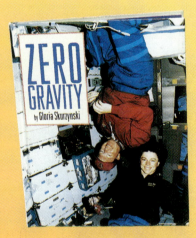

Zero Gravity
by Gloria Skurzynski
Bradbury Press, 1994

"While traveling in space, astronauts *look* different. In the absence of gravity, their body fluids move up toward the chest and head; this makes their faces puff up and their cheeks go higher. Hands swell, too."

What else happens to astronauts while they are orbiting the Earth? What is it like in the space shuttle? Find out the answers to these questions and learn more about life in space by reading the book *Zero Gravity* by Gloria Skurzynski. Come join astronauts on a fascinating journey in a space shuttle.

▲ A U.S. space station where astronauts studied the Sun

Star Light, Star Bright

The brightness of the Sun makes it harder to study than the Moon. You shouldn't look directly at the Sun, since it can badly damage your eyes. Looking at the Sun through an ordinary telescope can blind you. So astronomers use different equipment to get a close view of the Sun. For example, their telescopes have built-in cameras that take pictures of the Sun. People can then look at the photos without harming their eyes.

The Sun, like the Moon, can be viewed more closely with a space probe than with a telescope. Yet even machines can't get *too* close to the Sun. That's because its heat would destroy them! ■

INVESTIGATION 1 WRAP-UP

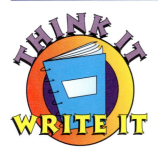

REVIEW

1. Describe two ways in which the Moon differs from Earth.

2. Why are images easier to see using the Hubble Space Telescope than using telescopes on Earth?

CRITICAL THINKING

3. Astronauts first walked on the Moon in 1969. Do you think their footprints are still there? Explain your answer.

4. In March 1998 the *Lunar Prospector* spacecraft found evidence of ice on the Moon. Do you think this means there could be life on the Moon? Explain your answer.

B17

INVESTIGATION 2

WHAT IS BEING ON THE MOON LIKE?

Imagine you live in the future and your home is on the Moon. How would your life be different than it is now? How would it be the same? In Investigation 2 you'll discover what living on the Moon might be like.

Activity

Lunar Olympics

Would you be a better gymnast or weight lifter on the Moon? Find out!

MATERIALS
- tape
- meterstick
- calculator
- heavy book
- string
- bathroom scale
- *Science Notebook*

Procedure

1. Find out how high you can jump on Earth. Stand and face a wall. Reach up and place a small piece of tape on the wall at the highest spot you can touch. Then jump up and see how high you can place a second piece of tape. Repeat the jump a few times to make sure your first jump was accurate.

2. Ask a group member to help you use a meterstick to **measure** the distance between the two pieces of tape. **Record** the result in your *Science Notebook*. The distance between the pieces of tape is the height you can jump on Earth.

Step 1

3. To learn how high you could jump on the Moon, use a calculator to **multiply** the height you can jump on Earth by six. **Record** this number.

 See SCIENCE and MATH TOOLBOX page H4 if you need to review **Using a Calculator.**

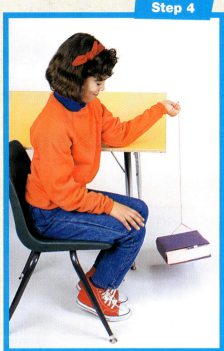

Step 4

4. Next, find out how many books you could lift on Earth. Place a heavy book on the floor next to a table. Tie a string around the book. Then with your elbow on the table, lift the book as shown. Use a scale to **measure** the weight of the book. **Record** the result.

5. Find out how much you could lift on the Moon. **Multiply** the weight of the book on Earth by six. **Record** the result.

Analyze and Conclude

1. Look at the data you've recorded. With your group, **hypothesize** what sports would be fun to play on the Moon. How might you want to change each sport's playing field or set of rules?

2. **Hypothesize** why you'd be able to play sports better on the Moon than on Earth. **Discuss** what's different about the Moon that would make this improvement possible.

INVESTIGATE FURTHER!

EXPERIMENT

Find out how far you could throw a ball on the Moon. First, throw a ball as far as you can on a playing field. Have another group member measure the distance you threw it. Then find out how far you could throw the ball on the Moon. Use a calculator to multiply the distance you threw it on Earth by 2.5.

Activity

A Moon Outing

MATERIALS
- Science Notebook

What things would you pack for a picnic on the Moon? In this activity you'll decide.

Procedure

1. Begin two lists in your *Science Notebook*. Title them "Things I Could Use on the Moon" and "Things I Could Not Use on the Moon."

2. Pretend you're going on an outdoor picnic on the Moon. Place each item at right on one of your lists.

3. Make a third list entitled "Things I Would Need on the Moon." Include things that aren't on the other two lists. Explain why you think you would need each one.

baseball and bat
bathing suit
bicycle pump
drums
fan
fishing pole
flashlight
insect repellent
kite
playground slide
playground swings
shovel
slingshot
sunglasses
umbrella
yo-yo

Analyze and Conclude

1. Look at your list of things that cannot be used on the Moon. For each item, **hypothesize** why the item wouldn't work on the Moon.

2. Based on all three of your lists, **infer** what conditions on the Moon are most important in deciding what you should bring there. **Discuss** your conclusions.

Which things could be done on the Moon? ▼

Spacesuits

Reading Focus Why do astronauts wear spacesuits on the Moon?

An astronaut is a person trained to go into space. When astronauts visit the airless Moon or take a "walk" in space, they have to wear spacesuits. A spacesuit is a set of clothing worn in space that can be tightly sealed to protect the person who wears it. Inside, each suit supplies everything a human being needs to survive.

Because of all the equipment it contains, each Moon spacesuit weighs about 91 kg (200 lb) on Earth. The same suit on the Moon would only weigh about 15 kg (33 lb).

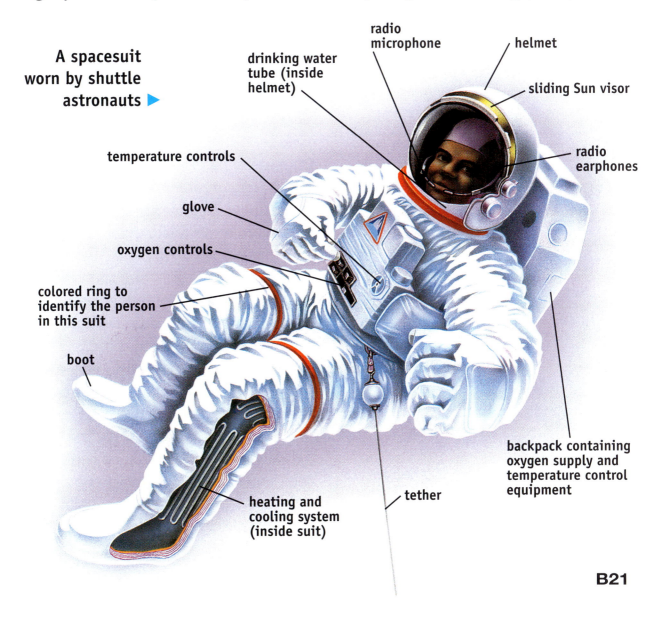

A spacesuit worn by shuttle astronauts ▶

- radio microphone
- helmet
- drinking water tube (inside helmet)
- sliding Sun visor
- radio earphones
- temperature controls
- glove
- oxygen controls
- colored ring to identify the person in this suit
- boot
- heating and cooling system (inside suit)
- tether
- backpack containing oxygen supply and temperature control equipment

B21

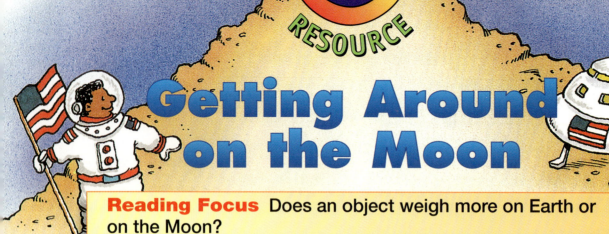

Getting Around on the Moon

Reading Focus Does an object weigh more on Earth or on the Moon?

Do you ever fly in your dreams? If so, when you awaken, it may take you a minute to realize that you can't keep right on flying out of bed! Why can't you just soar off the ground? It's because of **gravity** (grav'i tē), a pull that every object has on every other object.

The force of gravity keeps people and objects on the ground. It holds your pencil on your desk. It holds you in your chair. In space, it even holds the Moon in its place near Earth.

Jumping on the Moon

The "Lunar Olympics" activity on pages B18 and B19 shows that a person could jump six times higher on the Moon than on Earth. On the surface of Earth, gravity is six times stronger than on the surface of the Moon. That's because Earth has more mass than the Moon. Mass is the amount of material that makes up an object. The greater an object's mass, the stronger its gravity.

The force of gravity determines how much you weigh. The Moon's surface gravity is only one sixth that of Earth. So on the Moon you'd weigh only one sixth of what you weigh now. But you'd look the same.

The activity on page B20 lists some objects you use every day on Earth. Those objects would have to be used differently on the Moon. Imagine what a lunar playground would be like! You'd have an easier time going up in a playground swing, but you'd slide down a slide more slowly.

60 pounds   10 pounds

Using Math Objects weigh six times as much on Earth as they do on the Moon. How many tens are in 60?

Astronaut Buzz Aldrin jumps down from his ship in the Moon's low gravity. ▼

▲ **Astronaut Aldrin carries out experiments on the Moon.**

Moonwalkers

In 1969 two Americans, Neil Armstrong and Edwin "Buzz" Aldrin, became the first people to walk on the Moon. To learn about the Moon, they took photos, collected rocks and soil, and performed experiments. They had to go through a lot of training to learn how to do these jobs in only one sixth of the gravity they were used to on Earth.

The astronauts' visit to the Moon wasn't all work. They had a lot of fun hopping around like kangaroos in the Moon's low gravity. They had to be careful how they moved, though. What goes up must come down, even on the Moon! ■

INVESTIGATION 2 WRAP-UP

REVIEW

1. Describe the conditions on the Moon that require astronauts to wear spacesuits.

2. What holds the Moon in place near Earth?

CRITICAL THINKING

3. Explain why an astronaut on the Moon can easily carry a much heavier load than on Earth.

4. At first, when astronauts came back from walking on the Moon, they had difficulty walking on Earth. Explain why this happened.

INVESTIGATION 3

WHAT IS THE SUN LIKE?

You depend on the Sun's light to see other things. But you can't see the Sun itself very well, because looking directly at it can hurt your eyes. In this investigation you'll find out what the Sun is like up close.

Activity

Big Star, Small Earth

How big is the Sun? How far away is it? Compare Earth and the Sun in this activity.

MATERIALS
- paper model of the Sun
- drawing paper
- metric tape measure
- tape
- string
- Science Notebook

Procedure

1. Imagine that the Sun is the size of the model shown in the photo. **Draw** a circle to show how big you think a model of Earth should be. **Measure** the width of your circle and **record** the measurement in your Science Notebook.

2. Compare your estimate with those of other group members.

 Math Hint: To compare numbers, first line up the places of the numbers. Then compare the digits in each place, starting with the greatest place.

Step 1

B24

Step 5

3. Your teacher will tell you what size your Earth model should really be. **Record** the correct size. On a sheet of paper, **draw** a circle the size your teacher told you. Label this circle *Earth*.

4. Have a member of your group hold the Sun model at one end of a large open area. **Discuss** how far away the Earth model should be. Take your Earth model and stand that distance away from the Sun model. Have another group member **measure** the distance between the two models. **Record** the measurement.

 See **SCIENCE** and **MATH TOOLBOX** page H6 if you need to review **Using a Tape Measure or Ruler.**

5. Tape one end of a piece of string that is 59 m long to the Earth model. Tape the string's other end to the Sun model. Hold the models 59 m apart. This is how far apart Earth and the Sun would be if they were the sizes of the models.

Analyze and Conclude

1. How close was your drawing in step 1 to the size of the Earth model in step 3? What can you **infer** from this about the size of the real Sun?

2. How close was your guess in step 4 to the distance between the Earth and Sun models in step 5? What can you **infer** about the real distance between Earth and the Sun?

3. How did using models help you learn about the Sun's size and distance from Earth?

INVESTIGATE FURTHER!

Use the **Science Processor CD-ROM**, *Sun, Moon, and Earth* (Unit Opening, Which Is Which?; Investigation 1, Big and Small; Investigation 2, Earth and Moon) to compare characteristics and sizes of the Sun, Moon, and Earth.

Activity
Making Sunspots

Dark spots on the Sun were first observed more than 400 years ago. In this activity you'll make a model of sunspots.

MATERIALS
- goggles
- iron filings
- paper plate
- horseshoe magnet
- *Science Notebook*

SAFETY
Wear goggles during this activity. Don't try to look at real sunspots on the Sun.

Procedure

1. To **make a model** of sunspots, first sprinkle iron filings onto a paper plate so that they thinly cover the surface.

2. Have one group member hold the plate level. A second group member should hold a horseshoe magnet under the raised plate so that both ends of the magnet touch the plate's bottom.

3. Gently move the magnet around under the plate until all the iron filings have been collected.

4. **Observe** the plate from above. **Draw** a picture of what you see in your *Science Notebook*. Show where the filings are.

Step 2

Analyze and Conclude

1. **Compare** your drawing of the iron filings with the photograph of sunspots on page B30. Make a list of things that look the same. How is this model different from the photograph of the sunspots?

2. **Hypothesize** what might cause similar shapes to form in the iron filings and on the surface of the Sun.

Sun Power

Reading Focus What is the Sun and how does it help life on Earth?

A **sunspot** is a dark spot on the surface of the Sun.

A **prominence** is a huge loop of gas that appears on the edge of the Sun.

A **flare** is a bright area on the surface of the Sun.

▲ Features on the Sun

It's hot enough to melt any metal. It's so far away that its light takes eight minutes to reach your eyes. If it were a hollow ball, more than 1 million Earths could fit inside it. Do you know its name? It's the Sun!

Our Star

Like the twinkling dots that we see in the night sky, the Sun is a star. Compared to other stars, the Sun isn't very large. But to us it looks much bigger than the others because it's by far the closest star to Earth.

The activity on pages B24 and B25 shows that compared to Earth the Sun is huge!

A **star** is a ball of hot gases that gives off energy. Every day you experience two forms of energy given off by the Sun. You see its light, and you feel its heat.

The Sun is *very* hot. On the Sun's surface the temperature is about 5,500°C (9,900°F). When scientists speak about the surface of the Sun, they mean the top of the main body of its thickest gases.

B27

Features on the Sun

Astronomers can see different features that come and go on the surface of the Sun. There are dark spots known as sunspots and bright spots known as flares. There are huge loops of gas known as prominences. The picture on page B27 shows what these features look like.

In the activity on page B26, a magnet is used to make iron filings form a pattern. This pattern is similar to a region of sunspots. A sunspot region acts like a magnet, with north pole spots and south pole spots. These spots appear dark because they are cooler than surrounding areas of the Sun.

You Can't Live Without It

What are your favorite foods? Whatever your answer is, those foods come from the Sun. How is this so? Plants make their own food. To do this, they use sunlight. Some animals eat these plants. Other animals eat animals that eat plants.

Without sunlight, plants could not make food and they would die. The animals that eat plants—and the animals that eat those animals—would starve.

Almost all living things depend on the Sun for their food, as well as for heat and light. Life on Earth could not exist without it! ■

Almost all living things depend on the Sun for their food. ▶

Solar Storms

Reading Focus What are the effects of solar storms on Earth?

▲ A solar prominence

 You have probably seen electrical storms on Earth. What are some signs of such a storm? They include dark clouds, lightning, and thunder. The Sun also has storms—not storms of snow, wind, or rain, but storms of energy. These are called magnetic storms. That's because they are created by the pull of magnetic forces in the Sun.

Suppose you asked an astronomer to name some signs of a solar magnetic storm. (The term *solar* is used to refer to things related to the Sun.) The astronomer would say that sunspots, flares, and prominences are signs of solar storms.

Fireworks From Space

Do you think that storms on the Sun can affect things on Earth? You bet they can! On many nights, a beautiful display of light can be seen in the sky near Earth's North and South Poles. These two shimmering, colorful displays are called the northern lights and the southern lights. Solar storms produce these "fireworks." During the storms, invisible particles are given off by the Sun. When these particles reach Earth, they cause gases in Earth's atmosphere to glow.

The northern lights, as seen from the ground ▼

B29

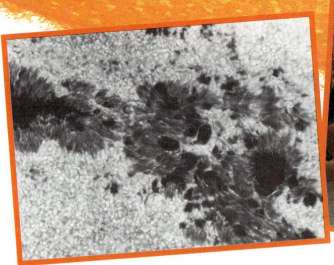

▲ Sunspots

▲ The northern lights, as seen from space

Dangers of Solar Storms

People who live in the Canadian province of Quebec will long remember ten days in March 1989. During that period, light bulbs went out. Elevators came to a halt between floors. Because televisions and radios went silent, it was hard to find out what was going on.

A giant solar flare had sent high-energy particles and radiation streaming out of the Sun toward Earth. The high-energy particles disturbed the running of electrical equipment. The result was a power blackout across Quebec as well as other problems all over the world.

A major flare like this one can harm astronauts if it catches them during a space flight. But smaller solar storms often give astronauts a spectacular view of the northern and southern lights—as seen from space! ■

Internet Field Trip
Visit **www.eduplace.com** to take a self-guided tour of the Sun.

INVESTIGATION 3 WRAP-UP

REVIEW

1. Describe the Sun. Include the three features that are signs of solar storms.

2. List several ways in which the Sun affects Earth.

CRITICAL THINKING

3. In the sky, the Sun and the Moon appear to be about the same size. Describe their real sizes. Which of the two objects is farther from Earth?

4. Write a brief science-fiction story about what would happen if Earth began to move closer to the Sun.

REFLECT & EVALUATE

Word Power

Write the letter of the term that best matches the definition. *Not all terms will be used.*

1. Material from space that lands on Earth
2. Pit shaped like a bowl
3. Device that makes faraway objects look larger
4. Pull that every object has on every other object
5. Ball of hot gases that give off energy
6. Scientist who studies objects in space

a. astronomer
b. atmosphere
c. crater
d. gravity
e. meteorite
f. star
g. sunspot
h. telescope

Check What You Know

Write the term in each pair that best completes each sentence.

1. The Moon has no (gravity, atmosphere).
2. A dark area on the surface of the Sun is a (flare, sunspot).
3. The force of gravity determines your (height, weight).
4. A bright area on the surface of the Sun is a (prominence, flare).

Problem Solving

1. If an object on the Moon weighs 42 pounds, how much would that same object weigh on Earth? Why?
2. What are some reasons that life can exist on Earth but not on the Moon? How are astronauts on the Moon provided with the things they need to stay alive?

Copy this drawing. Label each numbered feature on your drawing. Then describe each feature. How can these features affect Earth?

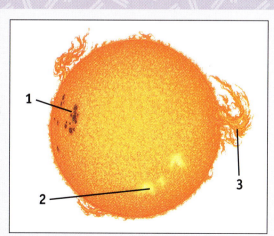

CHAPTER 2

MOTIONS OF EARTH AND THE MOON

"Twinkle, twinkle, little star, how I wonder what you are." Writers of poems, stories, and songs often describe what they see in the sky. Why are the Sun, Moon, and stars so interesting to writers and their readers?

Connecting to Science
CULTURE

Stars to Freedom More than 100 years ago in the United States, some people helped enslaved African Americans escape to freedom. One who helped was a one-legged man named Peg Leg Joe. He taught them a song called "Follow the Drinking Gourd." A gourd is a type of vegetable. People drank from hollowed-out gourds. Peg Leg Joe's song about the gourd, however, held a secret message.

One arrangement of stars in the night sky looks like a drinking gourd. Two of these stars point to the North Star. In this chapter you'll learn why the North Star is always found in the north. The secret message in the song was, "Follow the stars to the north." How did this help people travel to freedom?

Coming Up

INVESTIGATION 1
HOW DOES EARTH MOVE EACH DAY?
.... B34

INVESTIGATION 2
HOW DOES EARTH MOVE THROUGHOUT THE YEAR?
.... B42

INVESTIGATION 3
HOW DOES THE MOON MOVE?
.... B50

◀ Following the "drinking gourd" to freedom

How Does Earth Move Each Day?

Have you ever wondered why the Sun seems to move across the sky during the day? Or why the Moon and stars seem to change position overnight? In this investigation you'll explore changes in the sky that help explain how Earth moves.

Activity

A Shadow Stick Sundial

How does the Sun appear to move throughout the day? Watch a shadow to find out.

MATERIALS
- goggles
- magnetic compass
- straight stick or rod
- large sheet of paper
- black marker
- clay
- flashlight
- *Science Notebook*

SAFETY
Wear goggles during this activity. Never look directly at the Sun.

Procedure

1. On a sunny day, go outdoors with a magnetic compass, a straight stick or rod, and a large sheet of paper.

2. Using the stick, punch a hole in the center of the paper and then into the ground, as shown. Use the magnetic compass to find *north*, *south*, *east*, and *west*. Use a marker to write these directions on the paper.

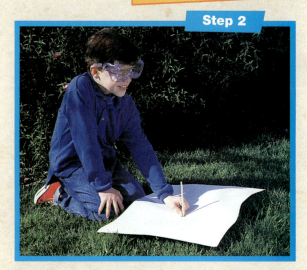

Step 2

B34

3. Locate the shadow of the stick on the paper. Use a marker to draw a line down the middle of the shadow. Make your line the same length as the shadow. **Label** your line with the time of day.

See **SCIENCE and MATH TOOLBOX** page H12 if you need to review **Measuring Elapsed Time.**

4. Repeat step 3 every hour for as long as you can. You have now made a sundial.

5. Go indoors and re-create your sundial, using a base of clay to hold the stick in position. Have your teacher darken the room.

6. Move a flashlight around your drawing until you can re-create each shadow that you drew outside. For each shadow, **observe** whether the flashlight is to the north, south, east, or west of your drawing. Note whether you have to hold the flashlight high or low.

7. In your *Science Notebook*, **draw** a copy of your sundial. Add a little picture of the Sun to show where you had to put the flashlight to re-create each shadow.

Analyze and Conclude

1. Is the Sun high or low in the sky when the shadows are the longest?

2. **Infer** in what direction the Sun appears to move across the sky throughout the day.

3. **Suggest a hypothesis** that would explain the way the Sun appears to move. What observations did you make during this activity that support your hypothesis? What else might explain what you observed?

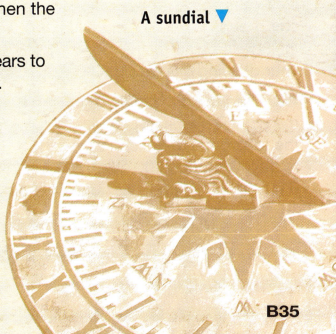

A sundial ▼

Activity

Making a Star Clock

MATERIALS
- copy of star clock patterns
- scissors
- paper fastener
- *Science Notebook*

Before people had clocks, they used the stars to tell time. In this activity you'll build your own star clock and use it to see how stars move during the night.

Procedure

1. Cut out the star clock's wheel and base.

2. Place the wheel on top of the base and fasten them together with a paper fastener through their centers, as shown.

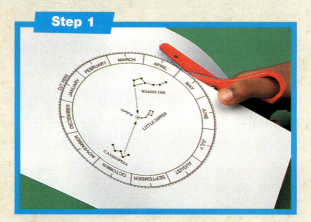
Step 1

3. The wheel tells the date, and the base tells the time. Set the mid-November point on the wheel next to the 6:00 P.M. point on the base.

4. The star clock now shows the positions in the sky of the Big Dipper, the Little Dipper, and Cassiopeia (kas ē ō pē′ə) at 6:00 P.M. in mid-November. **Draw** the positions of these star groups in your *Science Notebook*. Include the star Polaris (pō lar′is). **Label** your drawing *6:00 P.M.*

Step 2

5. Use your star clock to **predict** how the Big Dipper, the Little Dipper, Cassiopeia, and Polaris would look at the following times during the rest of that same night in mid-November: 9:00 P.M., 12:00 midnight, 3:00 A.M., 6:00 A.M. **Draw** and **label** each of your predictions.

People have imagined seeing pictures among the stars. What do you see when you look at these star groups? ▶

Analyze and Conclude

1. Study all five drawings. **Describe** how the Big Dipper moves during the night. Then use the pattern to **describe** how the Little Dipper and Cassiopeia move.

2. What did you observe about the position of the star Polaris during the night?

3. How long would it take the Big Dipper to circle the sky one complete time?

4. **Infer** how people could have used the pattern of the Big Dipper's movement to tell time.

5. Real stars appear to move the same way the stars on your star clock do. **Discuss** with your group what might cause these star motions. **Hypothesize** what might be happening that would make the stars appear to move.

INVESTIGATE FURTHER!

Use the **Science Processor CD-ROM**, *Sun, Moon, and Earth* (Investigation 3, What Is a Day?) to see how Earth's rotation causes the Sun to appear to move across the sky during a 24-hour cycle.

The Rotating Earth

Reading Focus How does the rotation of the Earth cause the cycle of day and night?

We say that the Sun rises in the east, sets in the west, and moves across the sky in between. When we say this, we are describing what we see. We aren't describing what really happens, though! The Sun just *looks* like it is moving because *Earth* is moving.

Around and Around We Go

You can't feel Earth's movement. To you, the ground feels perfectly still. Your home seems to stay in the same place day and night. Yet you are riding on the surface of a spinning Earth.

Scientists call this spinning motion **rotation** (rō tā′shən). The picture on the next page shows some important things about how Earth rotates. Notice the line that runs through Earth's North and South Poles in the picture. This make-believe line is called an **axis** (ak′sis). Earth spins like a top on its axis.

It takes 24 hours for Earth to spin all the way around—that is, to make one whole rotation. That's why there are 24 hours in one day.

As Earth rotates, one side of Earth faces the Sun while the other side faces away from the Sun. When your side of Earth faces the Sun, it's daytime. When your side of Earth turns away from the Sun, it's nighttime.

Look at the picture on page B39. Find the arrow that shows the direction of Earth's rotation. Find the spot that's marked, "Pretend you are here."

The Sun is setting. Is the photographer facing west or east? ▼

Picture yourself standing in that spot, looking at the sky. As Earth rotates once a day from west to east, you'll see the Sun, the Moon, and the stars seem to move across the sky from east to west.

The North Star

There's one star that hardly seems to move at all. Its name is Polaris. Notice that Polaris lies almost exactly over Earth's North Pole. That's why Polaris is known as the North Star.

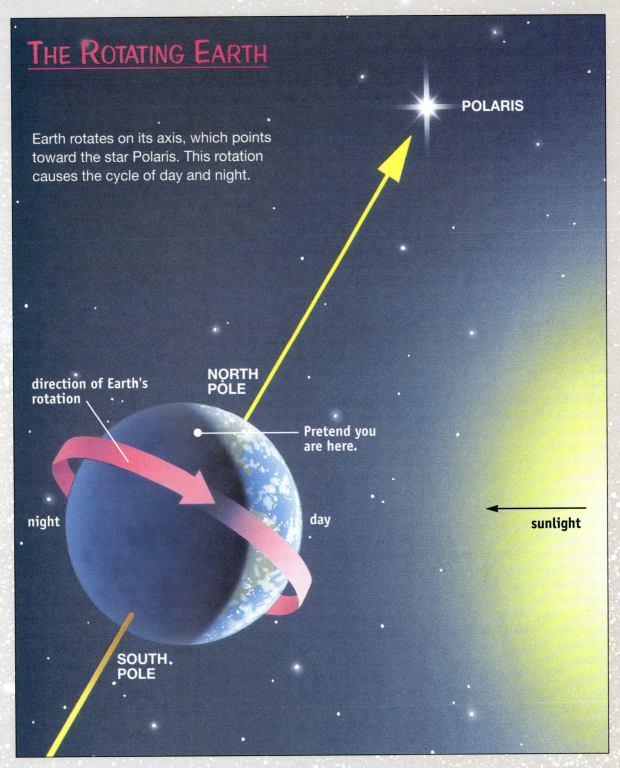

The Rotating Earth

Earth rotates on its axis, which points toward the star Polaris. This rotation causes the cycle of day and night.

All the other northern stars seem to spin counterclockwise around Polaris as Earth turns. This effect is shown by the star clock in the activity on pages B36 and B37.

If you lived in Australia or southern Africa, you'd see all the southern stars seem to spin around a point in space directly above the South Pole. But, there's no bright star right at that spot that people can call the South Star.

Find Your Way Home

The drawing below shows where you can find Polaris in the sky. It's in the star pattern called the Little Dipper. Find Polaris at the end of the dipper's "handle."

You can find Polaris by imagining a line from the two "pointer" stars in the Big Dipper. ▼

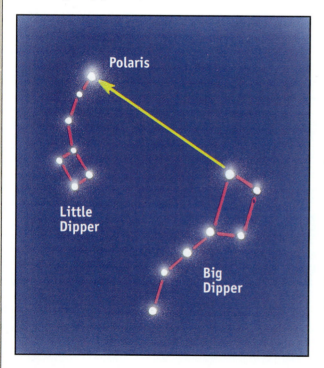

Italian clock

Chinese sundial

If you can locate Polaris, what direction can you find? North, of course! And if you know which way is north, you can then figure out all the other directions.

For hundreds of years, sailors have used Polaris to find their way home and steer different courses. Campers often use Polaris to find directions. Even the most modern spacecraft still steer by the stars.

Telling Time

Have you ever been outdoors playing and noticed that the Sun seemed to be very low in the sky? Did you think then that it was getting late and that you'd better hurry home? If you've ever had something like this happen, you've been using the Sun to tell time.

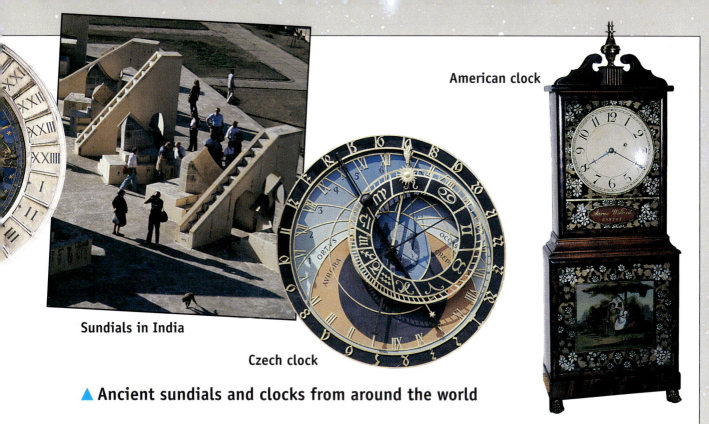

Sundials in India

Czech clock

American clock

▲ Ancient sundials and clocks from around the world

Earth's 24-hour rotation is the basis for the way we tell time. Before there were clocks, everyone used to tell time by the motion of the Sun and the stars across the sky. During the day, many people used sundials like the one that is made in the activity on pages B34 and B35. A sundial is a device that tells time by tracking shadows that the Sun makes. The shadows change as the Sun seems to move across the sky.

Even after people started to build clocks, they still had to check their work against the Sun and stars. Today's clocks keep very exact time. But scientists still check them against objects in the sky. There'd be a lot of confusion if our clocks didn't match the way that Earth moves! ■

 Internet Field Trip
Visit **www.eduplace.com** to find out more about sundials.

INVESTIGATION 1 WRAP-UP

REVIEW

1. What causes day and night?
2. Why is Polaris known as the North Star?

CRITICAL THINKING

3. Just before you go to bed at night, you see a certain star in the east. The next morning, just before dawn, you see the same star in the west. Explain what happened to make the star's position seem to change.

4. If Earth did not rotate, how would day and night be different?

How Does Earth Move Throughout the Year?

Does Earth's rotation on its axis explain the length of the year? Or does Earth also move in other ways? To find out, observe some more ways in which the Sun and the stars appear to move.

Activity

Sun Paths

Does the Sun follow the same path across the sky every day of the year? Find out!

MATERIALS
- Science Notebook

Procedure

1. Look at the pictures. They show the Sun's path across the sky on four different days during the year.

2. Use the pictures to provide the information asked for in steps 3 and 4. **Record** your response in your *Science Notebook*.

3. Name the months in which the Sun appears highest in the sky and lowest in the sky.

4. Name the month in which the Sun follows the longest path across the sky. Name the month in which it follows the shortest path.

Analyze and Conclude

1. Hypothesize what effects the changing path of the Sun would have throughout the year. How would the height that the Sun reaches and the length of its path affect conditions on the ground?

2. Infer which month is the hottest in the place shown in the pictures. **Infer** which month is the coldest. Explain your answers.

3. Infer whether the four months pictured all have the same number of hours of daylight. If not, which month has the longest day? Which has the shortest? Give reasons for your answers.

4. Do the motions of Earth that you've learned about so far explain why the Sun's path across the sky would change as it does in these pictures? **Hypothesize** what might cause such changes.

September

December

Activity

Constellations Through the Year

Does Earth move in some way besides rotating on its axis? This activity will help you find out.

MATERIALS
- lamp
- stool
- drawings of the constellations Leo, Scorpius, Pegasus, and Orion
- *Science Notebook*

SAFETY

Don't touch the lamp. You could burn yourself. Use caution when walking around the lamp cord.

Procedure

1. Place a lighted lamp on top of a stool. This represents the Sun.

2. Have four group members each hold one of the four drawings that your teacher will provide. These drawings show different constellations (kän stə lā'shənz), or star patterns.

3. The four group members should stand as shown. Have a fifth group member pretend to be Earth and stand anywhere inside the circle.

Step 3

4. The constellation Leo can be seen from the United States in springtime. **Discuss** where Earth would have to stand inside the circle to see the picture of Leo. Remember that stars can be seen only at night. Then have Earth stand where you think it should be. Make sure that Earth can see Leo.

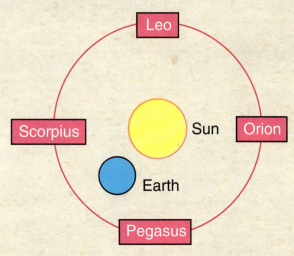

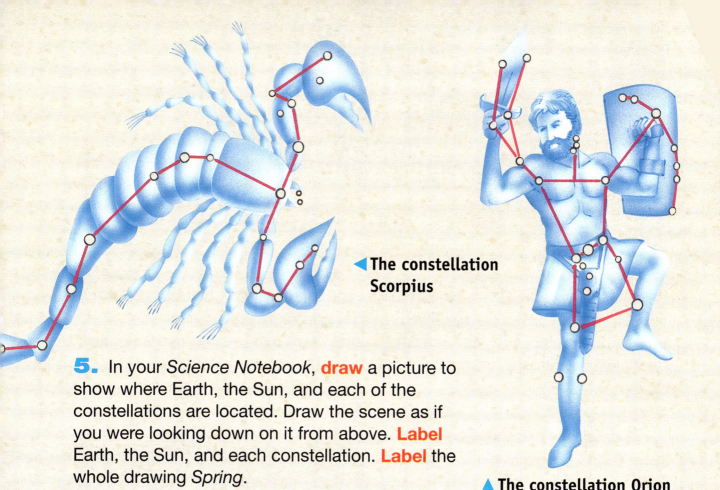

◀ The constellation Scorpius

▲ The constellation Orion

5. In your *Science Notebook*, **draw** a picture to show where Earth, the Sun, and each of the constellations are located. Draw the scene as if you were looking down on it from above. **Label** Earth, the Sun, and each constellation. **Label** the whole drawing *Spring*.

6. The constellation Scorpius can be seen in the summer. Decide where Earth should stand to see Scorpius. Try it out, then **draw** a picture as you did in step 5. **Label** the new picture *Summer*.

7. Pegasus can be seen in fall. Orion can be seen in winter. Decide where Earth should stand to see these constellations. **Draw** pictures labeled *Fall* and *Winter* that show these positions.

8. Think about where Earth stood to see the constellations in spring, summer, fall, and winter. Look at your four drawings to help you remember. Take turns walking from one position to the next until everyone has been to all four.

Analyze and Conclude

1. Based on your findings, **infer** how Earth moves during the year in relation to the Sun.

2. Explain how Earth's motion causes different constellations to be seen in different seasons.

INVESTIGATE FURTHER!

EXPERIMENT

Look up the names of the four constellations in this activity. Find out where each name came from and what it means. Then, with a parent's permission, go outside on a clear night and try to find the constellation or constellations that can be seen at this time of year.

Earth Moves Around the Sun

Reading Focus How does Earth's revolution around the Sun affect which constellations can be seen?

Native Americans who lived on the Great Plains observed that the Sun's path changes during the year. The Native Americans knew that the Sun's path followed a regular pattern. The pattern takes about 365 days to complete—and then it begins again. Our yearly 365-day calendar in based on the same pattern that the Native Americans observed.

Earth Circles As It Spins

Scientists too learn things by observing the Sun. They've figured out that the Sun's changing path shows something about Earth's motion. As Earth rotates on its axis, it also **revolves** (ri välvz′) around the Sun. This means that it travels around the Sun along its own path, called an **orbit** (ôr′bit). Earth's orbit is shaped roughly like a circle.

It takes Earth a year to complete one revolution around the Sun. In Chapter 3 you'll learn why this motion makes the Sun's path across the sky appear to change over the course of a year.

In the activity on pages B44 and B45, the person who pretends to be Earth sees a different **constellation**, or nighttime star pattern, at each season of the year. That too is a result of Earth's revolution around the Sun.

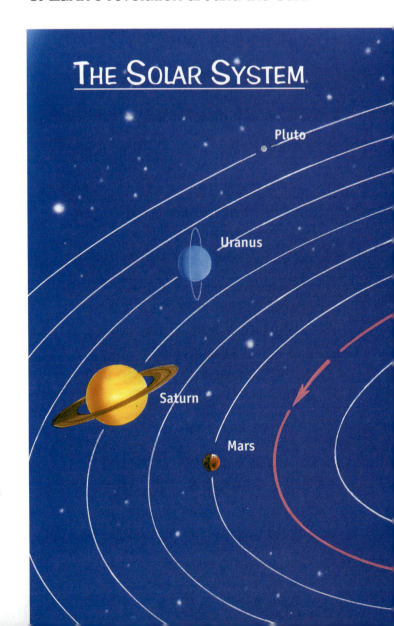

THE SOLAR SYSTEM

As Earth rotates, its night side faces away from the Sun. As Earth revolves around the Sun, that night side looks toward different parts of space at different times of the year. For that reason we see different constellations.

Our Solar System

Planets also move across the night sky. A **planet** is a large body that circles a star and doesn't give off light as a star does. Planets move across the night sky not only because of Earth's rotation, but because each planet is revolving around the Sun, too. Because of rotation and revolution, the nighttime sky changes all the time.

Look at the picture below. Earth is one of the nine known planets that revolve around the Sun. Together, the Sun and all the objects that orbit it make up our **solar system**. The planets in our solar system include Mercury, which is the planet closest to the Sun. Next to Mercury is Venus, then comes Earth, Mars, Jupiter, Saturn, Uranus, Neptune, and Pluto. How can you remember the planets in order from the Sun?

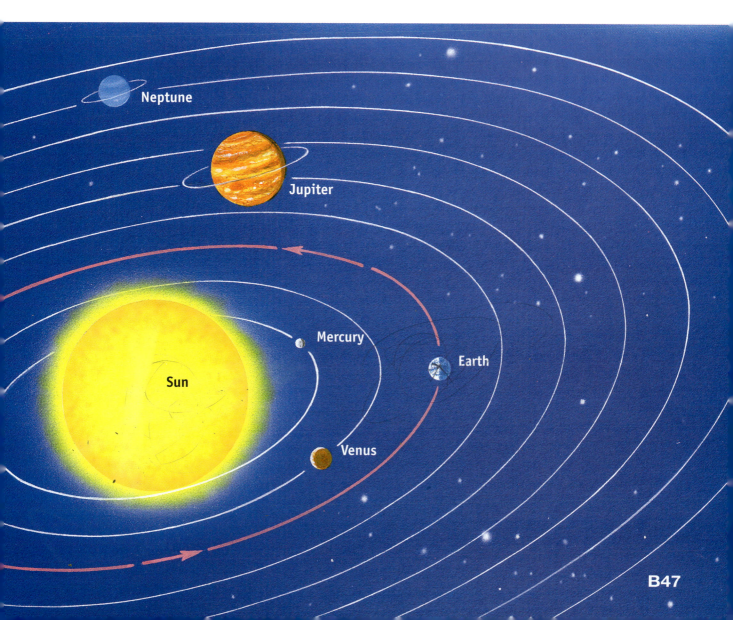

Earth and Sun— Ideas Through Time

Reading Focus What did early scientists think about how the Earth, the Sun, and the stars move?

People didn't always know that Earth revolves around the Sun. It took people a long time to figure out this fact. After all, we don't feel our planet moving through space. All we can tell from Earth is that the Sun and stars appear to move across the sky.

It's not surprising that early scientists thought Earth was standing still. In fact most of them thought that the Sun and stars revolved around Earth.

Aryabhata I, a mathematician in India, says that Earth rotates on its axis. But he still thinks the rotating Earth stays in one spot.

497

Most ancient societies—including those in China, Egypt, and India—think that Earth is flat and unmoving. The Sun and stars are thought to move across the dome of the sky.

3000 B.C.

A.D. 145
Ptolemy, an astronomer in Egypt, makes famous the hypothesis that Earth is round and that the Sun and other sky objects revolve around this unmoving Earth. Ptolemy's model is the one that most scientists accept for more than 1,000 years.

Through the years, however, different scientists developed better ways to explain the movements they saw in the sky. They formed different theories about Earth's relationship to the Sun. They based these theories on observations made with better tools. Some of those scientists and their ideas are shown in this time line. ■

1543
Nicolaus Copernicus, a Polish astronomer, challenges Ptolemy's theory. He says that the Sun is at the center of the solar system and that Earth and other planets revolve around the Sun. It takes a long time for people to accept this idea.

900
Al-Battani, an Arab astronomer, takes more careful measurements of the positions of the Sun, stars, and other objects in the sky. He realizes that Ptolemy's model doesn't fit all the movements he observes, but he doesn't propose a new theory.

INVESTIGATE FURTHER!

RESEARCH
Find out more about the theories of Ptolemy and Copernicus. Compare the two theories as to their strengths and weaknesses.

INVESTIGATION 2 WRAP-UP

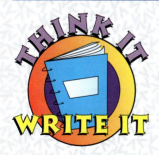

REVIEW

1. What effect does Earth's revolution have on the constellations seen from Earth?

2. Describe how Earth moves during the course of a year. Why is a year about 365 days long?

CRITICAL THINKING

3. How is Earth's revolution different from its rotation?

4. Why do you think people did not want to believe Copernicus when he first said that Earth revolved around the Sun?

How Does the Moon Move?

You've seen that the length of a day comes from Earth's rotation on its axis. You know that the length of a year comes from Earth's revolution around the Sun. Now you can investigate changes in the sky that occur over the course of a month.

Activity

Moon Phases

What makes the Moon change its appearance over the course of a month? In this activity you'll use models to find out.

MATERIALS
- bright lamp or flashlight
- white plastic-foam ball
- **Science Notebook**

SAFETY
Don't touch the lamp. You could burn yourself.

Procedure

1. Your teacher will turn off all the lights in a room except for one bright lamp or flashlight. This light will be a model of the Sun.

2. Stand in front of the Sun model. Hold a white plastic-foam ball at arm's length in front of you, as shown. This ball will be a model of the Moon.

Step 2

B50

3. Turn in place slowly and **observe** how the shaded part and the lighted part of your Moon model (ball) change. Try to make your Moon model look like each of the lettered pictures below. You can turn around in place as much as you wish, but stay in the same spot in front of the Sun model.

4. In your *Science Notebook,* **make a chart** like the one shown.

	A	B	C	D
How the Moon looks to me	●	◐	○	◑
How I was standing				

 See **SCIENCE and MATH TOOLBOX** page H10 if you need to review **Making a Chart to Organize Data.**

5. In your chart, **make a drawing** to show how you were standing when you saw that Moon. Draw the positions of the model Sun, model Moon, and yourself.

Analyze and Conclude

1. The light in this activity represents the Sun. The ball represents the Moon. **Identify** the object that you represent.

2. Based on your experiment, **infer** one way that the Moon moves in space.

3. If you continued to turn in circles, what pattern would you observe happening to the shaded parts and lighted parts of the ball?

UNIT PROJECT LINK

What would days and nights be like at your Moon base? Draw a dot on the Moon ball to show where your Moon base is. Then repeat step 3 of the activity to find out.

For more help with your Unit Project, go to www.eduplace.com.

Your Changing View of the Moon

Reading Focus What causes the phases of the Moon?

In the way that they move, Earth and the Moon are very much alike. Earth rotates on its axis and revolves around the Sun. In a similar way, the Moon rotates on its axis and revolves around Earth.

The Moon's Same Old Face

There's one special thing about the way the Moon rotates and revolves. It has to do with the time it takes for the Moon to make one complete rotation and one complete revolution.

For Earth, those two time periods are very different. It takes Earth 24 hours for one rotation. But it takes about 365 days for one revolution. The Moon takes the same amount of time to rotate once on its axis as it takes to revolve once around Earth—about 27 days.

The same side of the Moon always faces Earth (*below*). You never see the Moon's far side (*inset*).

To see what effect this has, look at the drawing on page B52. You can tell by the little flag in the picture that the Moon has rotated exactly once in the same time that it's revolved around Earth exactly once. But the flag has stayed facing Earth all that time!

That's what happens with the real Moon. The same side of it always faces Earth. Only astronauts have ever seen the far side of the Moon. Other people can only look at the far side in pictures.

Going Through Phases

If you were asked to draw a picture of the Moon, what would you draw? Would you show a Moon that looks like a full circle or only part of a circle? If you think about it, you'll realize that these are both correct ways to draw the Moon. Sometimes the Moon is full. At other times it looks like a crescent—a thin slice of a circle.

The changing shapes of the Moon that can be seen from Earth are known as **phases** of the Moon. These phases are modeled in the activity on pages B50 and B51.

Phases of the Moon occur because the Moon, like Earth, has day and night. As the Moon circles Earth, people on Earth see different amounts of the daylit half of the Moon.

Science in Literature

Zero Gravity Fun

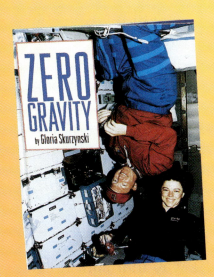

Zero Gravity
by Gloria Skurzynski
Bradbury Press, 1994

"When you jump on a bed, why don't you fly up to the ceiling and stay there? What makes you sink back down onto the mattress? It's a force called gravity. . . . Earth's gravity is felt far away, even farther away than our moon, which is about 240,000 miles from Earth. Our moon is held in its orbit by Earth's gravity."

If you've ever wondered what it would be like to live without gravity, then read the book *Zero Gravity*, by Gloria Skurzynski.

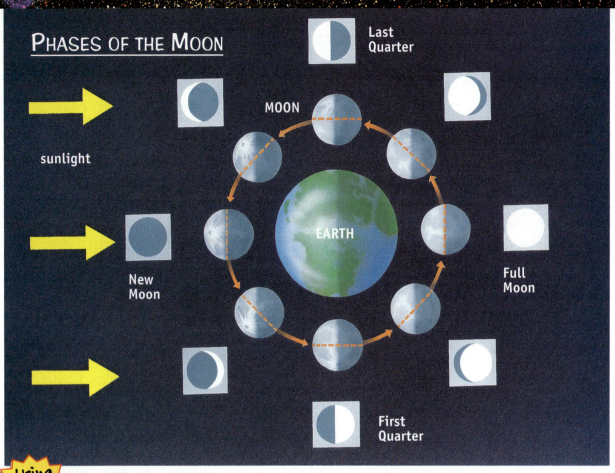

Using Math: The Moon goes through all of its phases in about 29 days. About how many full moons are there in one year? Use a calculator.

Sometimes you see only a tiny sliver of the daylit half of the Moon. When the Moon is full, you see the entire daylit half. You can understand phases better by looking at the drawing. Picture yourself standing on Earth to view the Moon in each position shown. What you see from Earth is shown in each box.

One thing you'll notice in the drawing is something called a new Moon. It's impossible to see a new Moon. That's because a new Moon occurs when the side of the Moon facing Earth receives no sunlight at all.

By the Light of the Moon?

A popular song of many years ago talked about dancing "by the light of the Moon." Can people really do anything by the light of the Moon? Not exactly.

It should be clear to you now that the Moon doesn't produce any light of its own as the Sun does. You can only see the Moon because sunlight bounces off or reflects off its surface into your eyes. This is similar to the way that light reflects off a mirror. So even on a moonlit night, you're really dancing by the light of the Sun!

The Moon: Fact and Fiction

Reading Focus How does the Moon affect Earth?

For thousands of years, people have seen pictures in the Moon. The ancient Chinese saw a rabbit and a toad. Some Europeans saw a crab. The Vikings saw a boy and girl in the Moon who they said were kidnapped when they went to get a pail of water. The boy and girl were Jack and Jill.

In the United States, people talk about "the man in the Moon." But many cultures, including the Maori (mä′ō rē) people of New Zealand, see a woman in the Moon instead.

It was once thought that the full Moon could cause strange behavior. The words *lunacy*, *loony*, and *moonstruck* come from this belief!

Look for the imaginary pictures in each Moon. ▼

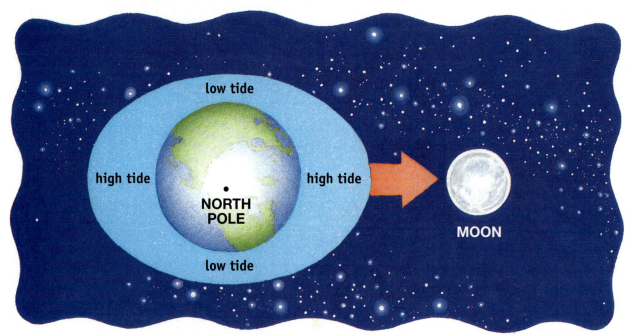

▲ The Moon's gravity causes Earth's tides.

The Real Power of the Moon

The Moon really does affect some things on Earth—the tides. Tides are the rising and falling of ocean water along coastlines.

Tides are caused by the gravity of the Moon. As Earth rotates on its axis, different sides of Earth face the Moon. The Moon's gravity pulls on the oceans on the side of Earth closest to the Moon, causing a high tide. At the same time, a second high tide occurs on the side of Earth that is farthest from the Moon. This high tide occurs because the solid Earth is pulled toward the Moon and away from the water on Earth's far side.

In between the two high tides are two low tides, as shown in the picture. During each 24-hour rotation of our planet, a given place on Earth will have two high tides and two low tides. That's a lot of changes caused by one faraway object! ■

INVESTIGATION 3 WRAP-UP

REVIEW

1. Describe how the motions of the Moon cause its phases.

2. What effect does the Moon have on Earth's oceans?

CRITICAL THINKING

3. You look for the Moon on a clear night, but it doesn't appear. Explain what could be happening.

4. Is it correct to call the far side of the Moon the dark side? Why or why not?

REFLECT & EVALUATE

Word Power

Write the letter of the term that best completes each sentence. *Not all terms will be used.*

a. axis
b. constellations
c. orbit
d. phases
e. planet
f. revolve
g. rotation
h. solar system

1. The spinning motion of Earth is ——.
2. The Sun and all objects that orbit it is called the ——.
3. Make-believe line that runs through Earth's North and South Poles is called the ——.
4. Nighttime star patterns are called ——.
5. Changing shapes of the Moon are called ——.
6. Earth's path around the Sun is called its ——.

Check What You Know

Write the term in each pair that best completes each sentence.

1. When you see the entire daylit half of the Moon, it is a (new Moon, full Moon).
2. Earth rotates once on its (axis, orbit) in 24 hours.
3. Tides are caused by the Moon's (rotation, gravity).
4. Earth makes one revolution around the Sun in a (day, year).

Problem Solving

1. Pretend that you're stranded on a desert island. How can you use the Sun to find north, south, east, and west? How can you use the Sun to tell time?
2. How could you use the stars to find north at night?
3. Where is the Moon located in relation to Earth and the Sun when you see a full Moon?

Copy this drawing. Label the two star patterns and the star Polaris. The yellow arrows show how the stars will appear to move. Tell which stars, if any, hardly seem to move at all.

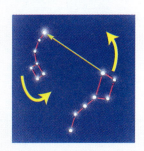

CHAPTER 3

EFFECTS OF EARTH AND MOON MOTIONS

In the Northern Hemisphere, or northern half of Earth, the longest day of the year is on or around June 21. On this day, the Sun follows its longest and highest path across the sky. What would you do to celebrate this day?

Connecting to Science
CULTURE

Celebrating the Shortest Night June 21 usually has the shortest night of the year in the Northern Hemisphere. In many parts of the world, people stay awake all through this shortest night. The Hopi people of Taos, New Mexico, race up a mountain to meet the Sun as it rises, singing

> There! There!
> Beautiful white-rising has dawned
> Beautiful yellow-rising has dawned
> There! There!

On June 21, people in Scandinavia build giant bonfires to stand for the Sun's great light and heat. In northern Mexico, beautiful head coverings are worn. In this chapter you'll find out more about the Sun and the ways it affects Earth.

Coming Up

INVESTIGATION 1
WHAT CAUSES SEASONS?
.... B60

INVESTIGATION 2
WHAT ARE ECLIPSES?
.... B72

◀ A Mexican headdress that celebrates the Sun

Investigation 1

What Causes Seasons?

What kinds of things do you like to do in the summer? Can you do the same things in the winter? For most people on Earth, there are differences between the seasons. In this investigation you'll find out how Earth's shape and movements cause the seasons.

Activity

Lines of Sunlight

Why is it warmer during the summer than it is during the winter? Find out what rays of sunlight have to do with the answer.

MATERIALS
- paper plate
- sheet of construction paper
- scissors
- sheet of lined paper
- tape
- Science Notebook

Procedure

1. Use a paper plate to make a circle. Turn the paper plate face down on a sheet of construction paper. Trace the edge of the paper plate. Cut out the circle.

2. This circle is a model of Earth. **Label** your model as shown in the diagram to the right.

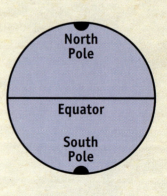

Step 2

 *Fold your paper circle in half. Draw your equator line on the fold.*

3. Place a sheet of lined paper on a table. Tape the paper in place.

B60

4. Place the circle on top of the lined paper as shown below. Imagine that the lines on the paper are rays of light from the Sun. **Draw** arrows to show where the sunlight is coming from. **Observe** how the rays of sunlight strike different parts of your model Earth. **Draw** a picture of your model in your *Science Notebook*.

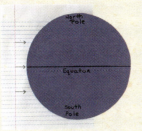

Step 4

5. Turn your model Earth so that the North Pole is tilted to the right, as shown. **Draw** how the Earth model and the Sun's rays look now.

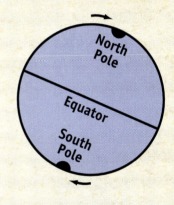

Step 5

Analyze and Conclude

1. Compare the drawings you did for steps 4 and 5. In each drawing, where do the rays hit the ground straight up and down? Where are they slanted?

2. Infer from your model how the angle at which sunlight hits the ground might affect the temperature on the real planet Earth.

3. Predict where on Earth it would be hottest and coldest in each of your drawings.

INVESTIGATE FURTHER!

Use the **Science Processor CD-ROM**, *Sun, Moon, and Earth* (Investigation 4, What Is a Year?) to learn about Earth's revolution and how it affects Earth's seasons.

Activity

Earth Tilts!

What does Earth's revolution around the Sun have to do with changes in the seasons? Find out in this activity.

MATERIALS
- modeling clay
- globe
- toothpicks
- lamp
- drawing of Polaris
- *Science Notebook*

SAFETY
Be careful not to burn yourself on the lamp.

Procedure

1. Press small balls of clay onto the North Pole and South Pole of a globe. Stick a toothpick into each piece of clay to represent Earth's axis.

2. Use a lamp as a model of the Sun. Place the lamp so that its light shines on the globe.

3. **Locate** the drawing of Polaris that your teacher has taped high up on a wall or ceiling. Position the globe so that its axis tilts, with the North Pole pointing toward the Polaris drawing.

Step 1

Step 3

B62

4. Observe which parts of your model Earth are now getting the most direct rays of sunlight. **Record** these observations in your *Science Notebook*.

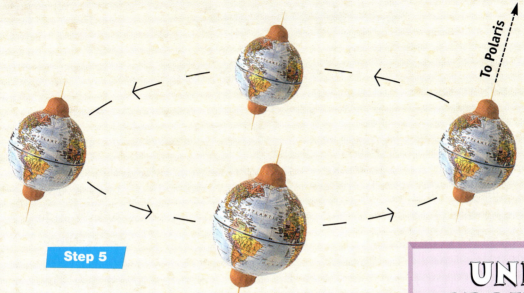

Step 5

5. Make your Earth model revolve around your Sun model. As you move your Earth model, always keep the North Pole pointing toward Polaris. At each of the four points shown in the picture above, **observe** and **record** which parts of Earth get the most direct rays of sunlight.

Analyze and Conclude

1. Locate your state on the globe. Where was the globe in its orbit around the Sun when your state got the most sunlight? Where was the globe when your state got the least sunlight?

2. Make signs that say *spring*, *summer*, *fall*, and *winter*. Then **infer** where the globe would be in its orbit during each of these seasons in your state. Place the signs in those parts of the room.

UNIT PROJECT LINK

Make a sky scene for your Moon base model. On large sheets of paper, draw what you'd see in the daytime sky from your base. Include the Sun, Earth, and stars. Show the day and night parts of Earth. Show the tilt of Earth's axis. What season is it in the United States on the Earth that you've drawn?

For more help with your Unit Project, go to www.eduplace.com.

# The Reason for Seasons

Reading Focus How are the seasons different in the Northern and Southern Hemispheres?

A construction-paper circle and a sheet of lined paper are used to make a model of sunlight hitting Earth. The activity on pages B60 and B61 shows that different parts of Earth get different amounts of sunlight. If Earth were flat instead of round, this wouldn't be the case!

Results of Roundness

Different parts of our planet get different amounts of sunlight because Earth is round. The parts that get the least light are the North Pole and the South Pole. The parts that get the strongest light are near the equator (ē kwāt′ər). The **equator** is an imaginary line that circles Earth halfway between the two poles.

How hot or cold a place is depends mainly on the angle at which sunlight strikes that place. The more direct sunlight a place gets, the warmer it is. Sunlight strikes the equator straight on most of the time, so it's warm there.

At the North Pole and the South Pole, however, sunlight always strikes the ground at an angle. This means that the light rays are spread out more thinly over a larger area, so it's colder there. In the activity on pages B60 and B61, the model light rays spread out at the surface near the poles of the Earth model.

Because Earth is round, sunlight strikes some parts of it more directly than others. ▼

B64

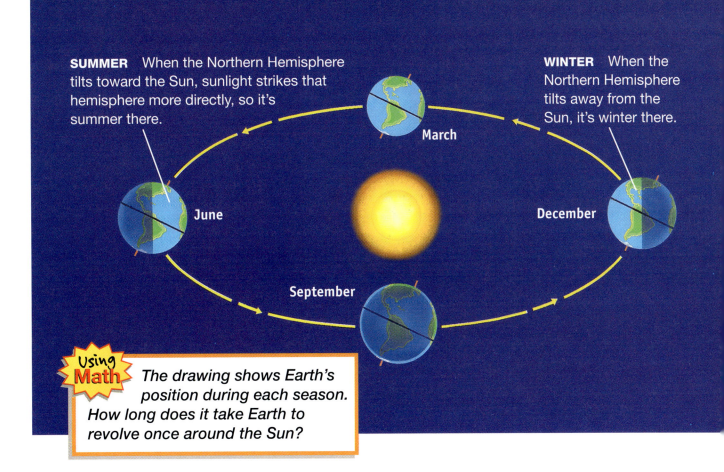

SUMMER When the Northern Hemisphere tilts toward the Sun, sunlight strikes that hemisphere more directly, so it's summer there.

WINTER When the Northern Hemisphere tilts away from the Sun, it's winter there.

Using Math The drawing shows Earth's position during each season. How long does it take Earth to revolve once around the Sun?

Earth's Tilting Axis

Find the axis on each picture of Earth in the drawing above. Do you notice anything strange about the axis? It's tilted!

Having a tilted axis means that Earth slants a little to one side as it revolves around the Sun. Look at the drawing. Notice that as Earth circles the Sun, the tilt always points in the same direction. The northern tip of the axis always points toward Polaris, the North Star.

The tilt of Earth's axis is what causes **seasons**—the four parts of the year. Spring, summer, fall, and winter are different from each other in most places on Earth. That's because the Sun's rays strike each place differently during the year. Sometimes the rays strike the ground more directly, causing summer. At other times they strike more at an angle, causing winter. This is shown in the activity on pages B62 and B63.

The United States is in the Northern Hemisphere (hem′i sfir), the northern half of Earth. Use the drawing to tell what season it is in the United States when the Northern Hemisphere tilts toward the Sun. When it's summer in the Northern Hemisphere, what season is it in the Southern Hemisphere?

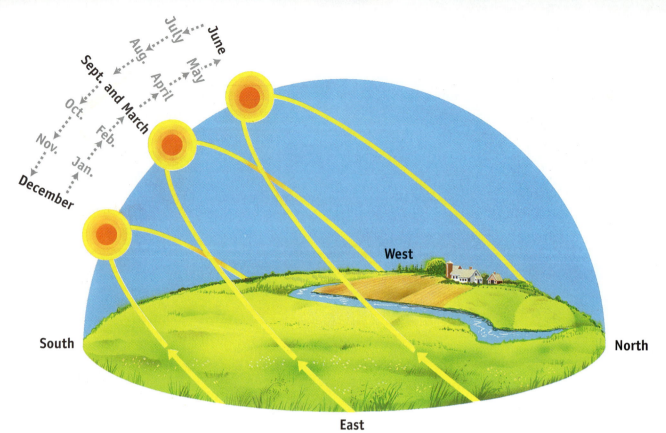

 The Sun's apparent path across the sky changes during different seasons. How many months are there in each season?

Rising Up, Sinking Down

You know that the Sun seems to follow a changing path across the sky. And you know that Earth revolves around the Sun. As Earth revolves, the tilt of Earth's axis affects the Sun's apparent path across the sky.

In summer, because your part of Earth is tilted toward the Sun, the Sun's path appears highest in the sky. The summer Sun path is also the longest, as shown above. Because it's the longest, there are more daylight hours in the summer months.

During winter in the Northern Hemisphere, the Sun's path appears lowest in the sky. This results in fewer daylight hours in the winter months.

What a lot of changes happen because of one little tilt! ■

INVESTIGATE FURTHER!

EXPERIMENT

Is the Sun always in the same place at different times of the year? Work with your group. Use a camera to take photos of an object and the shadow that it casts. Make a plan to show how the different positions of the Sun make the shadow change during different seasons. Show your teacher the plan and then carry it out. Share your results.

The First Calendar Makers

Reading Focus How are ancient calendars different from modern ones?

Do you know what day today is? Of course you do. In fact, you know what date, what month, and what year it is. That's because you use a calendar.

People have used calendars to keep track of time since they first began observing the Sun, Moon, and stars. People wanted calendars so they would know when to celebrate holidays. But even more important was the need of the farmers to know when to plant their crops.

Ancient Sky Watchers

The Mayas of ancient Central America designed a calendar. For centuries the Mayan calendar was more accurate than any other in the world. The Mayas used observatories like the one in the photograph below to measure the position of the Sun in the sky.

The ancient Mayan calendar had 18 months of 20 days each. It also had an extra 5 days that weren't attached to any month. These extra 5 days were probably used as holidays.

Part of an ancient Mayan calendar ▼

A Mayan observatory in Mexico ▼

The Chinese also have an ancient calendar. This calendar is very complicated. That's because it's based mainly on the phases of the Moon, not on the Sun's position. A Chinese year usually has 12 months of 29 or 30 days each. This adds up to fewer than 365 days. So a thirteenth month is added to some years. This keeps the calendar in line with Earth's revolution.

Creating the Modern Calendar

Calendar makers face a difficult problem. Earth doesn't take exactly 365 days to revolve around the Sun. Instead, it takes about $365\frac{1}{4}$ days. A calendar must account for the extra quarter-days. If it doesn't, these quarter-days add up over the years. Finally, in a few hundred years, the calendar no longer matches the seasons.

▲ Each year in the Chinese calendar is named after an animal—for example, this dragon.

Julius Caesar, who helped create the modern calendar ▼

When Julius Caesar became the ruler of ancient Rome, the Roman calendar was way out of step with the seasons. Caesar corrected this. He decided that the year we now call 46 B.C. would have 445 days. After this "year of confusion," the Romans began using a new 12-month calendar. It's the basis for the one we have today.

Most of the years in Caesar's calendar had 365 days. Every fourth year, however, was a *leap year* of 366 days. This extra day every four years made up for the extra quarter-day it takes Earth to revolve once around the Sun.

▲ Modern calendar makers work at the Royal Observatory in Greenwich, England.

Since Caesar's time, small changes have been made in his calendar. Astronomers have learned to calculate more exactly the time it takes Earth to revolve around the Sun. Scientists can even figure out when to add an extra *leap second* to a year! In this way, they keep the calendar in line with Earth's motion. ■

Science in Literature

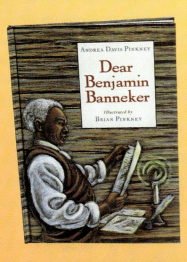

Dear Benjamin Banneker
by Andrea Davis Pinkney
Illustrated by Brian Pinkney
Harcourt Brace & Co., 1994

BANNEKER'S ALMANAC

"In colonial times, most families in America owned an almanac. . . . Folks read almanacs to find out when the sun and moon would rise and set, when eclipses would occur, and how the weather would change from season to season."

Find out more about the life of Benjamin Banneker by reading the book *Dear Benjamin Banneker* by Andrea Davis Pinkney. It is the story of a famous African American astronomer and writer who taught himself astronomy by observing the sky every night.

Near the Equator, Near the Pole

Reading Focus What are the seasons like in different parts of the world, and how do they affect life in those places?

Where do you live? Do you live on the East Coast or the West Coast of the United States? in the southwestern desert? near the Rocky Mountains? on the Great Plains? If you live in the United States, the weather in your area is probably sometimes warm, sometimes cool.

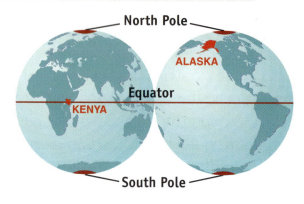

▲ The locations of Kenya and Alaska

As Hot As Summer

Suppose you lived near the equator in central Kenya in Africa. Look at the map on this page. Find the place where the line that represents the equator runs through Kenya.

Your life in Kenya would be quite different than it is in the United States. You wouldn't have four seasons with different temperatures. Living near the equator, you'd get summer weather all year round. It would therefore be very warm all the time.

In Kenya you'd wear shorts and light cotton shirts, and you wouldn't need a coat at all. You'd eat foods that grow well in warm lands, such as bananas and beans.

Kenyans wear lightweight clothing. ▼

Inuit people wear heavy clothing. ▼

B70

How an Eclipse Occurs

Reading Focus What are the positions of the Sun, Earth, and Moon during solar and lunar eclipses?

▲ People view a solar eclipse, using safety glasses and special cameras.

In 1991, astronomers from all over the world came to Mexico to visit an ancient Native American city called Monte Albán. Many of the scientists had traveled thousands of kilometers. They came to this place to observe in person what can be seen in the picture on page B72—a total eclipse of the Sun.

The people who live around Monte Albán felt lucky that the eclipse could be seen from their home. Total solar eclipses are rare, and each one can be seen from only a small area on Earth.

What's it like to observe a total eclipse of the Sun? One astronomer said, "You remember it for the rest of your life." A bright sunny day plunges into darkness. The temperature drops. Dogs may bark and roosters may crow. Daytime birds may stop singing. Flowers that only bloom at night may open. And most important of all, the Sun does its awesome "disappearing act"!

3. After your group agrees, **draw** in your *Science Notebook* the scene you created in step 2. **Label** the Sun, Earth, and the Moon.

4. Now let a globe represent Earth. Place the globe where the lamp can shine on it. With your group, **hypothesize** about where the Moon model should be to create a lunar eclipse, like the one in the photo. Test your hypothesis.

5. Draw the scene you made in step 4.

Step 4

▲ Stages of a total lunar eclipse

Analyze and Conclude

1. What are the positions of the Sun, Earth, and the Moon during a solar eclipse?

2. Hypothesize about what phase the Moon is in during a solar eclipse. Use the drawing from step 3 and the models to help you answer this question.

3. What are the positions of the Sun, Earth, and the Moon during a lunar eclipse?

4. Hypothesize about what phase the Moon is in during a lunar eclipse. Use your drawing and models to help you.

INVESTIGATE FURTHER!

EXPERIMENT

What question do you have about eclipses? Hypothesize what you think the answer would be. Plan an experiment to find the answer to your question. After your teacher approves your plan, try your experiment. Share your results with your classmates.

INVESTIGATION 2

WHAT ARE ECLIPSES?

Imagine you were living many centuries ago. Suppose that in the middle of a cloudless day the Sun suddenly started to disappear bit by bit. What would you think was happening? Such an event is called an eclipse. In this investigation you'll learn what causes two kinds of eclipses.

Activity

Homemade Eclipses

What positions of the Sun, the Moon, and Earth result in an eclipse? In this activity you'll use models to show solar and lunar eclipses.

MATERIALS
- lamp or flashlight
- plastic-foam ball
- globe
- *Science Notebook*

SAFETY
Don't burn yourself by touching the lamp.

Procedure

1. Place a bright lamp or flashlight on a table. Point the light out into the room, not toward the floor or ceiling. Turn off all other lights.

2. Pretend you are Earth, the lamp is the Sun, and a plastic-foam ball is the Moon. **Talk** with your group. **Hypothesize** where you should position your model Moon so that you create a solar eclipse, like the one shown in the photograph. **Test** your hypothesis.

Step 2

Stages of a total solar eclipse ▶

B72

As Cold As Winter

Suppose that you lived among the Inuit (in'ōō wit) people in northern Alaska. You'd never get direct sunlight that close to the North Pole. It would therefore be very cold all the time. You might go to school by riding on a snowmobile. Once you arrived, you'd probably get a hot breakfast to warm you up.

In northern Alaska you'd be in the Land of the Midnight Sun. This means that in the middle of summer, you would have 24 hours of sunlight each day. That's when the North Pole tilts toward the Sun. But in winter you'd see hardly any sunlight. That's when the North Pole tilts away from the Sun. Imagine a day when the Sun didn't rise!

During the long, dark winter, some people develop an illness. It's known as Seasonal Affective Disorder, or SAD. People with SAD become tired and unhappy. Bright lights make them feel better. The lights "fool" their bodies into thinking there's more daylight! ■

The path of the Midnight Sun, which never sets ▼

INVESTIGATION 1 WRAP-UP

REVIEW

1. Why is it warmer at the equator than at the North Pole and South Pole?

2. How does the tilt of Earth's axis help cause the seasons?

CRITICAL THINKING

3. The tilt of Earth's axis causes the four seasons. Where on Earth is the effect of the tilt hardly felt? How do you know?

4. Suppose you're planning a trip to the South Pole. What month would you choose to visit there? Explain the reasons for your choice.

▲ Wolves and dragons were once said to cause eclipses.

Predicting Eclipses

People in the past didn't know what caused eclipses. They made up stories to explain them. Some Asian cultures said that the Sun disappeared because a dragon was trying to eat it. The Vikings of northern Europe saw that the Moon turned red during a lunar eclipse. They said this happened because a wolf bit the Moon and made it bleed.

From past observations, some ancient astronomers learned to predict when an eclipse would take place. Today, scientists know the exact movements of the Moon and Earth. They can tell just when an eclipse will occur—and predict it centuries in advance!

Goodbye Sun, Goodbye Moon

The activity on pages B72 and B73 models a solar eclipse. A **solar eclipse** occurs when the Moon, as it revolves, moves directly between the Sun and Earth. In this position the Moon blocks the Sun from our view.

During a total solar eclipse, features such as prominences are visible around the edges of the Sun.

A solar eclipse occurs when the Moon blocks the light of the Sun from reaching Earth. ▼

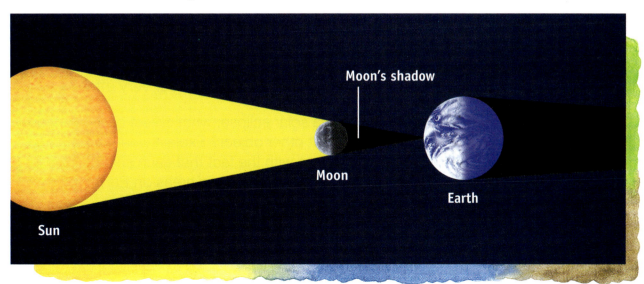

B75

▲ A lunar eclipse occurs when the Moon moves into Earth's shadow.

It's usually hard to see features on the Sun because of the Sun's glare. This is one reason astronomers will travel far to see a solar eclipse.

An eclipse of the Moon works a little bit differently. A **lunar eclipse** occurs when the Moon moves into Earth's shadow. This is modeled in the activity on pages B72 and B73. In this position, Earth blocks the Sun's light from reaching the Moon directly. A small amount of sunlight, however, does reach the Moon. That light bends around planet Earth as it passes through Earth's atmosphere. Lit by this little bit of sunlight, the Moon looks red or copper-colored.

Eclipses don't happen very often. That's because the Moon's orbit around Earth tilts a little. This makes it rare for the Sun, the Moon, and Earth to line up perfectly. You also have to be in just the right spot on Earth to see a total solar eclipse. Total solar eclipses are rare.

But anyone on the night side of Earth can see a total lunar eclipse. So watch for the next one! ■

INVESTIGATION 2 WRAP-UP

REVIEW

1. Draw the positions of the Sun, Earth, and Moon during a solar eclipse. Do the same for a lunar eclipse.

2. Why don't eclipses occur very often?

CRITICAL THINKING

3. In a solar eclipse, what object casts a shadow on what other object? Explain what this shadow has to do with the fact that each solar eclipse is visible only from certain areas on Earth.

4. Suppose the Moon were farther away from Earth than it is. How would a solar eclipse be different?

CHAPTER 3 REVIEW

REFLECT & EVALUATE

Word Power

Write the letter of the term that best matches the definition.

a. equator
b. lunar eclipse
c. seasons
d. solar eclipse

1. When the Moon moves into Earth's shadow
2. Spring, summer, fall, winter
3. Imaginary line that circles Earth halfway between the two poles
4. When the Moon moves directly between the Sun and Earth

Check What You Know

Write the term in each pair that best completes each sentence.

1. Earth's tilted axis causes (eclipses, seasons).
2. When the Northern Hemisphere tilts away from the Sun, the season there is (winter, summer).
3. When the Northern Hemisphere tilts toward the Sun, the season in the Southern Hemisphere is (spring, winter).
4. The path of the Sun appears (highest, lowest) in the summer sky.

Problem Solving

1. When it's winter in the Northern Hemisphere, what season is occurring in the Southern Hemisphere? Why?
2. How does the tilt of Earth on its axis affect the amount of sunlight that the South Pole receives at different times of the year?
3. Describe how the positions of the Sun, Earth, and Moon differ during a solar eclipse and a lunar eclipse.

Copy this drawing. Based on the drawing, what is the season in the place where the **X** is drawn? What month might it be? Explain. Draw a map to show what season it is today where you live.

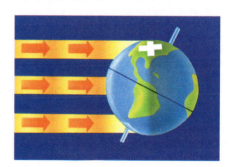

B77

Drawing Conclusions

Writers often imply, or hint at, more information than they actually state. They give you clues and expect you to figure out the rest, using what you already know. Suppose you read, "Mike picked up his umbrella as he headed out the door." You might infer, or conclude, that it was raining or that rain was forecast for the day.

Consider these questions as you draw conclusions.
- What does the author say?
- What do I know?

Read the paragraphs below. Then complete the exercises that follow.

The Moon: Fact and Fiction

For thousands of years, people have seen pictures in the Moon. The ancient Chinese saw a rabbit and a toad. Some Europeans saw a crab. The Vikings saw a boy and girl in the Moon. . . .

In the United States, people talk about "the man in the Moon." But many cultures, including the Maori people of New Zealand, see a woman in the Moon instead.

1. Which statement is a conclusion that you can draw from the paragraphs? Write the letter of that statement.

    a. The face of the Moon is always changing.

    b. The Maori people see a woman in the Moon.

    c. Different people see different things in the Moon.

    d. People in the United States see the Moon most clearly.

2. What was the most important clue?

Using MATH SKILLS

Using Math: Time Measurement

This calendar shows when the phases of the Moon occur.

October

Sunday	Monday	Tuesday	Wednesday	Thursday	Friday	Saturday
				1	2	3
4	5 ○ Full Moon	6	7	8	9	10
11	12 ◐ Last Quarter	13	14	15	16	17
18	19	20 ● New Moon	21	22	23	24
25	26	27	28 ◑ First Quarter	29	30	31

Use the data in the calendar to complete the exercises.

1. On which day of the week does full Moon occur?

2. How many days after full Moon is new Moon?

3. What phase happens one week after the appearance of full Moon?

4. How many phases of the Moon are shown on this calendar? What are the dates of those phases?

5. On which day of the week will November begin?

6. On which day does the month of September end?

7. How many Saturdays are there in October? How many Sundays are there?

8. What is the date two weeks before first quarter Moon?

9. What number would you add to the date of Friday, October 2, to find the date of the following Friday?

10. There are about 29 days from new Moon to new Moon. Estimate the date in November of the next new Moon.

UNIT B WRAP-UP!

On your own, use scientific methods to investigate a question about the Sun, Moon, or Earth.

THINK LIKE A SCIENTIST

Ask a Question

Pose a question about the Sun, Moon, or Earth that you would like to investigate. For example, ask, "How does the mass of an object affect the size of the crater it produces?"

Make a Hypothesis

Suggest a hypothesis that is a possible answer to the question. One hypothesis is that two objects of the same size but with different masses would produce craters of different sizes.

Plan and Do a Test

Plan a controlled experiment to find out how the mass of an object striking the Moon affects the size of the crater left behind. You could start with a meterstick, two balls (same size, different mass), and sand. Develop a procedure that uses these materials to test the hypothesis. With permission, carry out your experiment. Follow the safety guidelines on pages S14–S15.

Record and Analyze

Observe carefully and record your data accurately. Make repeated observations.

Draw Conclusions

Look for evidence to support the hypothesis or to show that it is false. Draw conclusions about the hypothesis. Repeat the experiment to verify the results.

WRITING IN SCIENCE
Science-Fiction Story

Write an entertaining story about characters staying at a resort on the Moon. Make your story scientifically accurate. Use these guidelines to write your story.

- Brainstorm for story ideas.
- Draft your story.
- Check your science facts.
- Revise and edit your story.

Matter, Energy, and Forces

Theme: Systems

THINK LIKE A SCIENTIST
SLIDERS C2

CHAPTER 1 — All About Matter C4
Investigation 1   What Is Matter? C6
Investigation 2   How Can Matter Be Changed? C16

CHAPTER 2 — Energy and Change C26
Investigation 1   What Is Energy? C28
Investigation 2   What Is Heat, and How Can It Move? .C40
Investigation 3   How Can Heat Change Materials? ... C52

CHAPTER 3 — Force, Motion, and Machines C58
Investigation 1   What Is a Force? C60
Investigation 2   How Do Machines Make Work Easier? C68

Using Reading Skills C78
Using Math Skills C79
Unit Wrap-up! C80

SLIDERS

If you live where it snows, you probably know the fun of sledding down a snowy hill. That's how the sport of luge (lōōzh) began. In this sport, a person zooms down a track while lying face up on a racing sled. A person who competes in a luge race is called a slider. A slider needs to understand the forces that will help the luge, or sled, go as fast as possible. In this photo a student slider in Bavaria, in Germany, races his luge down a track.

THINK LIKE A SCIENTIST

Questioning In this unit you'll study matter, energy, forces, and machines. You'll investigate questions such as these.
- How Can Matter Be Changed?
- How Do Machines Make Work Easier?

Observing, Testing, Hypothesizing In the Activity "Ramps and Rocks," you'll test how the steepness of a ramp affects the force needed to move an object. Then you'll hypothesize how to move heavy objects up a ramp.

Researching In the Resource "Machines—Force Changers," you'll find out how a machine can change the size or direction of a force.

Drawing Conclusions After you've completed your investigations, you'll draw conclusions about what you've learned—and get new ideas.

CHAPTER 1

ALL ABOUT MATTER

What do a skyscraper, a butterfly, and a puff of smoke have in common? They are very different, but they are all matter. How many kinds of matter are there, anyway? And how do you describe matter?

Connecting to Science
ARTS

Matter of Taste Think of all the different kinds of food you eat. Each of those foods is a different kind of matter. Since the beginning of time, people have caused changes in food. At first the changes were mainly physical—cutting, peeling, crushing, and grinding. Since the discovery of fire, people have also changed food chemically by cooking it.

Over the years food preparation has become an art. People involved with the culinary (kyo͞o′lə ner ē) arts, such as chefs and bakers, spend hours mixing different combinations of ingredients to make appetizing dishes. But you might not think about the amount of time spent making food look more appetizing. Today, the appearance of the food being served is almost as important as how it tastes.

Coming Up

What Is Matter?
.... **C6**

How Can Matter Be Changed?
.... **C16**

◀ This platter of assorted foods is a feast for the eyes as well as for the stomach.

C5

INVESTIGATION 1

WHAT IS MATTER?

How can you tell a dog from a cat? Dogs and cats have features in common. Yet, each has features that allow you to identify it. In this investigation you'll learn that the same is true for different kinds of matter.

Activity

Grouping Things

MATERIALS
- bag of assorted objects
- magnet
- *Science Notebook*

What do a marshmallow and a golf ball have in common? Not very much, it would seem. They are the same color—white. Color is just one property that can be used to group objects. You will explore some others in this activity.

Procedure

1. Your teacher will give your group a bag with several objects in it. Open the bag and remove the objects.

2. Observe the objects. The objects are different, but they have certain features, or properties, in common.

3. In your *Science Notebook*, **make a chart** like the one shown on the next page. **Record** the name of each object and give a brief description of each.

See **SCIENCE and MATH TOOLBOX** page H10 if you need to review **Making a Chart to Organize Data.**

Object	Description	Flexible		Magnetic	
		yes	no	yes	no

4. Now handle each object. Some of the objects are flexible (flek′sə bəl). This means that their shape can be changed in some way. Others are rigid. Their shape cannot be changed easily. Sort the objects into two groups and **classify** them as flexible and not flexible (rigid). **Record** the results in your chart.

Step 4

5. Next **infer** which, if any, of your objects will be attracted by a magnet. Based on your inferences, **classify** the objects as magnetic or nonmagnetic. **Record** your inferences on a separate sheet of paper.

6. Now use the magnet to **test** each object. **Record** the results in your chart.

7. Choose other properties, such as hardness, by which to classify the objects. **Classify** an object as hard if it can't be scratched by your fingernail. **Classify** it as soft if it can be scratched. Then scratch the hard objects with a penny. **Record** all your results in your chart.

Analyze and Conclude

1. What properties could you describe by just looking at the objects?

2. What kinds of materials did you **infer** would be attracted by a magnet? On what feature did you base your inferences? Were all your inferences correct? If not, what materials fooled you?

3. **List** some other features, or properties, you might use to group these objects.

Technology Link CD-ROM

INVESTIGATE FURTHER!

Use the **Science Processor CD-ROM**, *Forms of Energy* Spreadsheet and Writer Tools to record your predictions and data about the properties of the objects you observe.

Activity

Measuring Things

MATERIALS
- bag of assorted objects
- balance
- metric ruler
- *Science Notebook*

Some properties that are used to describe objects can also be measured. Can you think of some of these properties?

- -

Procedure

1. Your teacher will give you a bag with several objects in it. Open the bag and remove the objects.

2. The **mass** of an object is the amount of matter that object contains. Pick up each object to "feel" or "sense" its mass. **Infer** the mass of each object. Then order the objects from greatest mass to least mass. **Record** the order in your *Science Notebook*.

3. **Make a chart** like the one shown. Using a balance, **measure** the mass of each object in grams. **Record** the name of each object and its measurement in the first two columns of your chart.

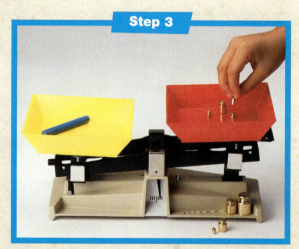

Step 3

Object	Mass	Length

See **SCIENCE and MATH TOOLBOX** page H9 if you need to review **Using a Balance**.

4. Although the objects have different shapes, some are longer than others. **Order** the objects from longest to shortest. Then use a metric ruler to **measure** the length of each object. **Record** those measurements in the third column of your chart.

Analyze and Conclude

1. Look at your list in which you ordered the objects by sensing their masses. **Compare** this order with the order that is based on measured masses. On the list, circle the name of each object that you put in the wrong order. **Discuss** why you thought these objects had more or less mass than they really did.

2. **Compare** the results of your length measurements with those of another group. Did you all measure each object the same way? **Discuss** any differences in the measurements.

3. Think of other ways you could measure and compare the lengths of the objects used in this activity. **Record** your ideas.

Science in Literature

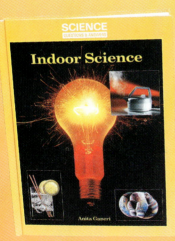

Indoor Science
by Anita Ganeri
Dillon Press, 1993

Skating on Water

"If you put pressure on ice, you raise its freezing point. This means that the outer layer stays liquid for a longer time. This is how ice skates work. As you skate, your weight presses down on the blades and on the ice. This extra pressure stops the ice from freezing so that there is a thin film of water under each skate."

This information is part of an article titled "How does water change to ice?" Learn more about water and other kinds of matter by reading the articles in *Indoor Science*, by Anita Ganeri. They're interesting and fun.

What's the Matter?

Reading Focus How can you tell if something is matter?

▲ How do the masses of the trucks compare? the masses of the balls?

Look outside. Everything you see—houses, clouds, trees, police cars, puppies, stop signs—is a kind of matter.

Now look around your classroom. You'll likely see desks, books, lunch boxes, clocks, chalk, and wastebaskets. All of these objects are made of matter. What about the dust on the windowsill and the water in the sink? You guessed it. The dust and water are matter, too.

Here, There, and Everywhere

Matter is anything that has mass and takes up space. Matter is everywhere. If you can see something or touch it or smell it, it's matter. In fact, you don't *have* to be able to see something for it to be matter. For example, you can't see air, but it's matter.

The Matter of Mass

In the activity on pages C8 and C9, a number of objects are arranged according to mass. In many cases it is not necessary to measure the mass of each object. You can just tell that some objects are heavier or harder to move than other objects. Heavier objects have more mass than lighter ones.

Mass is the amount of matter that something contains. The more matter that something has, the greater its mass.

Look at the two trucks in the picture above. Except for color, they are very much alike. Each truck contains the same amount of matter. So their masses are the same.

The two balls in the picture also look alike. But one contains more matter than the other. How can you tell which ball contains more matter?

Taking Up Space

In addition to having mass, matter takes up space. In the activity on pages C8 and C9, a number of objects of different shape are arranged by size. Each of the objects takes up a certain amount of space.

The amount of space that matter takes up is called **volume** (väl′-yōōm). Some objects, such as a skyscraper and a ship, take up lots of space. The volume of these objects is very large. Compared to a ship, a baseball has a much smaller volume. But even the tiniest bit of matter, smaller than a speck of dust floating in the air, has volume.

Now think about matter that you can barely see, such as the tiny dust particle in the air. It takes up space. And so do the even smaller invisible bits of matter that make up air. Look at the balloons in the picture at left. Which balloons take up more space? Do the unfilled or filled balloons take up more space? What does your answer about the balloons tell you about air? ∎

UNIT PROJECT LINK

For this project you will design, build, and test a model of an energy-efficient house. Work with your partners to create a Builder's Notebook. In the notebook, list the kinds of energy that will be used in your house. Then draw diagrams to show how your house will be built to save energy.

Technology Link
For more help with your Unit Project, go to www.eduplace.com.

▲ Compare the volumes of the balloons.

Properties of Matter

Reading Focus How are physical properties of matter different from chemical properties?

Everyone in Cheryl's family hangs their coats in the same closet. How can Cheryl tell which coat is hers?

Describing Matter

Cheryl can tell which one is her sister Jan's coat right away. It is the only blue one. Cheryl can also tell the coats belonging to her mother and father. Their coats are much longer than the others.

Cheryl's coat is the same size and color as that of her twin brother Gerald. But Gerald's coat is made of different material.

Cheryl uses the length and color of the coats to tell which one is hers. She might also use the feel, or texture, of the material. Length, color, and texture are all properties of the coats. A **property** is something that describes matter.

You use properties to describe different kinds of matter all the time. In the activity on pages C6 and C7 a number of properties of different objects are observed. For example, a magnet is used to test for the property of magnetic attraction. Only those objects that are attracted to, or picked up by, the magnet are made of matter that has this property. The other objects are not magnetic.

Measuring Properties

What is the length of a baseball bat? Which has more mass, a ballpoint pen or a piece of chalk? How much water will an aquarium hold? These are questions about the properties of objects. All are properties that can be measured.

Different tools are used to measure the properties of mass and length. A balance is used to measure the mass, in grams (g), of different objects.

▲ Measuring length

▲ Measuring mass

A tape measure or a metric ruler is used to measure length. These tools are also used to measure how wide and how tall something is. Tape measures and rulers are marked in centimeters (cm) and millimeters (mm).

Sometimes you need to measure the volume of liquid matter that you have. For example, to make fruit punch, you might need to measure a certain volume of orange juice. The picture shows students using three different tools for measuring the volume of a liquid. These tools have scales marked in milliliters (mL).

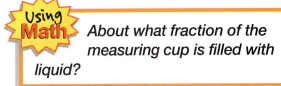

Using Math About what fraction of the measuring cup is filled with liquid?

C13

Harder to Measure

The objects in the picture have lots of different properties. Some of these properties are easy to measure. For example, you could measure the mass of the objects. You could measure the volume of the paints and the vanilla. You could measure the height of the bottles and the distance around them. You could find the length and width of the sandpaper.

Other properties of these objects would not be easy to measure. How would you measure the texture of the sandpaper or the scouring pad? What units of measure would you use to describe the colors of the paints, the odor of the vanilla, or the strength of the magnet? The tools that you have cannot be used to measure these properties.

Physical or Chemical?

All of the properties of matter discussed so far have been physical (fiz′i kəl) properties. A **physical property** is one that can be measured or observed with the senses without changing the matter into another kind of matter. For example, a frozen juice bar might be 20 cm long, have a mass of 50 g, feel cold, and smell and taste like a strawberry. These are all physical properties. The fact that the juice bar melts at a certain temperature (about 0°C) is also a physical property.

In addition to physical properties, matter has chemical (kem′i kəl) properties. A **chemical property** is one that describes how matter can change into another kind of matter. A chemical property can only be observed when one kind of matter changes into another kind of matter.

Suppose you had an iron bar, a wood log, and a building brick. Which of these items would you use as fuel for a campfire?

▼ **What properties can be used to describe each kind of matter?**

If you know anything about the chemical properties of the three items, you would choose the log. Why? Because it can burn. Being able to burn is a chemical property of wood. When matter burns, it changes into other kinds of matter. What other matter has the chemical property of being able to burn?

Making Matter Useful

You know that properties are used to describe matter. Properties make it possible to tell one kind of matter from another. Properties also make matter more or less useful for a given purpose.

Would you rather sleep on a pillow filled with pebbles or cotton? Why aren't shoes made of steel instead of leather? Why aren't windowpanes made of wood instead of glass? The answers to all of these questions have to do with properties of matter. Cotton is soft, leather bends easily, and you can see through glass. It's clear that the usefulness of a material depends on its properties. ■

What's wrong with this picture? ▲

INVESTIGATION 1 WRAP-UP

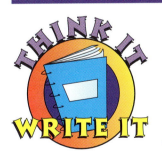

REVIEW

1. What tool would you use to measure the mass of a sample of matter? the volume?

2. How do physical properties differ from chemical properties?

CRITICAL THINKING

3. Why is it sometimes helpful to use a tape measure rather than a ruler to measure an object?

4. Without using standard masses, how could you use a balance to find out which of two objects had the greater mass?

INVESTIGATION 2

HOW CAN MATTER BE CHANGED?

If you saw a log in half, you get sawdust. Sawdust is the same matter as the log. When you burn a log, you get ashes. Are ashes the same matter as the log? In this investigation you'll find out some ways in which matter can be changed.

Activity

States of Matter

Will solids push liquids out of the way? Does a gas take up space? Find out.

MATERIALS
- measuring cup
- water
- narrow plastic jar
- grease pencil
- 4 large marbles
- clear plastic bowl
- paper towel
- clear plastic cup
- *Science Notebook*

Procedure

1. Your teacher will give you a measuring cup containing 200 mL of water. **Observe** the shape of the water in the cup.

2. Carefully pour the water into a narrow plastic jar. **Observe** the shape of the water. In your *Science Notebook*, **record** your observations and **make a drawing** of the jar and water.

3. Use a grease pencil to mark the level of the water on the side of the jar. Then carefully add two marbles, one at a time, to the jar. **Observe** the shape of each marble and the level of the water. Mark the new water level on the jar and on your drawing.

Step 3

4. **Talk with your group** and together predict what will happen if you add two more marbles to the jar. **Record** your prediction. Then check it by adding two more marbles. Mark the new water level and **record** your observations.

Step 5

5. Fill a bowl with water. Then crumple a paper towel and push it into the bottom of a clear plastic cup. Turn the cup over as shown to make sure the paper stays in the cup. **Predict** what will happen to the paper towel if you push the overturned cup straight down into the bowl of water. **Record** your prediction.

6. Carefully push the cup down into the water in the bowl as shown. Remove the cup and look at the paper to see if it is wet or dry. **Record** your observation.

Step 6

Analyze and Conclude

1. Based on your observations of the water and marbles, what can you **infer** about the shape and volume of matter in the liquid state and solid state?

2. What caused the water level to change when you added marbles to the water in the jar?

3. How did pushing the cup under water show that gases take up space? (Remember: Air is a gas.)

INVESTIGATE FURTHER!

EXPERIMENT

Measure how much the water level changed after adding four marbles. Next, predict how much the level will change if you add four more marbles. Tell what your prediction is based on. Then carry out the activity to check your prediction.

Activity

Change Without Change

In this activity you will change matter. But will the matter itself really have changed? Find out.

MATERIALS
- goggles
- bag of assorted materials
- hand lens
- scissors
- tweezers
- *Science Notebook*

SAFETY

Wear goggles during this activity.

Procedure

1. Empty the bag of assorted materials on your work surface. **Observe** each material with a hand lens.

 See **SCIENCE and MATH TOOLBOX** page H2 if you need to review **Using a Hand Lens**.

2. **Talk with your partner** to decide how you might change each of the materials. Such changes might include tearing, cutting, and bending.

3. After checking with your teacher, make changes to each material. In your *Science Notebook*, **record** the name of each material and how it was changed.

4. **Observe** each of the changed materials with the hand lens.

Step 1

Analyze and Conclude

1. What property or properties did you change?

2. Did any of the changes you made produce any new kinds of matter? How do you know?

The Nature of Matter

Reading Focus How does the movement of water particles differ in ice, liquid water, and water vapor?

You're hot and thirsty. You pour warm soda over some ice cubes in a glass. You watch as bubbles rise through the soda. When they reach the surface, the bubbles burst into the air. As you drink, the bubbles reaching the surface of the soda tickle your nose.

As you pour soda over ice, you observe an important fact about the nature of matter. The ice, soda, and bubbles represent the three basic forms of matter.

▲ How is the shape of a solid, such as a crayon, affected by the shape of the container it is in?

States of Matter

Think about all the different kinds of matter that exist. It may surprise you to learn that matter can be found in one of three forms—solid, liquid, or gas. These forms are called **states of matter**.

A **solid** is matter that has a definite volume and a definite shape. A solid can be turned or moved or placed in different containers, but its volume and shape stay the same.

◀ This glass of soda contains matter in its three basic forms.

▲ How is the shape of a liquid affected by the shape of the container it is in?

Too Small to See

The activity on pages C16 and C17 includes matter in all three states. Matter in each state is made up of very tiny particles. Any one of these particles is much too small to feel, taste, smell, or see. The smallest particle of matter is called an **atom**. How small is an atom? The period at the end of this sentence could contain more than 2 billion atoms.

Even when you break a solid into pieces, each piece has a definite shape and volume of its own.

A **liquid** is matter that has a definite volume but no definite shape. A liquid poured from one container to another takes up the same amount of space. But the shape of the liquid changes. As the pictures show, a liquid has the same shape as the container it is in.

A **gas** is matter that has no definite volume or shape. Like a liquid, a gas takes the shape of its container. However, a gas will spread out to fill every part of a container.

Look at the pictures of the bicycle pump. When the handle of the pump is pulled out, air from outside the pump fills the tube-shaped pump. When the handle is pushed in, the air is forced into the tire.

Using Math — What shape does the air in the tire take? What happens to the diameter of the tire as it fills with air?

Particles on the Move

The tiny particles that make up matter are always moving. The way they move depends on the state of the matter. Their motion is least in solids and greatest in gases. ■

In Picture 1, think of the children in the elevator as particles in a solid. Like the children, the particles are packed close together. They may want to move around, but there's little room. So they vibrate (vī′ brāt), or move back and forth, in a small space.

In Picture 2, as the elevator doors open, the children are more like particles of a liquid. They have a little more room to move about, and they can move past each other.

Finally, in Picture 3, the children have arrived at a large open playroom. Here they are like the particles of a gas, free to move about at high speeds. They seem to fill every available space in the room.

C21

Changes in Matter

Reading Focus How are physical changes in matter different from chemical changes?

You and a friend watch as a pizza cook crushes some fresh tomatoes to make a sauce. Then she cuts up some green peppers and mushrooms and shreds some cheese. The cook has caused changes in all these food items.

Next the cook spreads the sauce, vegetables, and cheese over flattened pizza dough. She places the dough and toppings in a hot oven. As the pizza bakes, more changes take place. The dough turns into crisp crust, the toppings cook, and the cheese melts.

A Different Look

Matter can change in two basic ways. In one of these ways, only the *look* of the matter is changed.

In the activity on page C18 clay is reshaped and paper is torn. Reshaping clay and tearing paper cause the look, or appearance, of the matter to change. However, the *kinds* of matter —clay and paper— stay the same.

Another way that the appearance of matter can change is by a change of state. Ice is water in the solid state. What would happen if you left a bowl of ice cubes on the kitchen counter for an hour or so? The ice would melt. You'd find a bowl of liquid water in place of the ice cubes. The state of the water would have changed from solid to liquid. But the matter in the bowl would still be water.

▲ How does the heat of an oven change the matter that makes up a pizza?

▲ Some physical changes in matter

Changed—But Not Changed

The reshaping of clay, tearing of paper, and melting of ice are examples of physical changes in matter. A **physical change** is a change in the size, shape, or state of matter.

Have you ever boiled water to make hot chocolate? If so, you probably noticed bubbles forming in the water and rising to the surface. The bubbles were water vapor, a gas. At the surface, the bubbles burst, sending water vapor into the air. Heat caused liquid water to change to a gas—a physical change.

It is important to remember that no new matter is formed when a physical change takes place. A tomato is still a tomato, whether it's whole or crushed to make pizza sauce. Water is still water, whether it's solid, liquid, or gas. Clay is still clay no matter how you change its shape. Look at the pictures above to see some examples of physical change.

What's New?

Think about a pizza, hot from the oven. The crust is brown and crispy. The toppings look, smell, and taste different than they did before the pizza was baked. The heat of the oven has caused a chemical change in the matter that makes up the pizza. A **chemical change** is a change in matter in which different kinds of matter are formed.

Look at the "before" and "after" pictures of a campfire. When wood burns, different kinds of matter are formed. Wood changes to ashes and smoke. The burning of wood causes a chemical change to take place.

How does wood change when it is burned? ▼

The rusting of iron is a slow chemical change. ▶

Slow but Sure

Some chemical changes happen very quickly. The burning of wood is one example of a rapid chemical change. Other chemical changes happen slowly.

Have you ever left a metal object, such as a bicycle, outside for a long time? If so, you probably know about the change shown in the picture. The bicycle, once shiny green metal, has rusted. You can tell that a chemical change has taken place. The rust is not the same kind of matter as the metal the bicycle was made of. One kind of matter—iron—has changed to another kind of matter—rust.

On a Sour Note

Milk is a healthful food that contains vitamins, minerals, and proteins. But under certain conditions proteins can cause milk to change. When this happens, the milk is said to turn sour.

Fresh milk has a smooth, even texture. Sour milk is lumpy. Fresh milk has a pleasant odor and a sweet taste. If you've ever smelled or tasted sour milk, you know it's different from fresh milk. When milk turns sour, it definitely undergoes a chemical change. ■

Internet Field Trip
Visit **www.eduplace.com** to learn more about changes in matter.

INVESTIGATION 2 WRAP-UP

REVIEW

1. Which state of matter has a definite volume but no definite shape?

2. Sawing a board into three pieces is an example of what kind of change? Explain your answer.

CRITICAL THINKING

3. How is shaping hamburger into patties different from broiling the patties on a grill?

4. Which solid, sand or building blocks, would you use to model a liquid? Explain your answer.

REFLECT & EVALUATE

Word Power

Write the letter of the term that best matches the definition. *Not all terms will be used.*

1. Matter that has no definite volume or shape
2. Is measured with a balance
3. Smallest particle of matter
4. The amount of space matter takes up
5. Something that describes matter
6. Matter that has a definite shape and volume

a. atom
b. gas
c. liquid
d. mass
e. matter
f. property
g. solid
h. volume

Check What You Know

Write the word in each pair that correctly completes the statement.

1. A state of matter that has no definite shape is a (solid, liquid).
2. Paper burning is an example of a (physical change, chemical change).
3. Color is a (physical property, chemical property).
4. Two objects that take up the same amount of space have the same (volume, mass).

Problem Solving

1. You have a large block of ice. Without breaking up the large block, how can you change it into smaller cubes of ice?
2. Give an example of a solid, a liquid, and a gas that you might find in a kitchen. Then describe both a physical change and a chemical change that would be likely to take place there.

The drawings show particles in matter in three different states. Tell which state each one shows. Then draw a picture that shows matter in each of three states. Label the picture.

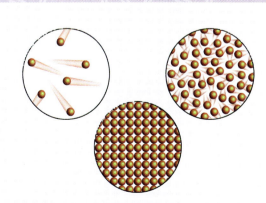

CHAPTER 2

ENERGY AND CHANGE

Has this ever happened to you? You're playing your favorite hand-held computer game and the screen begins to fade. In a few minutes the screen goes blank! The cause is power failure. What can you do to restore the energy for the game?

PEOPLE USING SCIENCE

Product Engineer The toys you see on these pages are powered by energy from the sun. This kind of energy is called solar energy. Would you like to play with a solar-powered plane, windmill, or bicycle? Michael DiLabio is an engineer who designs power systems for toys. His solar panels make these thrilling toys move.

To design these toys, Michael DiLabio needs to know how energy can change from one kind to another. When his solar panels are attached to a toy, the panels "catch the sunlight." They change the energy of the sunlight into electrical energy. The electricity powers the toy's motor and causes the toy to move.

What other things can energy do? Read this chapter and find out!

Coming Up

INVESTIGATION 1
WHAT IS ENERGY?
............C28

INVESTIGATION 2
WHAT IS HEAT, AND HOW CAN IT MOVE?
............C40

INVESTIGATION 3
HOW CAN HEAT CHANGE MATERIALS?
............C52

◀ Michael DiLabio checks out one of his solar-powered toys.

Investigation 1

What Is Energy?

Has anyone ever told you, "Eat your food so that you'll have energy (en′ər jē) to play" or "Turn out the lights, you're wasting energy"? In this investigation you'll find out what energy is by observing what it can do.

Activity

Mystery Can

Here's a fun toy to make that will show you a way that energy can cause motion.

Procedure

1. Cut a rubber band. Then thread it through the holes in one of the plastic lids from a coffee can.

2. Have a group member help you tie two washers to the rubber band. Study the diagram to help you.

3. Thread the rubber band through the holes in another lid. Then tie the ends together as shown.

4. Bend one plastic lid and push it inside a coffee can. Snap the other lid on the can.

MATERIALS
- scissors
- strong rubber band
- 2 plastic coffee can lids, each with two holes
- 2 washers
- coffee can with both ends removed
- *Science Notebook*

SAFETY
Be careful not to cut yourself on the edges of the can.

Step 1

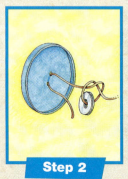
Step 2

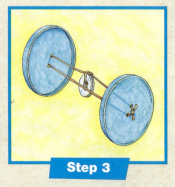
Step 3

C28

Step 5

5. Reach into the can and pull the bent lid through the can. Snap the lid in place.

6. Predict what will happen if you roll the can away from you across the floor. Explain why you made the prediction you did. **Record** your prediction in your *Science Notebook*.

7. Now try rolling the can a few times. **Observe** what happens and **record** your observations.

Analyze and Conclude

1. What happened when you rolled the can? How did your group's prediction compare with the results?

2. Infer what was happening inside the can. How would you explain your observations?

3. Energy is needed to make things move. Where did the energy come from to start the can rolling? **Infer** where the energy came from after the can stopped rolling away from you.

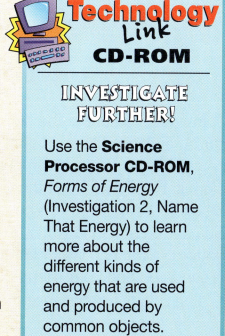

INVESTIGATE FURTHER!

Use the **Science Processor CD-ROM**, *Forms of Energy* (Investigation 2, Name That Energy) to learn more about the different kinds of energy that are used and produced by common objects.

Do You Have the Energy?

Reading Focus How can stored energy be changed to energy of motion?

Imagine you are in the first seat of a car on a water ride at an amusement park. You are slowly being pulled up a big hill. Finally you're at the top. *Swoosh!* Your car rushes downward. *Splash!* It enters the water at the bottom of the hill. Water sprays up around you and your friends.

The ride is fun because the car moves downhill very fast. Energy makes the ride possible. That's because all moving things have energy. In fact, energy is needed to make lots of things happen.

Energy Everywhere

Look around you. Outside, cars whiz by on the streets. Children at a playground glide through the air on swings. Inside your classroom, clock parts turn and bells clang. All these things involve energy.

▲ Is diving into a pool an example of energy of motion or stored energy?

At this moment a heater may be warming the air in your classroom, or an air conditioner may be cooling the air. This morning you may have watched soft bread crisp into toast. These changes use energy, too. But what is energy? **Energy** is the ability to cause a change in matter.

Recall that matter is anything that has mass and takes up space. In other words, just about everything is matter. So, energy is needed to stop a speeding truck or to lift a speck of dust and keep it floating through the air. A plant needs energy to grow. And so do you!

Energy of Motion

When matter is moving, it has energy. When you throw a ball, the moving ball has energy. So too do a speeding freight train and a snowflake drifting to Earth.

Wind can move objects, such as tree branches, because moving air has energy. Moving water also has energy. The energy that moving matter has is called **energy of motion**. Look around at your classroom and outdoors. What objects that you see have energy of motion?

Stored Energy

Although an object isn't moving, it can have the *ability* to move. Energy in matter that can cause that matter to move or change is called **stored energy**. A girl standing still on a diving board has stored energy. As she jumps off the diving board, she has energy of motion.

Energy can also be stored in fuels. Gasoline that makes a car move has stored energy. The food that you eat has stored energy, too.

Stored Energy Changes

If you store something, you know you can use it later. Stored energy can be used later, too. The girl jumping off the diving board is an example of stored energy being used.

In the activity on pages C28 and C29, rolling a coffee can across the floor causes a rubber band inside the can to wind up. As it winds up, the rubber band changes some of the can's energy of motion into stored energy. When the rubber band unwinds, the energy that was stored in the wound-up rubber band changes back to energy of motion.

FORMS OF ENERGY

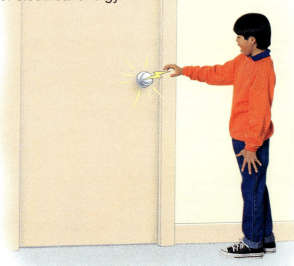

ELECTRICAL ENERGY Have you ever touched a metal doorknob and received a shock? Shocks, lightning, and the electricity that runs through the wires of your house are examples of electrical energy. ▼

▲ **HEAT** All matter is made of tiny particles that are constantly moving. The energy of motion of the tiny particles is heat. If you've ever washed your hands in hot water, you've felt the effects of heat energy!

MECHANICAL ENERGY Mechanical (mə kan′i kəl) energy is the energy of moving objects. The moving parts in a machine have mechanical energy. ▼

Although energy can be described as energy of motion and stored energy, there are many forms of energy. Look at the pictures on these pages and read about different forms of energy.

Everything you do is possible because of energy. Look around you. Are the lights on? Do you hear any sounds? Is anyone moving? Think about all the ways you use energy. Energy really is everywhere! ■

◀ **SOUND** Sound is a form of energy that you can hear. Sound energy comes from particles that are vibrating, or moving back and forth rapidly. Sound moves in waves through matter such as air or water.

LIGHT Light is a form of energy that you can see. Light energy from the Sun moves in waves through space. Light energy also comes from electric lamps and burning matches. ▼

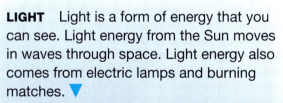

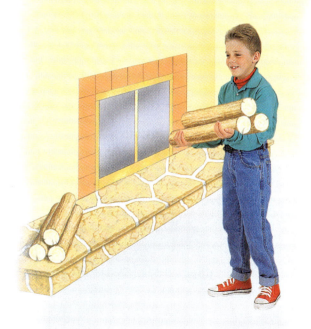

CHEMICAL ENERGY Chemical energy is stored in matter. Fuels such as gasoline, coal, and oil have stored energy. So do matches, wood, and food. Matter itself is not energy. Energy is stored in coal, for example, but coal is not energy. ▼

Internet Field Trip
Visit **www.eduplace.com** to learn more about some of the different forms of energy.

Energy You Can See

Reading Focus How do we see things that do not give off light of their own?

Think of some things that give off light. The Sun, stars, neon signs, and campfires are a few examples of things that give off light. How do you know that these things give off light? That's an easy question—you can *see* the light. Unlike most forms of energy, light is visible.

Reflect on It

Most things do not give off light of their own. Picture yourself in a very dark room. It's so dark that you can't see a thing. Suddenly, someone turns on a flashlight. After your eyes adjust to the brightness, what can you see in the room?

You see the light that the flashlight gives off as its bulb glows. But you also see things in the room that you couldn't see before—including the flashlight itself!

You see these things because light from the flashlight strikes them. Some or all of the light is reflected by, or bounces off, the objects in the room. Some of this reflected light enters your eyes, and you see the object.

I Have a Little Shadow

Light travels in straight lines from its source until it strikes some object or material. Some materials, such as air and clear glass, let light pass through them.

Most materials block light and keep it from passing through. Materials that block light are said to be **opaque** (ō pāk′). When light strikes an opaque object, a shadow forms behind the object. A shadow is an area that light does not reach.

A Mixture of Colors

Sunlight looks white. But it's not. Sunlight is a mixture of many colors. As the picture shows, a prism can separate white light into its different colors. What are the different colors that make up white light?

What Color?

You can name the different colors of yarn in the picture below. But can you explain why one ball of yarn looks blue and another looks red? The answer lies in the mixture of colors that make up white light.

When white light strikes a red object, the object absorbs, or takes in, all of the colors but red. It reflects the red light, so that is the color you see. A black object absorbs all of the colors that strike it. A white object reflects all of the colors that strike it. ■

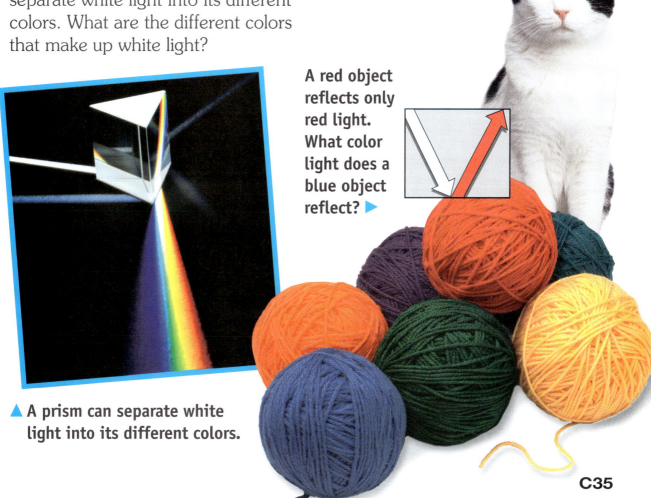

▲ A prism can separate white light into its different colors.

A red object reflects only red light. What color light does a blue object reflect? ▶

C35

Using Solar Energy

Reading Focus What energy change takes place in a solar collector?

The Sun is an important source of energy. The Sun's energy is called **solar energy**. One way people use solar energy is to collect it in the form of light energy and change it to heat energy. This heat energy can be used to heat water. It can also be used to heat homes.

The house below has a flat-plate solar collector on its roof. Study the drawing and read the steps to see how the solar collector helps provide heat for the house.

 The temperature inside the solar collector can reach as high as 94°C (201°F). How does this temperature compare to the boiling-point temperature of water, which is 100°C (212°F)?

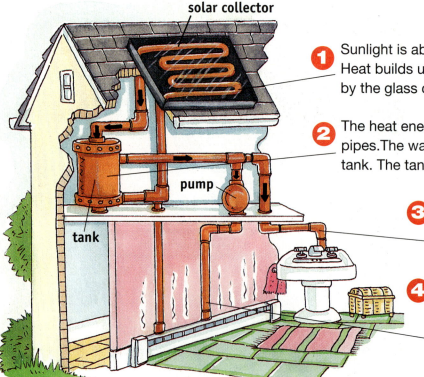

❶ Sunlight is absorbed by the solar collector. Heat builds up in the collector and is held in by the glass cover.

❷ The heat energy is absorbed by water in pipes. The warmed water is pumped into a tank. The tank stores the hot water.

❸ The tank may be connected to the pipes that carry water to the faucets in a home.

❹ The hot-water tank may also be connected to a heating system. The hot water is pumped through radiators, warming the air in the house.

Energy Changes Form

Reading Focus What are some examples of energy changing form?

What do sweating on a warm day, listening to the radio, riding on a bus, and eating have in common? They all are examples of energy changing form.

Nothing Lost, Nothing Gained

Have you ever seen a match burst into flame? You may have wondered what gives a match its special properties. After all, a match is just a thin wooden stick or a cardboard strip, with a rounded, colored tip.

The "secret" of the match is in the rounded tip. Chemical energy is stored in that tip. For the match to burst into flame, the tip must be rubbed on a rough surface. Rubbing causes the chemical energy stored in the tip to change to light energy and heat energy.

There are many ways in which energy can change form. And when energy changes form, heat energy is usually involved. On the next two pages, read about some ways that energy can change from one form to another. As you read, look for energy changes in which heat energy is involved.

◀ **From Electrical to Light Energy**
A light bulb uses electrical energy. In the bulb the electrical energy changes to heat. The wire in the bulb gets so hot that it glows brightly.

From Light to Heat Energy
How does it feel to stand in sunlight? It feels warm, doesn't it? That's because energy from the Sun is taken in by your body and changed to heat energy. ▶

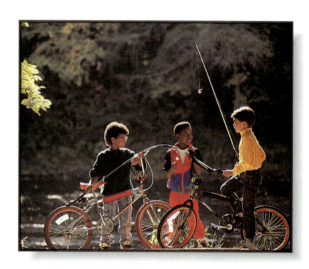

Science in Literature

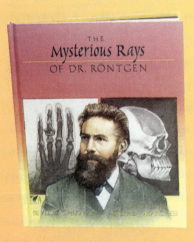

The Mysterious Rays of Dr. Röntgen
by Beverly Gherman
Illustrated by Stephen Marchesi
Atheneum, 1994

A New Kind of Ray

"Soon everyone wanted an X-ray picture. In New Jersey, Thomas Edison, the inventor of the electric light, began experimenting with X rays. Instead of taking permanent photographs, he used a fluorescent screen similar to a movie screen and people lined up for the novelty of seeing their bones displayed right through their clothing."

The discovery of X-rays led to one of the most important developments in medical history. Read about this discovery in *The Mysterious Rays of Dr. Röntgen* by Beverly Gherman.

◀ **From Light to Chemical Energy**
Plants use energy from the Sun to make food. Using light energy, plants change water and air to chemical energy in food.

From Electrical to Heat Energy ▶
This stove uses electrical energy. The stove changes electrical energy to heat energy. What other kind of energy can you see?

◀ **From Chemical to Heat Energy**
Fuels like coal, wood, and oil are used to heat homes. When these fuels are burned, they give off heat. Chemical energy is changed to heat energy. Look at the picture. What other form of energy is given off?

INVESTIGATION 1 WRAP-UP

REVIEW

1. List five forms of energy in use in your classroom. Explain how each is being used.

2. What feature of light energy makes it different from other kinds of energy?

CRITICAL THINKING

3. A skier waiting at the top of a hill has what kind of energy? How can she change that energy?

4. Explain the energy changes that occur when you turn on a fan.

INVESTIGATION 2

WHAT IS HEAT, AND HOW CAN IT MOVE?

Why are some things warm and other things cold? How does heat get from one end of a teaspoon to the other end, or from a campfire to your toes? You'll find the answers to these questions in this investigation.

Activity

Bottle Thermometer

Temperature is a measure of how hot or cold something is. It is measured with a thermometer. In this activity you'll see how a thermometer works.

MATERIALS
- goggles
- clear plastic bottle
- water
- food coloring
- modeling clay
- metric ruler
- clear plastic straw
- dropper
- grease pencil
- 2 plastic bowls
- ice cubes
- timer
- *Science Notebook*

SAFETY
Wear goggles during this activity. Clean up spills immediately.

Procedure

1. With your group, fill a clear plastic bottle with water. Add a few drops of food coloring to the water.

2. Wrap a small piece of modeling clay around a straw, about 5 cm from the end, as shown.

3. Put the shorter end of the straw into the bottle of colored water. Seal the straw in place with the clay.

4. Use a dropper to add more water to the straw until the water level is halfway up the straw. Make sure there are no air bubbles in the straw. Use a grease pencil to draw a line on the straw at the level of water.

Step 2

straw — clay — 5 cm

C40

5. In step 6 you will put your bottle thermometer into a bowl of ice water and then into a bowl of warm water. **Talk with your group** and **predict** what would happen to the water level in the straw. Be sure you can explain why you made the predictions you did. **Record** your predictions in your *Science Notebook*.

Step 6

6. Put the bottle thermometer into a bowl of water. Add ice to the water. Wait three minutes. Then mark the straw at the level of the water. **Record** your observations.

 See **SCIENCE and MATH TOOLBOX** page H12 if you need to review **Measuring Elapsed Time.**

7. Now put the bottle thermometer into a bowl of warm water. Wait three minutes. Mark the straw at the level of the water. **Record** your observations.

Analyze and Conclude

1. Describe what happened to the water in the bottle thermometer when you cooled it. What happened when you warmed it? How did your predictions compare with your results?

2. Infer whether warm water takes up more space or less space than cool water. How do your observations support your inferences?

3. Hypothesize how your bottle thermometer is similar to a real thermometer.

INVESTIGATE FURTHER!

EXPERIMENT

Predict what will happen if the bottle thermometer you made is placed in sunlight. Try it. Mark the straw to show your results each time. Share your results with your classmates.

Activity

Side by Side

MATERIALS
- red paper (one sheet per student)
- plastic bag
- *Science Notebook*

In this activity you'll play a game to model how heat moves through solids.

Procedure

1. Each student should get a sheet of red paper and crumple it into a ball. These balls are models of heat.

2. One student should collect all the paper balls and be the "heat source." The other students stand in a line, with arms touching, next to the "heat source." These students are models of the particles that make up a solid.

3. The "heat source" should pass paper balls ("heat"), one at a time, to the next student in line. That student should pass the "heat" to the next student, and so on.

Analyze and Conclude

From the model, **infer** how a pan warms up when it's placed on a stove burner. **Record** your inference in your *Science Notebook*.

Step 3

Activity

Heat Takes a Trip

Why do the handles of some pots get too hot to touch safely? Find out.

MATERIALS
- goggles
- hot water
- plastic jar
- metal spoon
- wooden craft stick
- plastic spoon
- timer
- *Science Notebook*

SAFETY
Wear goggles during this activity. Clean up spills immediately.

Procedure

1. Suppose you place a metal spoon, a wooden craft stick, and a plastic spoon in hot water. With your group, **predict** what the dry end of each object will feel like after five minutes. **Record** your predictions in your *Science Notebook*.

2. Your teacher will pour hot water into a plastic jar. Place the metal spoon, wooden stick, and plastic spoon into the jar of hot water. Wait five minutes.

3. With the objects in the water, feel the dry end of each one. **Record** your observations.

Analyze and Conclude

1. Which object felt the warmest after five minutes in hot water? Which object felt the coolest?

2. **Compare** your predictions with your results. Were you surprised by the results? Explain.

3. Heat energy moves through solids. Some kinds of solids allow heat to move better than other kinds of solids. From your results, **infer** why pots are made of metal and why pot handles are often made of wood or plastic.

Step 2

Heat Waves

> **Reading Focus** What is the difference between heat and temperature?

You put a slice of cold pizza into a microwave oven and "zap" it. In a minute the crust is hot and the cheese is melted. To understand this change, you need to find out how heat changes matter.

Moving Particles

You know that all matter is made of tiny particles too small to be seen. These particles are always moving. They have heat energy.

Recall that matter can be found as a solid, a liquid, or a gas. A solid has a definite shape and takes up a definite amount of space. In a solid the particles are close together, and strong forces between particles hold them in place. So the particles can't move much. They simply vibrate back and forth.

A liquid does not have a definite shape, but it takes up a definite amount of space. The particles in a liquid have a little more space between them than the particles in a solid. Also, the forces holding the particles together are weaker. These differences allow the particles to flow past each other, so a liquid takes the shape of its container.

A gas doesn't have a definite shape or take up a definite amount of space. It takes the shape of its container and will move out of an open container. In a gas the particles are much farther apart than those in a liquid, and there are no forces holding them in place.

Compare the arrangement of particles in a solid, a liquid, and a gas. ▶

Heating and Cooling Matter

As you know, matter is made up of particles that move. When heat is added to matter, the particles in the matter move faster. The faster the particles of matter move, the more heat energy the matter has and the hotter it is. The more slowly the particles move, the less heat energy the matter has and the cooler it is.

When heat is added to the bottle thermometer in the activity on pages C40 and C41, the particles of water move faster and slightly farther apart. So the colored water takes up more space and the level of colored water rises into the straw.

Using Math What temperature readings are shown on this thermometer?

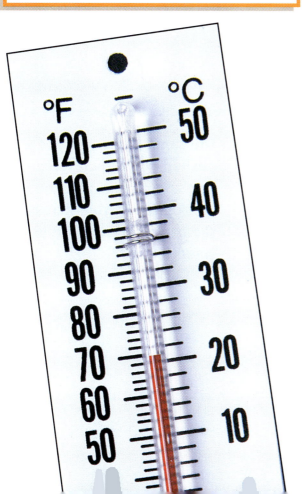

Heat and Temperature

On a cold day the air inside your house feels warm. When you step out of a hot shower, the same air feels cool. Your body isn't a very good thermometer. A bottle thermometer doesn't measure exact temperature either.

Temperature is a measure of how hot or cold something is. Temperature is measured with a thermometer. But a thermometer does not measure heat. Heat and temperature are not the same thing.

Think back to a time when you were splashed by a drop of hot water. Now imagine how it would feel to be splashed by a cup of hot water. The cup of water would cause a much more painful burn. The drop of hot water and the cup of hot water are the same temperature. But the cup of hot water has more moving particles, so it has more heat energy than the drop.

▼ **Which has more heat energy?**

drop of water
95°C (203°F)

cup of water
95°C (203°F)

C45

Making Matter Hot

Think back to the microwave oven that heated your cold pizza slice. A part inside the oven gives off invisible waves of energy called microwaves. The waves cause the tiny particles of water in the food to move faster, so your pizza gets hot.

Microwaves make particles in matter move faster. But there are other ways to do this. **Friction** (frik′shən) is a force that makes it hard for two objects to move past each other when the objects touch. When two objects rub against one another, their particles move faster, and heat is produced.

Friction makes it hard for objects to move past or over each other. There is more friction if the surfaces that are rubbing are rough rather than smooth. When there is more friction, movement takes more effort and more heat is produced. That's why your hand feels warmer when you rub it over a rough surface, such as a carpet, than when you rub it over a smooth table top. ■

These students are using a rubber band to push a block of wood across a smooth floor. ▼

▲ **The same block of wood is pushed with equal force across a carpet. Will the block slide farther across the carpet or across the smooth floor?**

Heat on the Move

Reading Focus In what ways does heat move, and how do the ways differ?

Imagine your hands are cold. To warm them, you wrap them around a cup of warm cocoa. How does the heat move from the cocoa through the cup to your hands?

A Touching Story

The activity on page C42 involves "heat" passing among people who are touching, or are in direct contact with each other. **Conduction** (kən-duk′shən) is the movement of heat by direct contact between particles of matter. The pictures show the movement of heat by conduction through a metal pot.

❶ In solids the tiny particles of matter are touching each other and have little movement.

❷ When the particles in the solid are heated, they move faster and bump into particles next to them.

❸ Then those particles start moving faster. After a while, all the particles in the solid are moving faster.

Heat energy always moves from an area of higher temperature to an area of lower temperature. That's why your cold hands are heated by a warm cup of cocoa.

CONDUCTION OF HEAT THROUGH A POT

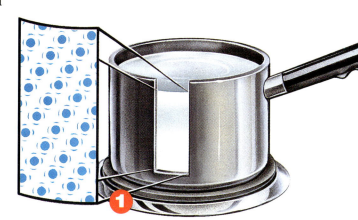

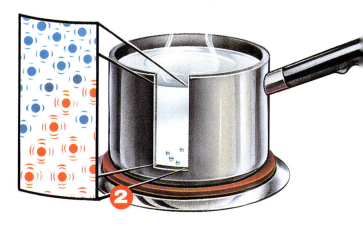

▲ Air is a good insulator. That's why two doors help keep a house warm.

▲ Fiberglass insulation helps keep heat from moving into and out of a house.

A Good Conductor

Some solids conduct heat more easily than other solids. A material that heat travels through easily is called a **conductor** (kən duk′tər).

In the activity on page C43, the metal spoon heats faster than the wooden stick or the plastic spoon. That's because metals are good conductors of heat energy. The wood and plastic do not heat as quickly. That's because these materials are not good conductors. An **insulator** (in′sə lāt ər) is a material that does not conduct heat well. Fiberglass is a material that is often used to insulate homes.

Fluid Motion

Since the particles in liquids and gases are moving around, they don't touch each other as often as do the particles in solids. Heat travels through liquids and gases by convection (kən vek′shən). **Convection** is the movement of heat through liquids and gases by the movements of particles from one part of the matter to another.

Liquids and gases are called fluids (flōō′idz). The particles in a fluid have greater freedom to move about than do particles in a solid. When heat energy is added to a fluid, the particles near the heat move faster and farther apart. Then there are fewer particles in the warmer part of the fluid than in other parts. The warmer part of the fluid becomes "lighter" and moves upward. Find out more about the movement of heat by convection in the drawing on page C49.

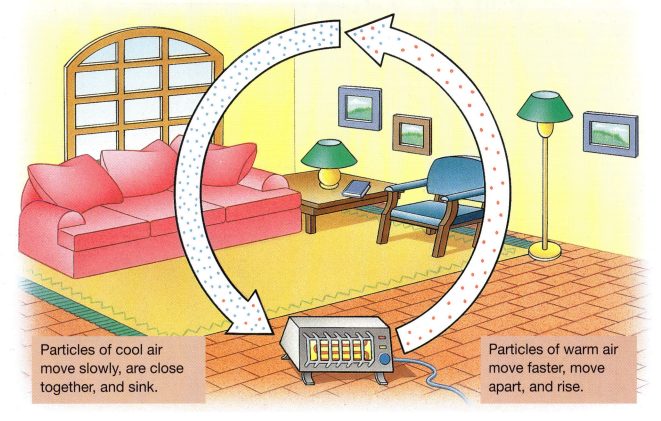

Particles of cool air move slowly, are close together, and sink.

Particles of warm air move faster, move apart, and rise.

▲ Follow the movement of air in this convection current.

Direct Rays

Conduction and convection both depend on particles of matter to carry heat from one place to another. Heat can also move through space that has little or no matter to carry it. Space that has no matter in it is called a vacuum (vak'yo͞om).

There is almost no matter in space between the Sun and Earth. If heat couldn't travel through this near vacuum, much of the Sun's energy would not reach Earth.

The Sun gives off energy called radiant (rā'dē ənt) energy. Some of this energy is in the form of light, which you can see. But much of the Sun's radiant energy is in the form of invisible waves.

These waves can travel through the near vacuum of space, where there is no matter to carry heat. The movement of heat energy in the form of waves is called **radiation** (rā dē ā'shən). Any light that shines on you can warm you by radiation. ■

UNIT PROJECT LINK

Think about how to use insulation to control how heat travels in your model home. In your Builder's Notebook, draw pictures to show how insulation would work in your model home. Begin building your model home.

Technology Link
For more help with your Unit Project, go to **www.eduplace.com**.

C49

Keeping Warm!

Reading Focus Why do materials that trap air make good cold-weather clothing?

Look at the bird standing in the snow. How does it keep warm? If you look closely, you'll see that the bird's feathers are fluffed. The fluffed feathers trap air between them. Air is a good insulator. The trapped air and the feathers help keep the bird warm.

People aren't as lucky as birds. They don't have feathers. In cold winter weather it's important to hold in body heat. Wearing layers of clothing helps to trap air and keep heat in. But some kinds of clothing are better insulators than others.

▲ How is this robin keeping warm?

Look at the pictures of different materials and fibers used for winter clothing. Fibers are single, threadlike structures from which materials used for clothing are made.

Down feathers are small, soft feathers. Down jackets contain feathers from geese. Down feathers trap air, which is a good insulator. ▼

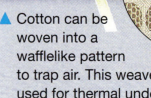

▲ Cotton can be woven into a wafflelike pattern to trap air. This weave is used for thermal underwear.

HALF PRICE BOOKS

RETURN POLICY

Cash refunds and charge card credits on all merchandise are available within 7 days of purchase with receipt. Merchandise charged to a credit card will be credited to your account. Exchange or store credit will be issued for merchandise returned within 30 days with receipt. Cash refunds for purchases made by check are available after 12 business days, and are then subject to the time limitations stated above. Please include original packaging and price tag when making a return. Proper I.D. and phone number may be required where permitted. We reserve the right to limit or decline refunds.

Gift cards cannot be returned for cash, except as required by law.

The personal information you provide is confidential and will not be sold, rented or disclosed to a third party for commercial or other purposes, except as may be required by law.

◀ Wool is often used in making winter clothing. Wool fibers have a rough, scalelike surface that traps air.

Recycled plastic bottles can be stretched into thin strands of fiber. These strands trap air well when they're used to fill jacket linings. The recycled plastic fibers can also be woven into cloth. ▼

INVESTIGATION 2 WRAP-UP

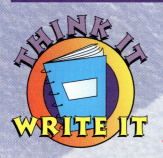

REVIEW

1. What is the difference between heat and temperature?

2. Name and describe the three ways that heat moves from one place to another.

CRITICAL THINKING

3. What happens to the temperature of a bowl of hot soup that's left out on a counter for several hours? Explain why this happens.

4. Houses are often built with insulating materials between the outside and inside walls. Explain why this is done.

Investigation 3

How Can Heat Change Materials?

If you leave a carton of ice cream on a kitchen counter, it'll soon melt into a soupy mess. What does heat have to do with this change? In this investigation you'll see how heat changes matter.

Activity

MATERIALS
- plastic cup of water
- *Science Notebook*

Cool Fingers

How does your skin feel when you climb out of a swimming pool on a breezy day? Find out why it feels that way.

Procedure

Dip one finger into a cup of water. Then blow on the wet finger and a dry finger at the same time. In your *Science Notebook*, **record** the difference in how the two fingers feel.

Analyze and Conclude

1. **Compare** the feeling of the wet finger to the dry finger when you first started blowing on them. Explain why you think the fingers felt different.

2. What happens to the water on your finger? Where do you think it goes?

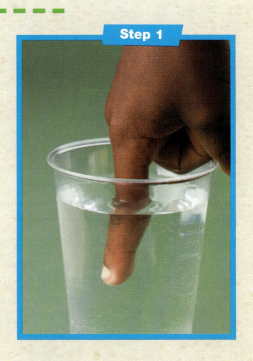

Step 1

Activity

Wet or Dry

Find out why a dry swimsuit feels warmer than a wet one.

MATERIALS
- 2 thermometers, labeled A and B
- 2 squares of cotton cloth
- water
- timer
- *Science Notebook*

SAFETY
Be careful when handling glass thermometers. Clean up spills immediately.

Procedure

1. Label two thermometers *A* and *B*. Place the thermometers side by side on your work surface.

2. **Read the temperature** shown by each thermometer. In your *Science Notebook*, **record** the temperature reading of each thermometer.

 See **SCIENCE and MATH TOOLBOX** page H8 if you need to review **Using a Thermometer.**

3. Dampen one square of cotton cloth with water. Lay the damp cloth over the bulb of thermometer *A* and a dry cloth over the bulb of thermometer *B*.

4. Allow the thermometers to sit for 15 minutes. Then **read** and **record** the temperatures again.

Analyze and Conclude

1. Did either cloth take heat from its surroundings? How do you know?

2. **Infer** why you feel cooler in a wet swimsuit than in a dry one.

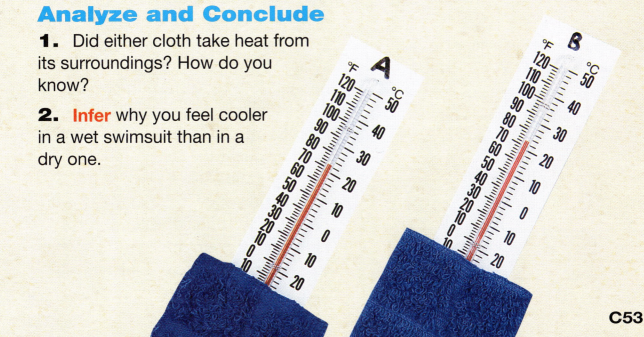

Adding and Subtracting Heat

Reading Focus What are two ways that matter can change when heat is added or subtracted?

You know that heat moves from warmer matter to cooler matter. Ice cream will melt in a warm kitchen because heat energy from the warm air moves to the cold ice cream.

Melt Away

When heat is added to a solid such as ice, the particles of the solid speed up. When the particles are moving fast enough, the solid melts. **Melt** means "to change from a solid to a liquid."

Solids melt at different temperatures. Ice cream will melt at room temperature. A chocolate bar will melt in your hand, while an iron bar will melt at 1,530°C (2,786°F).

Ice cream melts at temperatures warmer than 0°C. ▼

▲ What causes the clothes to dry?

Up, Up, and Away

When heat is added to a liquid, the particles move faster. If enough heat is added, the particles will move fast enough to escape from the liquid. The liquid will evaporate (ē vap′ə-rāt). **Evaporate** means "to change from a liquid to a gas."

Evaporation takes place in the activity on page C52 and the one on page C53. As liquid water absorbs heat from the air, the liquid changes to a gas called water vapor.

Out of Thin Air

Have you ever seen water droplets form on the outside of a pitcher of cold juice? Water vapor from the air has condensed (kən denst′) on the pitcher. **Condense** means "to change from a gas to a liquid." The particles of water vapor near the pitcher moved more slowly as they cooled. They came closer together and changed to liquid on the glass.

 Is the temperature of the iron shown greater than or less than 1,530°C?

Recall the example of melting iron on page C54. If the temperature of liquid iron goes below 1,530°C (2,786°F), the iron will become solid. This change from liquid to solid iron is another example of freezing.

Well Mixed

Heat energy can help matter mix. When a solid mixes with a liquid and becomes invisible, the solid is said to dissolve. Hot water can dissolve more of a solid, such as sugar, than an equal amount of cold water can. The particles in hot water move faster, making it possible for more sugar to dissolve.

▲ Where do the drops come from?

Liquid to a Solid

If enough heat is taken away from a liquid, it will freeze. **Freeze** means "to change to a solid." When liquid water loses heat energy, the particles of water move more and more slowly. When the particles are moving slowly enough, the forces between particles take over and the water freezes, or changes to the solid state.

Which will dissolve more sugar? ▼

C55

▲ **Why are bridges built with spaces between sections?**

The Story Expands

Particles of matter move faster and slightly farther apart when heat is added. So when matter is heated, it expands, or takes up more space.

When heat is taken away, most matter contracts, or takes up less space. As heat is taken away, particles move more slowly and move closer together. As the particles move closer, the matter gets smaller.

Water is an exception to the rule. Most matter contracts when heat is taken away. Water is different because water expands when it freezes.

Changing Forever

Recall that when heat is added to some kinds of matter, those kinds of matter change forever. Think about an egg. It looks quite different before you cook it than it does after you cook it. Other materials, such as wood, change to ash when they're burned. You can't change a cooked egg back into a raw egg any more than you can change ash back into wood. That's because heat caused chemical changes in the egg and in the wood. ■

Heat changes some matter forever. ▶

INVESTIGATION 3 WRAP-UP

REVIEW

1. What happens to a solid if you heat it to a high-enough temperature?

2. Compare what happens when a liquid evaporates with what happens when a gas condenses.

CRITICAL THINKING

3. Why is iron usually found as a solid?

4. Infer and explain why sidewalks are made with spaces between the sections of concrete.

Chapter 2 Review: Reflect & Evaluate

Word Power

Write the letter of the term that best completes each sentence. *Not all terms will be used.*

1. The ability to cause a change in matter is called ___.
2. A material that heat does not travel through easily is called a/an ___.
3. The movement of heat through liquids and gases is called ___.
4. To change from a liquid to a gas is to ___.
5. The measure of how hot or cold something is called its ___.
6. The movement of heat by direct contact of particles is called ___.

a. condense
b. conduction
c. conductor
d. convection
e. energy
f. evaporate
g. insulator
h. temperature

Check What You Know

Write the word in each pair that correctly completes each sentence.

1. Heat travels through empty space by (convection, radiation).
2. When matter changes from a gas to a liquid, it (condenses, freezes).
3. Air is a good (conductor, insulator).
4. The state of matter that has no definite volume is a (gas, liquid).

Problem Solving

1. Why isn't it a good idea to place a glass of water in a freezer?
2. Which would keep a room warmer in cold weather, a window made of two panes of glass with air trapped between them or a window with a single pane of glass? Explain.

Look at the two drawings. Name the kinds of energy present in each drawing. Then describe how the energy shown in drawing *A* is changed to the energy shown in drawing *B*.

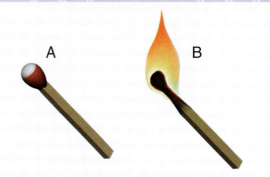

C57

CHAPTER 3

FORCE, MOTION, AND MACHINES

Suppose you had a task to perform, such as opening a stuck window or cracking a nut. You'd have to apply some force to the window or the nut. What would you do if you weren't able to apply enough force? You'd use a machine.

Connecting to Science
CULTURE

Ancient Machines Much of what we know about ancient cultures comes from studying buildings and other structures they left behind. Examples of such ancient structures are the pyramids of ancient Egypt and the giant rocks of Stonehenge, in England. Someday, historians may study our structures to learn about the culture of our times.

Today, workers use dozens of different machines, such as cranes and bulldozers, to move heavy materials. But how did the Egyptian workers move blocks weighing more than 2 tons to the top of a pyramid some 150 m (490 ft) high? They used simple machines, such as ramps and levers.

In this chapter you'll use some of these same machines. And you will find out how these machines make it easier to complete a task.

Coming Up

INVESTIGATION 1

WHAT IS A FORCE?
............C60

INVESTIGATION 2

HOW DO MACHINES MAKE WORK EASIER?
..............C68

The giant ramp shown here is a type of simple machine. ▼

Investigation 1

What Is a Force?

The player in left field is ready to catch a long fly ball hit in her direction. A sudden gust of wind comes along, and the ball lands behind her! What happened? In this investigation you'll find out how the movement of an object can be changed.

Activity

Roll On!

Think about pushing a classmate on a playground swing. Then think about pushing an adult on the same swing. If you push each with the same force, which person will swing higher? Why?

MATERIALS
- goggles
- 2 pencils
- rubber band (strong)
- 6 washers
- small toy truck
- masking tape
- meterstick
- Science Notebook

SAFETY
Wear goggles during this activity.

Procedure

1. Work on the floor in an open area. While two members of your group each holds a pencil as shown, stretch a rubber band around the pencils. The pencils should be held just far enough apart to hold the rubber band in place without stretching it.

2. Place six washers in a toy truck and tape them in place.

Step 1

3. Place the back of the toy truck against the rubber band. Pull the truck backwards to stretch the rubber band as shown. Place a small piece of masking tape on the floor to mark the exact spot where the front of the truck stops.

4. Release the truck and **observe** its motion. Use a meterstick to **measure** how far the truck rolled from the piece of masking tape. Be sure to measure to the front of the truck. **Record** this measurement in your *Science Notebook*.

Step 3

 See **SCIENCE** and **MATH TOOLBOX** page H6 if you need to review **Using a Tape Measure or Ruler.**

5. Remove the washers from the truck. Place the empty truck against the rubber band. Pull it back to exactly the same place that you pulled the loaded truck. Then repeat step 4.

Analyze and Conclude

1. What gives the truck the push needed to make it move?

2. Was the push on the loaded truck as strong as the push on the empty truck? How do you know?

3. When did the truck have more mass, in step 4 or step 5? When did the truck travel farther?

4. Based on the results, what can you **infer** about how far a given push will move objects of different masses?

INVESTIGATE FURTHER!

EXPERIMENT

Try this activity again, but this time change the size of the push instead of the mass of the truck. Use a loaded truck for both tests. Talk with your group and predict how far the truck will travel when the rubber band is stretched 10 cm and then 15 cm. Record your predictions in your *Science Notebook*. Then do the tests. Record the results.

C61

Activity
Gravity Roll

MATERIALS
- smooth board
- several books
- masking tape
- meterstick
- small toy truck
- *Science Notebook*

Imagine you are on a skateboard at the top of a hill. How would the steepness of the hill affect the distance you would travel once you reached the bottom of the hill? Find out.

Procedure

1. Make a ramp about 20 cm high by placing one end of a smooth board on a stack of books. Use masking tape to mark a line on the ramp 20 cm from the top.

 Math Hint Your science book is about 2.5 cm thick.

2. In your *Science Notebook*, **make a chart** like the one shown. **Measure** the height of the ramp from the floor to the strip of masking tape. **Record** the height in your chart.

Trial Number	Height of Ramp	Distance Traveled
1		

3. Place a toy truck on the ramp. The front of the truck should be at the starting line. Release the truck and **observe** how far it travels from the bottom end of the ramp. Use a meterstick to **measure** this distance. **Record** the results in your chart in the column labeled *Distance Traveled* for Trial 1.

Step 1

4. **Talk with your group** and **predict** how increasing the height of the ramp will change the distance the truck will travel. **Record** your prediction. Add enough books to the stack to make the strip of masking tape about 30 cm high. **Measure** the height and **record** it in the row for Trial 2.

5. Repeat step 3. **Record** the distance for Trial 2.

6. Lower the height of the ramp to about 10 cm. **Measure** the height and **record** it. Repeat step 3. **Record** the distance in the row for Trial 3.

Analyze and Conclude

1. What force pulls the trucks down the ramp?

2. **Make a bar graph** to show the information in your chart. Show the heights of the ramp along the bottom of the graph and the distances traveled by the truck along the side.

 See **SCIENCE** and **MATH TOOLBOX** page H3 if you need to review **Making a Bar Graph**.

3. **Draw a conclusion** about how the height of the ramp is related to the distance the truck travels. **Record** your conclusion.

INVESTIGATE FURTHER!

EXPERIMENT

Repeat this activity with one important change—place a second toy truck at the foot of the ramp. Have one toy truck move down the ramp and strike the second toy truck. Measure and record the changes in motion that occur to both trucks.

Step 3

Force, Energy, and Friction

Reading Focus What happens to the motion of an object when a force is applied to the object?

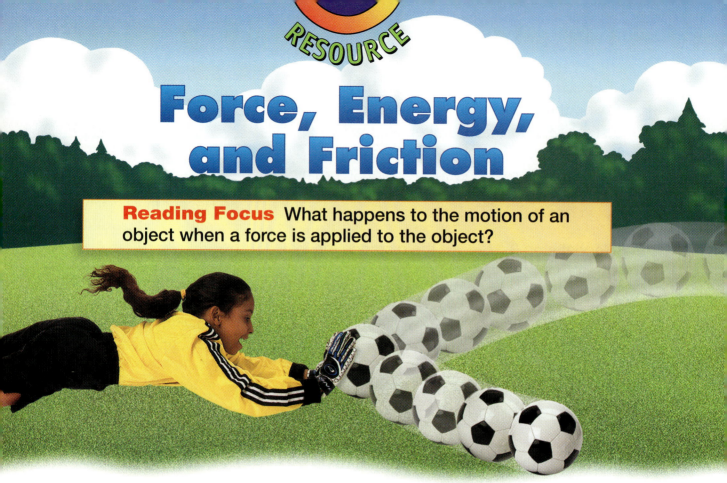

There are 20 seconds left in the soccer game. Your team is ahead by a goal. A member of the other team sends the ball speeding toward your team's goal. Your goalie dives. Her hands barely touch the ball, but just enough to push it wide of the goal. She has made the save!

Pushes and Pulls

When the goalie pushed the ball away from the goal, she applied a force to the ball. A **force** is a push or a pull. When a force is applied to an object, the force can cause a change in the object's motion.

A force on an object can cause it to change direction. This is what happened when the goalie pushed the soccer ball. A force can also change an object's speed, or how fast the object is moving. Think about what happens when you kick a slow-moving soccer ball. The force (push) of your kick causes the ball to move faster. It may also cause the ball to move in a different direction.

It Takes Energy

When you push or pull an object, you apply a force to that object. It takes energy to apply a force. Recall from Chapter 2 that energy is the ability to cause changes in matter.

In the activity on pages C60 and C61, energy is used to stretch a rubber band by pulling it back with a toy truck. This energy is stored in the rubber band. The stretched rubber band is then used to apply a force to the toy truck. When the truck is released, the rubber band

◀ Kicking or pushing a soccer ball can cause it to change direction.

applies a force to the truck. This force causes the truck to speed away from the rubber band.

Familiar Forces in Nature

If you drop something, it falls. If you apply the brakes on your bicycle, the bicycle slows down or stops. These are familiar experiences. Since motion is changing in both of these examples, forces must be at work. The forces at work are gravity and friction.

Gravity (grav'i tē) is a force that pulls objects toward each other. The size of the force depends on the masses of the objects pulling on each other. The greater the masses, the greater the force of gravity. In the activity on pages C62 and C63, Earth's gravity causes the toy truck to roll down the ramp. The steeper the ramp is made, the more Earth's gravity affects the truck.

Earth is so big and has so much mass, it exerts a strong pull on everything on and near its surface. When you drop something, Earth's gravity pulls that object down toward Earth's surface. You've felt the effects of gravity if you've ever fallen off your bicycle after jamming on the brakes. Gravity pulled you to the ground.

Earlier in this unit you learned about friction. Friction is a force that makes it hard for two objects in contact to move past each other. When you apply the brakes on your in-line skates, you cause the brake pads to rub against the surface on which you're skating. Friction between the brake pads and the surface causes the skates (and you) to slow down and then stop. ■

Friction helps the skater stop. ▼

The Greatest Invention

Reading Focus How has the wheel been improved throughout history?

What is the most important invention in history? Of course, there is no single right answer to this question. But if you said "the wheel," many people would agree with you. The wheel is certainly *one* of the most important inventions.

The next improvement was the development of the spoked wheel. The earliest spoked wheels had wooden rims connected to the center by several (usually 4 or 6) spokes. Spoked wheels were lighter and stronger than solid wheels.

2000 B.C.

The first wheel appeared in Sumer, an area of Mesopotamia (mes ə pə tā′mē ə) near present-day Iraq. The earliest wheels were probably used for making pottery.

5000–3000 B.C.

2500 B.C.
Logs were used as rollers in ancient Egypt to help move giant stone statues. During the same period, Sumerians were using solid wooden wheels on their carts and chariots.

C66

In China and Japan, large wheels with iron rims and as many as 20 spokes were used on carts transporting goods throughout Asia. Two hundred years later, similar wheels were on the covered wagons used by settlers of America's West.

A.D. 1600

This century has seen a constant development of new and better materials for tires and wheels, like the aluminum alloy automobile wheel shown here.

20TH CENTURY

1700–1900

Many different kinds of wheels were used in machines invented during the Industrial Revolution. Spoked metal wheels protected by air-filled tires were used on early versions of the automobile.

1000 B.C.

Steel rims, or "tires," were added to wheels to make them last longer. Celtic chariots had the first lightweight spoked wheels with steel rims.

INVESTIGATION 1 WRAP-UP

REVIEW

1. What is a force?

2. Name two ways that a force can change the motion of an object.

CRITICAL THINKING

3. Suppose you are standing on a dock next to a large ocean liner. Which exerts the stronger pull of gravity on your body, Earth or the ocean liner? Explain.

4. Why is friction considered to be a force?

C67

How Do Machines Make Work Easier?

Have you ever swung a baseball bat or raked leaves? If so, you have used a machine. You may be surprised to learn that these objects are machines. In this investigation you'll find out about machines and learn how they help us move things.

Activity

The Ups and Downs of a Seesaw

A seesaw is a type of lever. To make your end go up, someone needs to push down on the other end. How much force must that person use? Where should he or she sit? Find out.

MATERIALS
- tape
- 3 round pencils
- 2 small paper cups
- metric ruler
- modeling clay
- paper clips
- *Science Notebook*

Procedure

1. Tape three pencils together as shown.

2. Tape a paper cup to each end of a metric ruler. Place the ruler on the pencils so that the middle of the ruler rests on the top of the pencils. The point where the ruler touches the pencils is called the **fulcrum** (ful′ krəm).

Step 1

 To find the middle of a 30-cm ruler, divide 30 by 2.

C68

3. Place a piece of clay the size of a large marble in the cup at the zero end of the ruler.

4. Add paper clips, one at a time, to the cup at the other end until the clay end of the ruler is lifted. Then count the paper clips.

5. In your *Science Notebook*, **make a chart** like the one shown. **Record** the distance from the fulcrum to the cup with the paper clips. Then **record** the number of paper clips needed to lift the clay.

Distance From Fulcrum to Paper Clips	Number of Paper Clips Needed to Lift the Clay
15 cm	

6. Move the ruler so that the fulcrum is 10 cm from the cup with the clay. Repeat steps 4 and 5.

7. Move the fulcrum to the 5-cm mark. **Talk with your group** and **predict** how many paper clips will be needed to lift the clay. **Record** your prediction. Then repeat step 4 and **record** your data.

INVESTIGATE FURTHER!

EXPERIMENT

Suppose you and a friend are going to ride on a seesaw. How would you change your position on the seesaw if you were using it with a friend who weighs less than you do? with a friend who weighs more than you do? The next time you're on a playground, check your predictions.

Analyze and Conclude

1. **Talk with your group** and **predict** how many paper clips you would need if the fulcrum were at the 8-cm mark and at the 20-cm mark. Then check your predictions.

2. What can you **infer** about how the lever makes the job of lifting the clay ball easier?

Step 4

Activity

Ramps and Rocks

Suppose you had to help move a heavy rock from the ground onto the back of a truck. Would it be easier to lift the rock straight up or to slide it up a ramp? Find out.

MATERIALS
- goggles
- string
- small rock
- paper clip
- thin rubber band
- metric ruler
- smooth board
- several books
- *Science Notebook*

SAFETY
Wear goggles during this activity.

Procedure

1. Tie a piece of string around a small rock. Bend a paper clip into a double hook. Connect it to the rock as shown.

2. In your *Science Notebook*, **make a chart** like the one shown. **Measure** the length of an unstretched rubber band. **Record** the length in your chart.

LENGTH OF RUBBER BAND		
Unstretched	Lifting Rock	Pulling Rock Up Ramp

 See **SCIENCE and MATH TOOLBOX** page H6 if you need to review **Using a Tape Measure or Ruler.**

3. Hook the rubber band to the paper clip and rock. With a smooth, even motion, use the rubber band to lift the rock straight up. Have a member of your group **measure** the length of the stretched rubber band. **Record** this length in your chart.

4. Make a ramp by placing one end of a smooth board on a stack of books. Place the rock at the bottom of the ramp.

Step 1

5. Slowly pull on the hook and rubber band until the rock starts to move up the ramp. Continue to pull at a slow, steady rate so that the rubber band remains stretched at the same length. Have a group member **measure** and **record** the length of the stretched rubber band as you pull on it.

6. Make the slope of the ramp steeper by adding two or three more books to the stack. **Talk with your group** and **predict** how a steeper ramp will affect the length of the stretched rubber band as you pull the rock up the ramp. **Record** your prediction. Then repeat step 5 using the steeper ramp.

Analyze and Conclude

1. Did you have to apply more force to lift the rock or to pull it up the ramp? How do you know?

2. How did making the ramp steeper affect the amount of force needed to pull the rock up the ramp? How did this result compare with your prediction?

3. **Draw a conclusion** about how using a ramp affects the job of raising a heavy object.

UNIT PROJECT LINK

Look back at your list of the many kinds of energy that people use at home. Think of ways people can conserve, or save, each kind of energy. In your Builder's Notebook, draw pictures with labels to show how these energy-saving ideas would work in your model home.

For more help with your Unit Project, go to www.eduplace.com.

Step 5

Machines— Force Changers

> **Reading Focus** In what two ways can a simple machine change a force applied to it?

Have you ever seen someone try to remove the lid from a can of cocoa, such as the one shown in the pictures?

The boy is pulling up on the lid with his bare fingers. He finds that he can't apply enough force to move the lid. The girl is using a machine to help her perform the task. A **machine** is something that makes a task easier to do.

Keeping It Simple

What do you think of when you hear the word *machine*? You probably think of some big, noisy device powered by electricity or a gasoline engine. Many machines are like that.

Machines can also be very simple, with few moving parts. In the activity on pages C68 and C69, paper clips were added to one end of a seesaw to lift a ball of clay at the other end.

How does a machine make the girl's task easier?

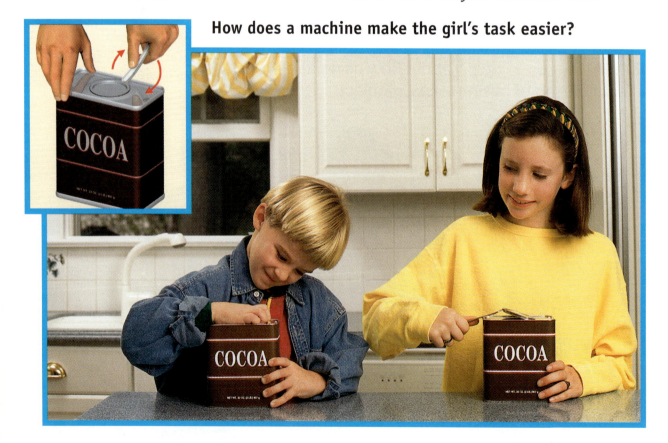

You used the seesaw as a simple machine called a lever (lev′ər). A **simple machine** is a device that changes the size or direction of a force.

A **lever** is a simple machine made up of a bar that turns, or rotates, around a fixed point. The fixed point around which a lever turns is called a **fulcrum** (ful′krəm). The girl in the picture is using the spoon handle as a lever. She is pushing down on the bowl of the spoon and the handle is pushing up on the lid at the other end. The edge of the can acts as the fulcrum. Used in this way, the lever changes both the size and direction of the girl's force. ∎

▲ Levers in action

Science in Literature

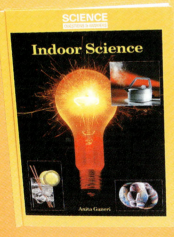

Indoor Science
by Anita Ganeri
Dillon Press, 1993

A Tough Nut to Crack

"We use lots of different machines and tools around our homes. Many of them make life easier for us. Some, such as washing machines and television sets, are very complicated. . . . But other machines, such as nutcrackers, are much simpler. They use a person's own muscle power to make them work."

What kind of a simple machine is a nutcracker? Find out about this and other simple machines in *Indoor Science* by Anita Ganeri. See how many of these simple machines you have used.

More About Machines

Reading Focus What are some examples of simple machines you use every day?

Other Simple Machines

Look at the picture of the playhouse. There are two ways to reach the playhouse. You can climb straight up the ladder. Or, you can walk up the ramp. Which way to the playhouse is easier?

You would use less force walking up the ramp. A ramp is an example of a simple machine called an inclined plane. An **inclined plane** is a simple machine with a slanted surface. *Inclined* is another word for "slanted." In the activity on pages C70 and C71, the ramp makes it easier to raise a rock.

▲ A wedge *(top)* and a screw *(bottom)* are inclined planes that move.

Some kinds of inclined planes move. The screw and the wedge are examples of inclined planes that move. The threads of a screw are like an inclined plane wrapped around the center of the screw. The threads move as the screw is turned. A wedge is two inclined planes placed back-to-back. When a wedge is struck on a log, the wedge moves into the wood and pushes it apart, making it split.

Using Math Look at where the ladder and the ramp meet the playhouse. Which one makes an angle that is more like a right angle?

Is a doorknob a simple machine? If you've ever tried opening a door without one, you know that a doorknob helps make the task easier. A doorknob is an example of a wheel and axle.

A **wheel and axle** is a simple machine that is made up of two wheels that turn together. Force is usually applied to the larger wheel. This force causes the smaller wheel, which is called the axle, to turn.

Without a pulley, how would you raise a flag to the top of the flagpole? ▼

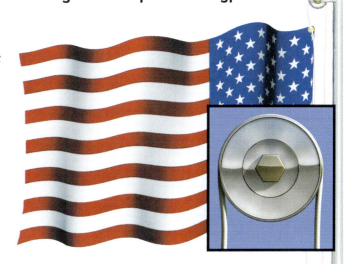

▲ **The doorknob is the wheel; it turns the axle that runs through the door.**

As you may have guessed, the "wheels" in a wheel and axle often don't look like wheels.

Each day, across our country, people raise flags to the tops of flagpoles. Most of them use a simple machine called a pulley. A **pulley** is a wheel around which a rope or chain is passed. The fixed pulley shown here changes the direction of a force. You pull down on the rope. The flag moves up. In other types of pulley setups, the force is applied in the same direction as the object moves.

As you have learned, we use simple machines all the time. So the next time you walk up a ramp, turn a faucet handle, or use a can opener, think about how your task is being made easier.

▲ **A faucet handle is a wheel.**

Internet Field Trip
Visit **www.eduplace.com** to learn more about simple machines and how they work.

Working Together

What do you suppose happens if you combine two or more simple machines? If you guessed that such a machine makes tasks even easier, you are right.

A machine that is made up of two or more simple machines is called a **compound machine**. Study the picture to find out the simple machines that are combined in a familiar compound machine—the bicycle.

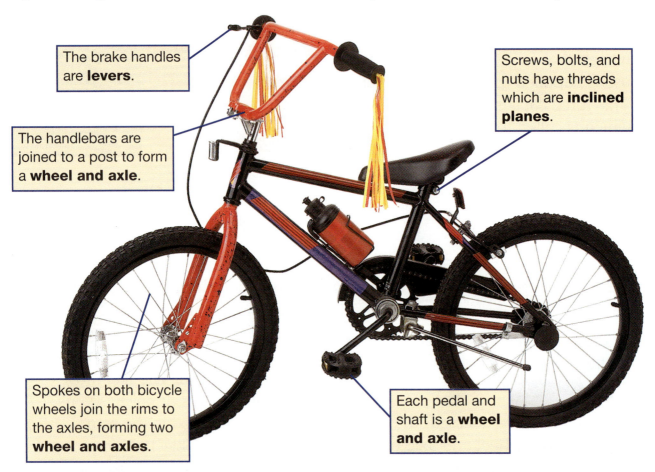

The brake handles are **levers**.

The handlebars are joined to a post to form a **wheel and axle**.

Screws, bolts, and nuts have threads which are **inclined planes**.

Spokes on both bicycle wheels join the rims to the axles, forming two **wheel and axles**.

Each pedal and shaft is a **wheel and axle**.

INVESTIGATION 2 WRAP-UP

REVIEW

1. In what two ways can a simple machine affect a force applied to it?

2. Give one example of each simple machine: lever, inclined plane, and wheel and axle.

CRITICAL THINKING

3. Suppose you turn the handle of a pencil sharpener. What kind of simple machine is the handle? Explain.

4. How does making an inclined plane steeper affect the amount of force needed to move a load up the plane? Explain your answer.

REFLECT & EVALUATE

Word Power

Write the letter of the term that best matches the definition. *Not all terms will be used.*

1. Simple machine with a slanted surface
2. A bar that rotates around a fixed point called a fulcrum
3. Any device that makes a task easier to do
4. A push or a pull
5. Force that pulls objects toward each other
6. Wheel around which a rope or chain is passed

a. force
b. friction
c. gravity
d. inclined plane
e. lever
f. machine
g. pulley
h. wheel and axle

Check What You Know

Write the word in each pair that correctly completes each sentence.

1. A ramp is an example of (a lever, an inclined plane).
2. A force applied to an object can change the object's (mass, motion).
3. A bicycle is a (simple machine, compound machine).
4. A force that pulls objects toward Earth is (friction, gravity).

Problem Solving

1. To move a heavy object, you use a crowbar as a lever, with a rock as the fulcrum. Where would you place the rock? Explain.
2. When you hit a baseball, does the bat exert a force on the ball? How do you know?
3. A rope passed through a wheel is used to move a heavy object up a ramp. What kind of machine is used here? Explain.

Study the drawing. Identify each type of simple machine shown. Then explain how each machine helps make a task easier to do.

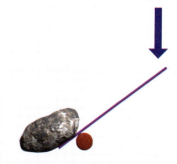

UNIT C Using READING SKILLS

Detecting the Sequence

Sequence is the order in which things happen. Sometimes a paragraph contains signal words, such as *first*, *then*, *next*, and *later*. When a paragraph doesn't contain signal words, look for other clues, such as numbers in the text or numbered steps in a drawing.

Look for these clues to detect the sequence.
- Signal words: *first, then, next, later*
- Numbers in the text
- Numbered steps in a drawing

Read the selection below. Then complete the exercises that follow.

Changes in Matter

You and a friend watch as a pizza cook crushes some fresh tomatoes to make a sauce. Then she cuts up some green peppers and mushrooms and shreds some cheese. The cook has caused changes in all these food items.

Next the cook spreads the sauce, vegetables, and cheese over flattened pizza dough. She places the dough and toppings in a hot oven. As the pizza bakes, more changes take place.

1. Which statement tells the last step in making a pizza? Write the letter of that statement.

    a. The pizza cook crushes some fresh tomatoes.

    b. She cuts up some vegetables and shreds some cheese.

    c. She spreads the sauce, vegetables, and cheese over pizza dough.

    d. She places the dough and toppings in a hot oven.

2. Which clue helped you keep track of the sequence?

Using Math Skills

Bar Graph

A seesaw is a simple lever. This bar graph shows the lengths of various types of seesaws, from tiny to jumbo.

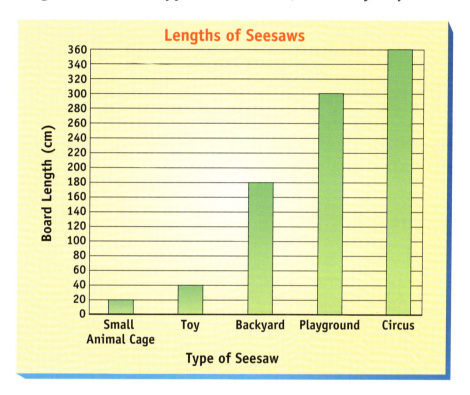

Use the data in the bar graph to complete the exercises.

1. How long is the longest seesaw? the shortest?
2. How much longer is the backyard seesaw than the toy seesaw?
3. How much longer is the playground seesaw than the toy seesaw?
4. Which seesaw is twice as long as the backyard seesaw? What is its length?

You may wish to use a calculator for Exercise 5.

5. Which three seesaws when placed end to end will be exactly 500 centimeters long?

UNIT C WRAP-UP!

On your own, use scientific methods to investigate a question about matter, energy, or forces.

THINK LIKE A SCIENTIST

Ask a Question

Pose a question about matter, energy, or forces that you would like to investigate. For example, ask, "How does the angle of a ramp affect the force acting on a toy car moving down the ramp?"

Make a Hypothesis

Suggest a hypothesis that is a possible answer to the question. One hypothesis is that the greater the angle of the ramp, the greater is the force acting on the toy car.

Plan and Do a Test

Plan a controlled experiment to find the effect that increasing the angle of the ramp has on the force acting on the toy car. You could start with a toy car, a board, and a timer. Develop a procedure that uses these materials to test the hypothesis. With permission, carry out your experiment. Follow the safety guidelines on pages S14–S15.

Record and Analyze

Observe carefully and record your data accurately. Make repeated observations.

Draw Conclusions

Look for evidence to support the hypothesis or to show that it is false. Draw conclusions about the hypothesis. Repeat the experiment to verify the results.

WRITING IN SCIENCE
Summary

Write a summary of "Heat on the Move," pages C47–C49. Use these guidelines in writing your summary.
- State the main ideas.
- List only the most important supporting details.
- Sum up the content in a statement.

Earth's Resources

Theme: Systems

THINK LIKE A SCIENTIST
FLOATING BERRIES D2

CHAPTER 1 **Air as a Natural Resource** D4
Investigation 1   What Are Natural Resources? D6
Investigation 2   How Is Air Used? D12

CHAPTER 2 **Water on Earth** D20
Investigation 1   Where Is Water Found on Earth,
                 and Why Is Water Important? D22
Investigation 2   How Can Sources of Fresh
                 Water Be Protected? D34

CHAPTER 3 **Land as a Natural Resource** D46
Investigation 1   How Do the Forces of Nature
                 Change Earth's Surface? D48
Investigation 2   Why Are Rocks and Soil
                 Important? D54

Using Reading Skills D62
Using Math Skills D63
Unit Wrap-up! D64

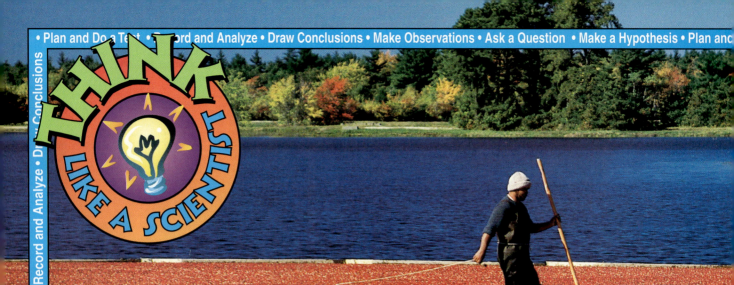

FLOATING BERRIES

This colorful photo shows cranberries being harvested in a bog in Massachusetts. Bogs are wet, marshy areas with acid soil. Ripe cranberries are harvested in an unusual way. First, the growers flood the bogs with fresh water. Then machines, called water reels, are used to stir up the water. This movement causes the cranberries to fall off their vines. Wooden boards are used to push the floating berries to the shore.

THINK LIKE A SCIENTIST

Questioning In this unit you'll study natural resources. You'll find out why air, water, and soil are so very important to people on Earth. You'll investigate questions such as these.

- How Can Sources of Fresh Water Be Protected?
- Why Are Rocks and Soil Important?

Observing, Testing, Hypothesizing In the Activity "Let's Clear This Up," you'll find out how filtering water is the first step in cleaning water. You'll also hypothesize how filtering changes muddy water.

Researching In the Resource "Wee Beasties," you'll find out why water that looks clean may still have germs in it. You'll learn what can be done to clean such water.

Drawing Conclusions After you've completed your investigations, you'll draw conclusions about what you've learned—and get new ideas.

CHAPTER 1

AIR AS A NATURAL RESOURCE

Imagine a spring morning, when the air is crisp and clean and sweet smelling. On such a day you might breathe deeply just because it feels good. Unless people take care of Earth's air, a perfect spring morning could become a thing of the past.

PEOPLE USING SCIENCE

Environmental Management Engineer

All people need industries to produce goods, such as food, clothing, and cars. But in making these goods, the companies also produce wastes which pollute the environment and affect people's health. That's where Dr. Corazon Claudio comes in. She advises companies on how to prevent pollution. She also suggests ways to reduce, reuse, or recycle wastes.

Dr. Claudio studied both engineering and business management in the Philippines and at Stanford University, in California. Today, she lives in the Philippines, where she works hard helping industries and communities protect Earth's resources. What are Earth's resources? You'll find out as you read this chapter.

Coming Up

INVESTIGATION 1
WHAT ARE NATURAL RESOURCES?
.... D6

INVESTIGATION 2
HOW IS AIR USED?
.... D12

◀ Dr. Corazon Claudio advises companies about pollution prevention in the Philippines and in other Asian countries.

INVESTIGATION 1

WHAT ARE NATURAL RESOURCES?

"Don't burn leaves! That will foul the air." "Dumping motor oil down the drain could ruin the water supply." "Littering can poison the soil." Why should people care about Earth's air, water, and land? In this investigation you'll find out.

Activity

Be Resourceful

Count the ways people use air, water, and land.

MATERIALS
• Science Notebook

Procedure

In your *Science Notebook*, **make a chart** like the one shown. **Observe** how air, water, and land is used in and around your school. **Record** a tally mark in your chart each time you see one of these resources being used.

Use of Resources		
Air	Water	Land

 See **SCIENCE and MATH TOOLBOX** page H5 if you need to review **Making a Tally Chart**.

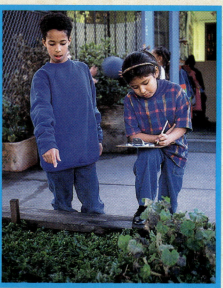

Analyze and Conclude

1. Which resource—air, water, or land—seems to have the most uses?

2. Describe ways air, water, and land are used.

Activity
Working Air

MATERIALS
- materials such as straws, paper, scissors, and glue
- *Science Notebook*

Some natural resources help to supply energy. For example, a waterfall can move parts of a machine called a turbine to make electricity. Experiment to find out how air can also move things.

Procedure

1. With your group, **plan an experiment** to show that air can move things. Your experiment can use materials such as those on the list as well as others. **Record** your plan in your *Science Notebook*.

2. Have your teacher approve your plan. **Predict** the results of your experiment. **Record** your prediction. Then carry out your experiment.

3. **Record** the results of your experiment.

Analyze and Conclude

1. How did your results compare with your prediction?

2. How did you show that air can move things?

3. **Infer** how moving air can be a natural resource.

Technology Link CD-ROM

INVESTIGATE FURTHER!

Use the **Best of the Net—Science CD-ROM**, Physical Sciences, *Energy Quest,* to find out how natural resources such as wind, water, sunlight, and fossil fuels are used for energy.

Step 1

Earth Matters

Reading Focus What are the three basic Earth materials, and why are they called natural resources?

Earth has sometimes been described as a giant spaceship. Indeed, Earth supplies people with the things they need as they travel through space on this big blue ball.

A Big Blue Ball

If you could see Earth from space, it would look like a big ball. You would see the brown of its land and the white of its clouds. But what you would likely see most clearly is the striking blue of its oceans. That's because most of Earth's surface is covered by water. Surrounding the Earth is a blanket of air called the **atmosphere** (at'məs fir). So Earth is a ball of water and land surrounded by air.

Living things on Earth, including human beings, depend on air to live. Air is a mixture of invisible gases. Animals need to breathe the gas oxygen (äks'i jən) from the air. Plants need oxygen as well as carbon dioxide (kär'bən dī äks'īd), another gas in air. Plants use carbon dioxide to make food.

Living things found in water and in soil also need oxygen and carbon dioxide to survive. Because there is air both in water and in soil, living things can thrive in these places.

The gases of its atmosphere make Earth the only planet known to be able to support life. ▶

Linked Together

Earth's three basic materials—air, water, and land—interact with each other. Some interactions you can see and even feel. For example, you can feel when the wind picks up sand and blows it in your eyes. Wind also causes waves on the ocean. Large ocean waves crash to shore—sometimes removing sand from the beach, sometimes moving it onto the beach. Some interactions you can't see. For example, every second of every day, some water from Earth's oceans enters the atmosphere as an invisible gas. Because Earth's air, water, and land are linked, activities that affect one resource can end up affecting the others.

Natural Resources

A **natural resource** is any material found on or in Earth that is used by people. Air, water, and land are Earth's basic natural resources. People need air to breathe, water to drink, and land on which to grow food. Some uses of these basic natural resources are investigated in the activity on page D6.

No living thing can live very long without enough air and water. And land is needed by many living things. So having enough air, water, and land matters to one and all. ■

Air interacts with land. ▼

Air interacts with water. ▼

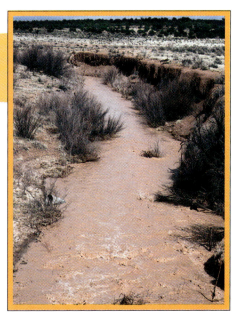

▲ **Water interacts with land.**

D9

Here Today, Gone Tomorrow?

Reading Focus What are the three types of natural resources?

Air, water, and land are Earth's basic resources. But there are other natural resources that people use.

Resources From Resources

A **mineral** (min′ər əl) is a solid found in nature that has a definite chemical makeup. Most minerals are obtained from Earth's land, often by mining them. Examples of minerals are salt, chalk, metal ores, and gems, such as diamonds. Think of ways people use minerals.

People drill down through solid rock to bring up oil and natural gas. They also dig deep mines to haul coal from Earth. Oil, natural gas, and coal are natural resources called **fossil fuels** (fäs′əl fyoo′əlz). Fossil fuels are substances that formed when plants and animals living millions of years ago decayed. Fossil fuels are very useful natural resources. They supply energy to heat and light our houses and to run our factories.

The living things of today are also natural resources. Plants and animals are used as food. Wood from trees is used for building materials and to make paper.

How many natural resources can you find in this picture? Which are living things? ▼

Three Types of Resources

The table shows how natural resources can be classified as one of three types. Resources can be renewable, nonrenewable, or inexhaustible (in eg zôs′tə bəl).

NATURAL RESOURCES

Type of Resource	Example
A **renewable resource** is one that can be replaced within a person's lifetime.	• Trees reproduce and can be planted to replace those cut down for timber. • Water that is dirty can be cleaned at treatment plants. • Air is recycled by nature.
A **nonrenewable resource** is one that cannot be replaced within a person's lifetime. The supplies of renewable resources decrease as they are used.	• Fossil fuels are being used up faster than they are forming. • Minerals such as diamonds are found in limited amounts. • Rain can wash away soil that takes thousands of years to form.
An **inexhaustible resource** is one that does not decrease, or become used up, as people use it.	• Wind can drive windmills to produce electricity. • Sunlight can be used to make hot water and to heat homes. • Waterfalls can turn turbines (machines) to produce electricity.

INVESTIGATION 1 WRAP-UP

REVIEW

1. What is a natural resource? Why are air, water, and land natural resources?

2. Classify trees, fossil fuels, minerals, soil, wind, and water as renewable, nonrenewable, or inexhaustible resources.

CRITICAL THINKING

3. Are renewable resources also inexhaustible resources? Explain your thinking.

4. Many cities and towns recycle metals, glass, and other materials. Why is it important to recycle resources?

Investigation 2

How Is Air Used?

The atmosphere, the blanket of air that surrounds Earth, is made of different gases. People take in oxygen from the atmosphere when they breathe. In this investigation you'll find out about oxygen and other gases in the atmosphere. And you'll see why these gases are important to people.

Activity

Greenhouse Gas

Some gases in the atmosphere are called greenhouse gases. How do greenhouse gases affect Earth?

MATERIALS
- materials for models: rocks, soil, plants, water
- goggles
- 2 clear plastic bottles (2 L), with tops cut off
- 2 paper clips
- 2 thermometers
- plastic wrap
- rubber band
- timer
- *Science Notebook*

SAFETY
Wear goggles during this activity.

Procedure

1. In your *Science Notebook*, **make a chart** like the one shown.

Time	Temperature (°C) Covered	Temperature (°C) Uncovered
Start:		

2. Use rocks, soil, and plants to **make a model** of an environment in the bottom part of a large plastic bottle. Make another model, just like the first one. Add water to moisten the soil in each bottle.

D12

3. Your teacher will help you use a paper clip to hang a thermometer inside each model.

4. Use a sheet of plastic wrap to cover the top of one model. Use a rubber band to hold the plastic wrap in place. Leave the other model uncovered.

Step 4

5. Put both models in a sunny place. **Predict** what will happen to the temperature of each model environment. Then **measure** and **record** the temperature of each model.

 See **SCIENCE and MATH TOOLBOX** page H8 if you need to review **Using a Thermometer**.

6. After ten minutes, **measure** and **record** the temperature of each model again. Repeat this every ten minutes for one hour. **Compare** your data with the data of other students in your class.

Analyze and Conclude

1. Which model is more like the Earth? How is this model different from the Earth.

2. What pattern, if any, do you see when you compare your data with that of other students in your class?

3. **Describe** what happened to the temperature in each model. In what way did the two models behave differently?

4. **Suggest a hypothesis** to explain any differences you observed in the two models.

UNIT PROJECT LINK

For this Unit Project you will plan and hold an Environmental Fair. With your class, plan and carry out a way you can help care for Earth's air. Then with your group, make a poster to show what you did to protect Earth's air.

 Technology Link

For more help with your Unit Project, go to **www.eduplace.com**.

It's Got Atmosphere

Reading Focus How is Earth's atmosphere important to all living things?

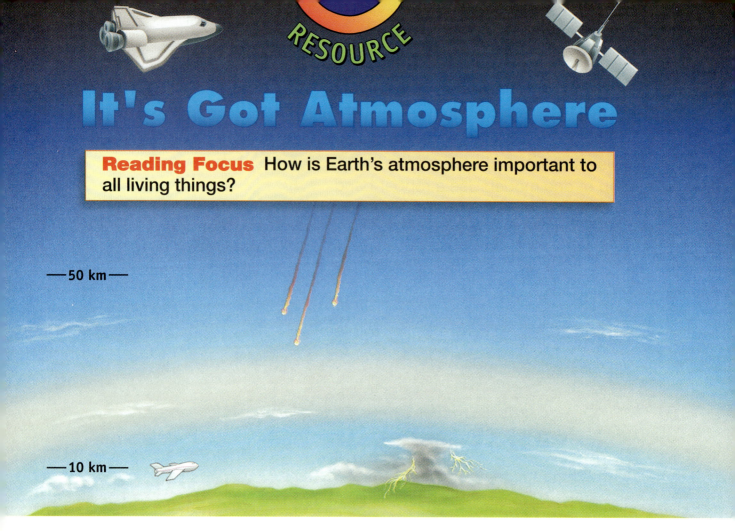

▲ Earth's atmosphere extends more than 700 km above Earth's surface.

Some young children keep a favorite blanket with them all the time. Such a blanket is called a security blanket. *Security*, in this sense, means "safe." In a way, Earth has a security blanket, too.

Earth's Security Blanket

Earth's security blanket is its atmosphere. The atmosphere begins at Earth's surface. Imagine you could rise from the surface upward through the atmosphere. If you could, you would find that breathing became more difficult. As you go higher in the atmosphere, the air particles spread out and the air becomes thinner. Why is there less air? Gravity holds the air around Earth. As the distance from the center of Earth increases, the effects of gravity decrease.

You can compare gravity's "grip" to the force of a magnet. Think of how a magnet's ability to attract a steel paper clip decreases as the magnet and clip are moved farther apart. Likewise, as you move farther away from Earth, the pull of gravity becomes less, too. In fact, at about 700 km (435 mi) above Earth, the air is so thin that you'd probably say the atmosphere was gone.

Warming Earth

You know that people need air to live. But the atmosphere does other things for people, too. The atmosphere allows much of the Sun's energy to reach Earth's surface. Earth's surface absorbs this energy and then releases much of it back into the air. This energy warms the atmosphere.

Some gases, such as carbon dioxide, are good at absorbing the energy released by Earth's surface. Such gases are called greenhouse gases. Greenhouse gases help warm the atmosphere, as is modeled in the activity on pages D12 and D13.

The warm air near Earth's surface warms the land and water. The movement of air around Earth helps carry heat all over the world.

The atmosphere also acts as a filter, as shown in the drawing below. It allows much of the Sun's light to come through. But it blocks many invisible rays of energy coming from the Sun. Some of these rays could harm living things.

Gases Back and Forth

As you have learned, air is a mixture of invisible gases. Among the most important are oxygen, carbon dioxide, and water vapor.

Animals, including people, breathe oxygen. The oxygen you breathe is used by the body to break down food. This activity releases energy that the body can use. A waste product of this activity is carbon dioxide. So people and animals breathe out some carbon dioxide.

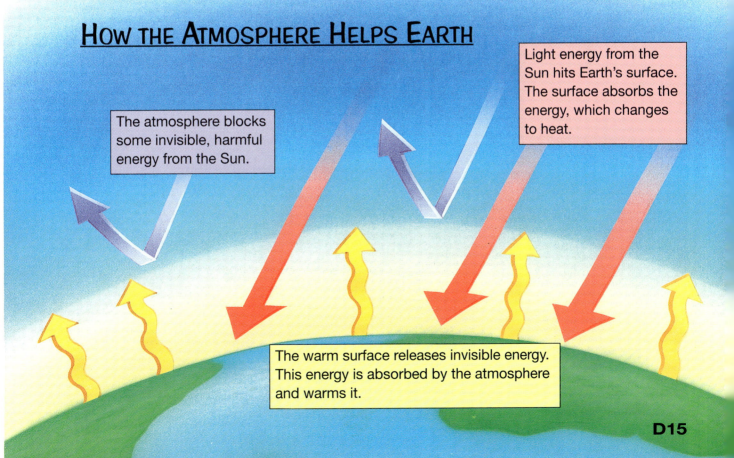

HOW THE ATMOSPHERE HELPS EARTH

The atmosphere blocks some invisible, harmful energy from the Sun.

Light energy from the Sun hits Earth's surface. The surface absorbs the energy, which changes to heat.

The warm surface releases invisible energy. This energy is absorbed by the atmosphere and warms it.

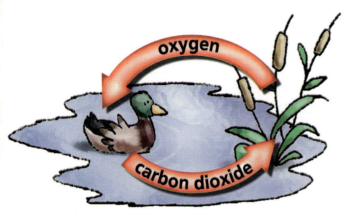

▲ **How would this system change if there were no plants?**

In another process plants take in carbon dioxide gas to make food. In this process plants give off oxygen. How do plants and animals help each other? Together plants and animals renew and recycle the air. And that's one reason why air is a renewable resource.

Water vapor is another gas that is found in the air all the time. Water vapor is water that has evaporated (ē vap ə rā′təd) or changed from a liquid to a gas. At times the air has a lot of water vapor in it. Then some of the water vapor changes back into liquid water, forming clouds and perhaps rain.

Gases in the atmosphere are needed to keep living things alive. The atmosphere keeps Earth, and all the living things on it, warm. It also protects living things from the Sun's harmful rays. The atmosphere is truly Earth's security blanket. ■

Science in Literature

DON'T YOU DARE POLLUTE THE AIR!

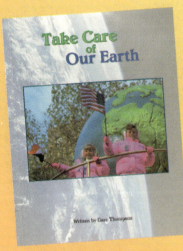

Take Care of Our Earth
by Gare Thompson
Steck-Vaughn Company, 1998

"Air is everywhere. . . . Sometimes the air smells fresh and sweet. At other times, the air may smell dirty and polluted. Polluted air hurts plants and people. Plants don't grow well in polluted air. People may find it hard to breathe, or they might get sick from polluted air."

Did you know that you can perform your own experiment to see whether or not your air is polluted? You can do this and other activities to detect pollution by reading *Take Care of Our Earth* by Gare Thompson.

A Fresh, Clean Start

Reading Focus What are some of the causes of air pollution?

On some days the air is clean and clear. How does such air become dirty?

Make the Dust Fly

You've learned the atmosphere is made up of invisible gases. But is there anything else in the air? You might be surprised if you looked at a sample of "invisible" air under a microscope. You might see bits of dust, pollen, and even tiny insects.

When the air contains harmful materials of any kind, it has become polluted (pə lōō'təd). **Pollution** (pə lōō'shən) is any unwanted or harmful material found in the environment. **Air pollution** is any unwanted or harmful material found in the air.

A forest fire adding to air pollution ▼

Where does air pollution come from? Some pollution is due to natural causes. Wind, for example, can pick up and carry dust and pollen.

Smoke is another source of pollution. Lightning striking a tree can start a forest fire. The smoke from the burning trees can hang in the air like a dark cloud over the land.

▲ Air pollution from erupting volcano

From time to time, a volcano (väl kā'nō) erupts somewhere in the world. A volcano can spew hot gases and ashes high in the air. These materials can drift thousands of kilometers, affecting air around the world.

The activities of people also cause air pollution. Much air pollution comes from the burning of fossil fuels—coal, oil, and natural gas. These fuels are used to run cars, heat homes, and run factories and power plants. The waste gases and smoke given off when fossil fuels burn result in harmful air pollution.

Air pollution can cause health problems for people. It can make breathing difficult. In some places, air pollution alerts are given to warn people that the air is unhealthful.

A Fresh Start

Plants, wind, and rain help clean the air. This is one reason why air is a renewable resource. But if too much pollution is put into the air too fast, nature can't keep up.

Today, people worldwide are working to clean the air and prevent air pollution. For example, cars are now made with parts that reduce air pollution from auto waste gases. Power plants are designed to clean waste gases before they are released into the air.

Power plants have been built that use energy from the Sun, from wind, and from moving water. These power plants provide energy without burning fossil fuels. What wise choices can you make to help prevent air pollution? ■

This car uses the Sun's energy to power it. How can the use of such cars help prevent air pollution? ▼

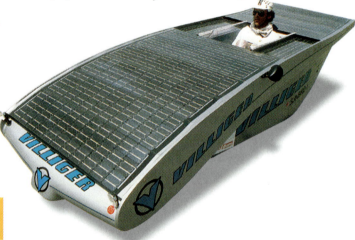

Internet Field Trip
Visit **www.eduplace.com** to find out more about natural resources.

INVESTIGATION 2 WRAP-UP

REVIEW

1. How is the atmosphere important to living things on Earth?

2. What are some natural causes of air pollution? How do people cause air pollution?

CRITICAL THINKING

3. Why is the atmosphere called Earth's security blanket?

4. How do plants and animals help make the air a renewable resource?

D18

REFLECT & EVALUATE

Word Power

Write the letter of the term that best completes each sentence. *Not all terms will be used.*

1. A resource that can be replaced within a person's lifetime is a ___.
2. A solid found in nature that has a definite chemical makeup is called a ___.
3. The blanket of air surrounding Earth is called the ___.
4. Fuels that formed when plants and animals decayed millions of years ago are called ___.
5. Unwanted or harmful materials found in the environment are called ___.

a. atmosphere
b. fossil fuels
c. mineral
d. natural resource
e. nonrenewable resource
f. pollution
g. renewable resource

Check What You Know

Write the term in each pair that best completes each sentence.

1. Energy from the Sun is (renewable, inexhaustible).
2. Earth's surface is covered mostly by (land, water).
3. The resources coal, oil, and natural gas are (renewable, nonrenewable).

Problem Solving

1. Suppose the amount of a greenhouse gas, such as carbon dioxide, in the air changed. Infer how Earth might be affected.
2. Sunlight and wind are inexhaustible resources. Explain why they aren't used to produce all of our energy.

Make a chart like the one shown. Paste pictures of resources from old magazines on your chart.

Renewable Resources	Nonrenewable Resources	Inexhaustible Resources

D19

CHAPTER 2

WATER ON EARTH

Have you ever cooled off under an open fire hydrant or a lawn sprinkler? Where does the water come from? How is water made safe for people to use? Next time you cool off under a sprinkler, think about all the ways you use water.

Connecting to Science ARTS

Water Poem Fire hydrants, a familiar sight across the country, seem an unlikely subject for a poem. But here is one about the joy of an open fire hydrant on a hot summer day in the city.

OPEN HYDRANT

Water rushes up
and gushes,
cooling summer's sizzle.
In a sudden whoosh
it rushes,
not a little drizzle.

First a hush and down
it crashes,
over curbs it swishes.
Just a luscious waterfall
for
cooling city fishes.
—Marci Ridlon

In Chapter 2 you'll discover some of the wonders of water. You'll even find out how people can drink sea water!

Coming Up

WHERE IS WATER FOUND ON EARTH AND WHY IS WATER IMPORTANT?
............D22

HOW CAN SOURCES OF FRESH WATER BE PROTECTED?
............D34

◀ Marci Ridlon writes children's books from her home in Ohio.

INVESTIGATION 1

WHERE IS WATER FOUND ON EARTH, AND WHY IS WATER IMPORTANT?

What makes Earth a great place to live? Water! Our planet is the only one that is known to have liquid water. In fact, Earth is sometimes called the water planet. You'll find out why as you investigate.

Activity

The Water Planet

Which covers more of Earth's surface—land or water? In this activity, you'll make an estimate of how much water covers Earth.

MATERIALS
- metric ruler
- paper plate
- map of the world
- colored markers
- tracing paper
- scissors
- graph paper
- Science Notebook

SAFETY
Be careful when using scissors.

Procedure

1. Using a ruler, **draw** two lines on a paper plate to make four equal sections as shown in the photo. This is your circle graph.

2. Look at a map of the world. **Talk with your group** and **estimate** what part of Earth's surface is covered with water—$\frac{1}{4}$, $\frac{1}{2}$, or $\frac{3}{4}$. **Record** your estimate in your *Science Notebook*. Shade one or more sections of your circle graph to show your estimate.

 Math Hint Shading $\frac{2}{4}$ of the paper plate is the same as shading $\frac{1}{2}$ of it.

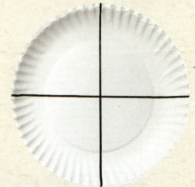

Step 1

Step 4

3. Now check your estimate. Lay tracing paper over a map of the world and then trace the water and land areas. Cut out the shapes. Write *water* on the cutouts that are water and *land* on the cutouts that are land.

4. Lay the cutouts of land and water on graph paper. Think of a way to arrange them to **compare** the amount of water to the amount of land. **Record** how you did it.

Analyze and Conclude

1. Look at all the circle graphs made by your class. What fraction of water do most of the graphs show?

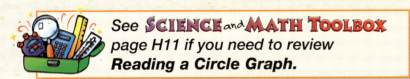

See **SCIENCE and MATH TOOLBOX** page H11 if you need to review **Reading a Circle Graph.**

2. **Compare** your estimate with what you found in step 4.

3. **Infer** why Earth is called the water planet.

Technology Link CD-ROM

INVESTIGATE FURTHER!

Use the **Science Processor CD-ROM**, *Earth's Water* (Unit Opening Investigation, Water Everywhere) to view planet Earth and see how much of it is covered by water. You will also find out how much of Earth's water is drinkable.

D23

Activity

Water Ups and Downs

Liquid water disappears from a cup and goes into the air. Find out how you can get the liquid water back again.

MATERIALS
- goggles
- plastic jar
- aluminum foil
- hot tap water
- rubber band
- ice cubes
- *Science Notebook*

SAFETY
Wear goggles during this activity. Clean up spills immediately.

Procedure

1. With your group, make a pan-shaped cover from aluminum foil for a plastic jar. Make sure the cover fits tightly over the jar's opening.

2. Remove the foil cover.

3. Your teacher will add hot tap water to the jar until it is one-third full. Then your teacher will put the foil cover back on the jar and secure it with a rubber band.

4. Quickly place a few ice cubes in the foil cover. Watch closely! **Observe** what happens on the underside of the foil. **Record** your observations in your *Science Notebook*.

Step 4

Analyze and Conclude

1. You've **made a model** of the movement of water between Earth's surface and the air. The warm water represents a lake or an ocean. The air above the water represents the air around Earth. The air high above Earth is cold. The ice on the foil cover cooled the air higher in the jar. How is your model different from the actual movement of water on Earth?

2. **Hypothesize** how water gets into the air and how it can return to Earth.

RESOURCE
A Watery World

Reading Focus Where is fresh water found on Earth, and how is it used by people?

We live in a watery world. The activity on pages D22 and D23 shows that Earth is covered by more water than land. In fact, about three fourths of Earth is covered by water.

Water on Earth

Pretend that all the water on Earth could be poured into 100 cups. Of the 100 cups, 97 would be filled with salt water, water that contains salt. Most of this salt is table salt, the kind used to flavor food. The salt comes from rocks and soil carried by rivers and streams into the ocean. Because of the large amount of salt, you'd become sick, or even die, if you drank a lot of sea water. Your body cannot use salt water for its functions.

If 97 of the 100 cups contain salt water, that leaves 3 cups of fresh water. Fresh water is water that people and animals can drink. But of these three cups of water, two are frozen into ice. These two cups of ice represent water frozen in icecaps, glaciers, and icebergs. That leaves only one cup of fresh water for all the living things on Earth to use. So, fresh water is very valuable.

EARTH'S WATER

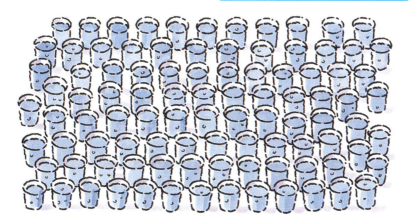

Ice

Liquid

97 cups salt water

3 cups fresh water

Using Math *Make a bar graph that compares the data shown above.*

D25

Water in Living Things

Using Math: What fraction of your body is not water? What fractions of the elephant, the potato, and the tomato are not water?

Water covers most of Earth's surface. But large bodies of water, such as oceans and rivers, are not the only places water is found. All living things contain a large amount of water. Nearly two thirds of your body is water. Look at the drawing above. How much water makes up an elephant, a potato, and a tomato?

What Is Water?

You may have heard someone say that water is "H - 2 - O." What does that mean? The *H* stands for hydrogen (hī′drə gən). Hydrogen is a gas that burns. It is used as a fuel. The *O* stands for oxygen. Oxygen is the gas in air that we need to live. When oxygen and hydrogen come together, they form water.

Look at the drawing below. Scientists use the capital letter *O* for oxygen and the capital letter *H* for hydrogen. The small number 2, called a subscript, means that there are two particles of hydrogen and one particle of oxygen in one particle of water.

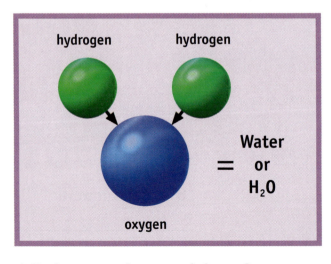

▲ Hydrogen and oxygen join to form water.

Using Water

Like air and soil, water is a natural resource. You know that a natural resource is a useful material from Earth. All living things need water to stay alive. A healthy person might live for more than a month without food, but the same person could survive only about three days without water.

While people need water just to survive, they also use water in many other ways. Look at the pictures below to see some uses of water. ■

WATER USES IN THE UNITED STATES

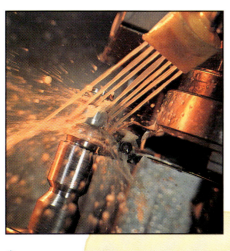

▲ **INDUSTRY** Water is used as a source of power and to make many products. This machine is cooled by water.

HOMES You use water every day. You use water when you bathe, cook, clean, and water plants. ▼

▲ **FARMING** Water is used for livestock and to grow crops. In dry places, farmers must irrigate their fields.

TOWNS Water is used to put out fires, treat sewage, and clean streets. ▼

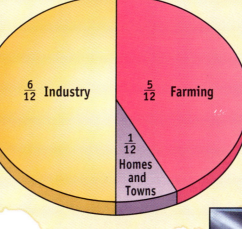

6/12 Industry
5/12 Farming
1/12 Homes and Towns

RESOURCE

Nature Recycles

Reading Focus How does nature recycle water, and what are sources of fresh water?

What constantly changes yet always stays the same? If you don't know, you're about to find out!

Think back to the last time you had a drink of water. Did you know that some of that water could have been the same water a dinosaur drank? The same amount of water has been on Earth for millions of years. But the form, or state, of water is always changing.

Amazing Water

Water, like all the things around you, is matter. Matter exists in one of three states—as a solid, a liquid, or a gas. Water is the only substance that is commonly found in nature in all three states.

How can you change the state of water? As shown in the drawing, to change the state of water you have to add or take away heat energy.

What must happen for water to change state? ▼

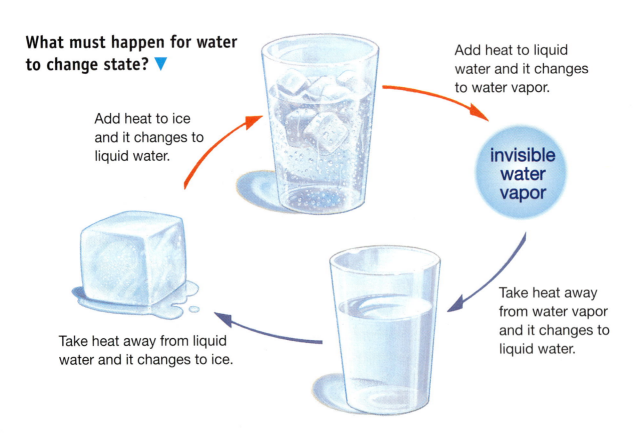

Add heat to ice and it changes to liquid water.

Add heat to liquid water and it changes to water vapor.

invisible water vapor

Take heat away from water vapor and it changes to liquid water.

Take heat away from liquid water and it changes to ice.

D28

If you put liquid water in a freezer, the water turns to a solid called ice. The freezer *takes away* heat energy from the water.

When you boil water, you are *adding* heat energy to water. Heating liquid water changes it to a gas. When liquid water changes to a gas, that water is said to **evaporate** (ē vap′ə rāt). When water is a gas, it is called **water vapor**. You can't see water vapor but there are times when the air seems heavy and wet. Your skin feels "sticky." On such days there's a lot of water vapor in the air.

When you add ice to a glass of lemonade, droplets of water often form on the outside of the glass. Water vapor in the air loses heat energy as the water vapor comes into contact with the cold glass. The water vapor changes to liquid water on the glass.

When water vapor changes to liquid water, it is said to **condense**. In the activity on page D24, water condenses on the underside of an aluminum-foil cover. How do the ice cubes on the top of the foil cover help water condense?

Internet Field Trip
Visit **www.eduplace.com** to find out more about Earth's water.

Science in Literature

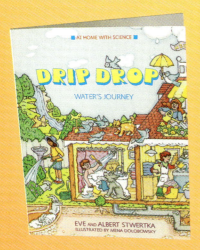

Drip Drop: Water's Journey
by Eve and Albert Stwertka
Illustrated by Mena Dolobowsky
Julian Messner, 1991

TINY BALLOONS!

"You cannot see water vapor. Sometimes, though, the vapor meets air that is cooler. Then the vapor changes again. It turns into drops of water that hang in the air like tiny balloons."

Did you ever wonder where the water comes from when you turn on the faucet? Where does it go after it runs down the drain? How is water cleaned and how is it moved through pipes? To find answers to these and many other questions, read *Drip Drop: Water's Journey* by Eve and Albert Stwertka.

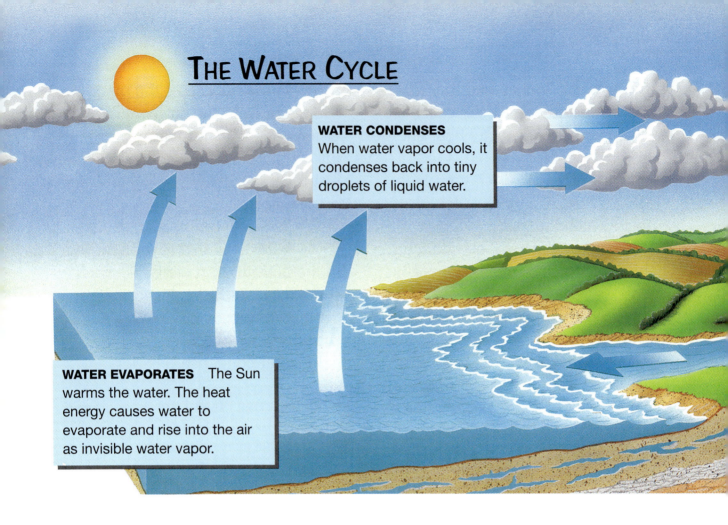

THE WATER CYCLE

WATER CONDENSES When water vapor cools, it condenses back into tiny droplets of liquid water.

WATER EVAPORATES The Sun warms the water. The heat energy causes water to evaporate and rise into the air as invisible water vapor.

A Never-Ending Cycle

Remember the riddle that appeared on page D28? It asked, "What constantly changes yet always stays the same?" Do you know the answer yet? It's water! The "constant changes" referred to in this riddle are changes in the state of water. These changes are part of a process called the water cycle. The **water cycle** is the path that water follows as it evaporates into the air, condenses into clouds, and returns to Earth as rain, snow, sleet, or hail.

Look at the drawing of the water cycle. Why is this path called a cycle? As you look at the picture, read what is happening in the different parts of the water cycle.

On the Waterfront

You know that the water cycle brings fresh water to Earth in the form of precipitation. But where does rainwater and melting snow go? Rainwater and melting snow flow downhill and collect in rivers and lakes or soak into the ground. This water is the source of fresh water for many cities.

A source of water that already exists on the land, such as a lake or a river, is called **surface water**. Cities that use surface water pump the water out of rivers and lakes, clean it, and send it to homes, schools, and businesses.

In some places, dams have been built across moving rivers or streams.

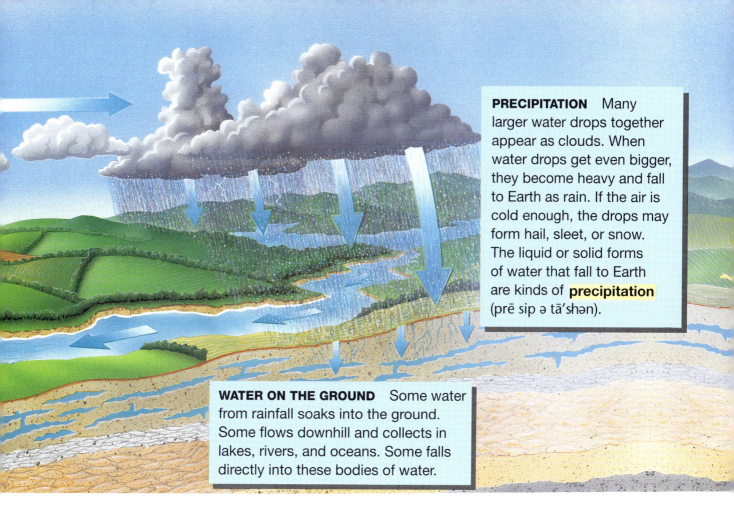

PRECIPITATION Many larger water drops together appear as clouds. When water drops get even bigger, they become heavy and fall to Earth as rain. If the air is cold enough, the drops may form hail, sleet, or snow. The liquid or solid forms of water that fall to Earth are kinds of **precipitation** (prē sip ə tā′shən).

WATER ON THE GROUND Some water from rainfall soaks into the ground. Some flows downhill and collects in lakes, rivers, and oceans. Some falls directly into these bodies of water.

A dam is a barrier that stretches across a river or stream and blocks the water's movement. The place behind the dam where the water collects and is stored is called a **reservoir** (rez′ər vwär). The water collected in reservoirs by dams on the Colorado River is one source from which Los Angeles, California, gets its water.

If there is no surface water nearby, people use water from under the ground. Water that soaks into the ground and fills the spaces between soil and rocks is called **ground water**.

An underground layer of rock where ground water collects is called an **aquifer** (ak′wə fər). Aquifers are important sources of water. To get water out of an aquifer, people often dig wells. Miami, Florida, and San Antonio, Texas, have wells dug into aquifers to get fresh water.

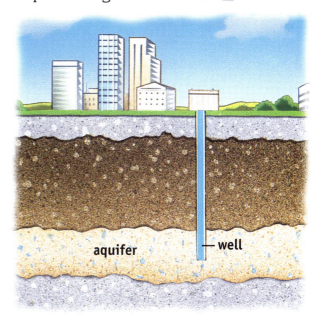

▲ **People dig wells to get water.**

The Salty Problem

Reading Focus How can people get fresh water from salt water?

What if the rain stopped and never fell again? You can imagine how dry everything would be. Suppose collecting rainwater was your only way to get fresh water. If it never rained, you would have quite a problem, wouldn't you?

Look at the map. Cape Verde (vurd), a group of islands off the western coast of Africa, has had almost no rain since 1968! That's long before you were born. So where do the people of Cape Verde find fresh water to drink?

Fresh Water From Salt Water

Many islands, like the Cape Verde Islands, don't have sources of fresh water. But they are surrounded by oceans, which are salt water. You know that people can't drink salt water without becoming ill. But can it be used as a source of fresh water?

Think about the water cycle. When salt water evaporates, only the water changes into water vapor, not the salt. Evaporation of salt water is part of the process of desalination (dē sal ə nā′shən). In desalination, salt is removed from ocean water to produce fresh water. One way this can be done is shown in the drawing on the next page.

It's very costly to desalinate ocean water. It takes a great deal of energy to pump the water through pipes and to heat it. But people who live on islands are happy to have fresh water—even if they must pay a lot in order to have it!

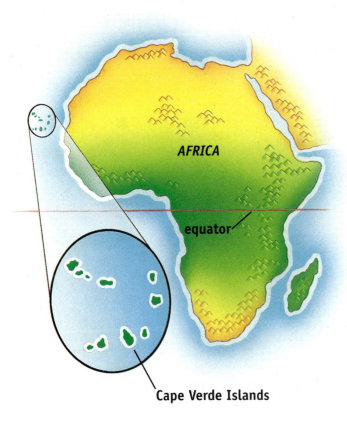

▲ Rainfall is scarce in Cape Verde.

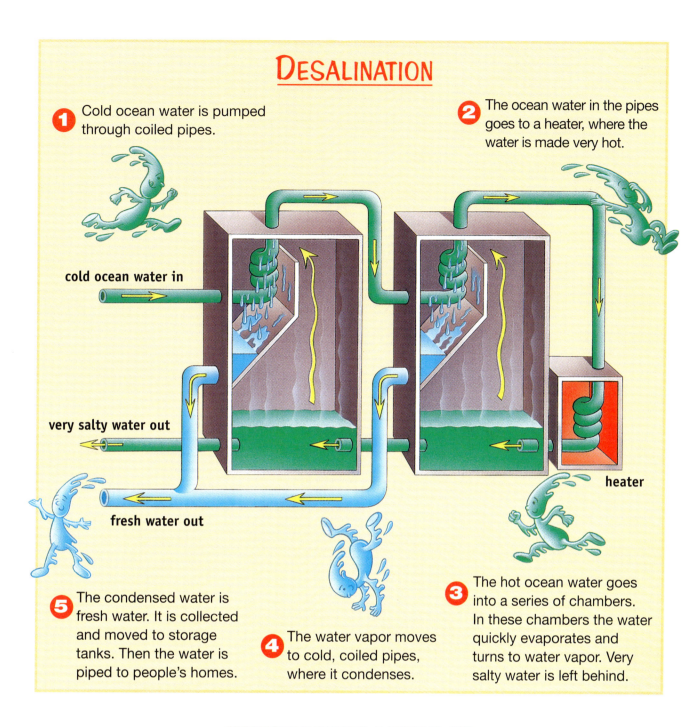

DESALINATION

1 Cold ocean water is pumped through coiled pipes.

2 The ocean water in the pipes goes to a heater, where the water is made very hot.

cold ocean water in

very salty water out

fresh water out

heater

5 The condensed water is fresh water. It is collected and moved to storage tanks. Then the water is piped to people's homes.

4 The water vapor moves to cold, coiled pipes, where it condenses.

3 The hot ocean water goes into a series of chambers. In these chambers the water quickly evaporates and turns to water vapor. Very salty water is left behind.

INVESTIGATION 1 WRAP-UP

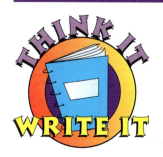

REVIEW

1. Why is Earth called the water planet?

2. Draw a picture of the water cycle. Then explain the changes that a drop of water goes through as it moves through the cycle.

CRITICAL THINKING

3. Does desalination occur in nature? Explain your answer.

4. If water runs downhill to the oceans, why don't oceans overflow?

INVESTIGATION 2

HOW CAN SOURCES OF FRESH WATER BE PROTECTED?

What kinds of harmful things are in fresh water? How can water be made safe for drinking? You'll investigate these questions and find their answers.

Activity

Let's Clear This Up

Freshwater sources are usually muddy and dirty. Why is filtering water an important step in cleaning water?

MATERIALS
- goggles
- newspaper
- plastic soda bottle, cut in half
- cheesecloth
- rubber band
- fine gravel, sand
- tap or pond water
- plastic jar with lid
- spoon
- soil, twigs, leaves
- *Science Notebook*

SAFETY
Wear goggles during this activity.

Procedure

1. Cover your work area with newspaper. Then **make a model** of a water-filtering system. Use the top part of a plastic soda bottle as a funnel. With a group member, use a rubber band to attach a piece of cheesecloth to the end of the funnel.

2. Set the funnel in the bottom part of the bottle. Put a layer of fine gravel into the funnel. Then add a layer of sand over the gravel. The materials in the funnel are part of your filtering system.

Step 2

Step 3

3. Pour water into a plastic jar until it is three-fourths full. Add two spoonfuls of soil and a few twigs and leaves to the water. Screw the lid tightly on the jar. Shake up the mixture to make muddy water. This mixture is like the water that may be in a reservoir or river.

 Math Hint *A jar that is three-fourths full is one-fourth empty.*

4. Talk with your group and **predict** what will happen if you pour the muddy water through the filter. **Record** your prediction in your *Science Notebook*.

5. Slowly pour the muddy water through the filtering system in the funnel. **Observe** the material that passes through the funnel into the base of the plastic bottle. **Record** your observations.

Analyze and Conclude

1. Compare your prediction with your results.

2. Filtering helps make surface water safe. **Hypothesize** how filtering changes muddy water.

3. How is what happens to the muddy water in your model of a water-filtering system like what happens to rainwater when it falls on the ground? How is your model different?

INVESTIGATE FURTHER!

EXPERIMENT

Observe a drop of your filtered water under a microscope. Draw what you see. Infer whether you think the things you see are nonliving or living. Hypothesize what would have to be done to this water to make it clean enough to drink.

D35

Activity
Testing Clear Water

Is clear water always clean water?

Procedure

1. Use a grease pencil to label a clear plastic cup *Tap Water*. Pour 50 mL of tap water into the cup. Label a second cup *Aquarium Water*. Pour 50 mL of aquarium water into this cup.

 See **SCIENCE** and **MATH TOOLBOX** page H7 if you need to review **Measuring Volume.**

2. Fertilizer is food for living things. **Talk with your group** and **predict** what will happen to the water if you put fertilizer into each cup. **Record** your prediction in your *Science Notebook*.

3. Use a dropper to place 20 drops of liquid fertilizer into each cup. Cover each cup with clear plastic wrap, and secure with a rubber band. Place the cups in a window.

4. After two days, **observe** the water in each cup with a hand lens. **Record** your observations. **Compare** your results with those of your classmates.

MATERIALS
- goggles
- grease pencil
- 2 clear plastic cups
- metric measuring cup
- tap water
- aquarium water
- liquid fertilizer
- dropper
- clear plastic wrap
- 2 rubber bands
- hand lens
- *Science Notebook*

SAFETY
Wear goggles during this activity. Wash your hands when you have finished.

Step 3

Analyze and Conclude

1. What did you observe in each cup? How did your prediction compare with your results?

2. Changes to the water occurred because of the presence of tiny living things. **Infer** why they might be present in one cup but not the other.

Wee Beasties

Reading Focus What harmful things are found in water, and how can water be cleaned?

They're everywhere and they're multiplying! What are they? They're germs! People use the word **germ** when they're talking about tiny living things that make them sick.

Germs Everywhere

There are different kinds of germs. One group of germs includes protists (prōt′ists). Protists are neither animals nor plants, but they are alive. Many kinds of protists live in water and wet soil. Another group of germs includes bacteria (bak tir′ē ə). Bacteria are neither animals nor plants. Bacteria live in soil, air, and water.

Protists are so small that they can't be seen with just the eyes. But bacteria are even smaller. About 500 bacteria could fit inside one protist! Fifty million bacteria could live in a single drop of pond water!

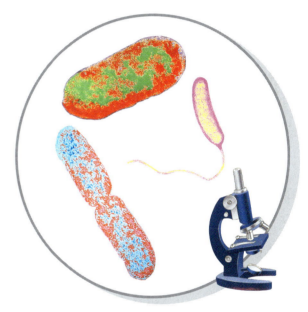

▲ These bacteria are shown about 10,000 times larger than they actually are.

Anton's Discovery

If germs are too small to see, how have people learned about them? To find the answer, you need to know what happened more than 300 years ago. That's when "wee beasties" were discovered.

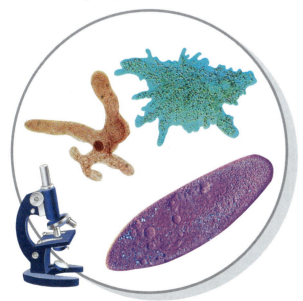

▲ These protists are shown about 100 times larger than they actually are.

In the second half of the 1600s, a young man named Anton van Leeuwenhoek (lā′vən hoŏk) lived in Holland. He was interested in microscopes (mī′krə skōps). A microscope is a device that makes very small things look bigger than they really are. Leeuwenhoek looked at many things through his microscopes. One day he looked at a drop of lake water through a microscope. He saw many tiny things moving around in the water. He called them "wee beasties" because they looked like little animals to him.

What a Treat

We know that the living things Leeuwenhoek saw were *not* animals. We now know they were protists.

WATER TREATMENT PLANT

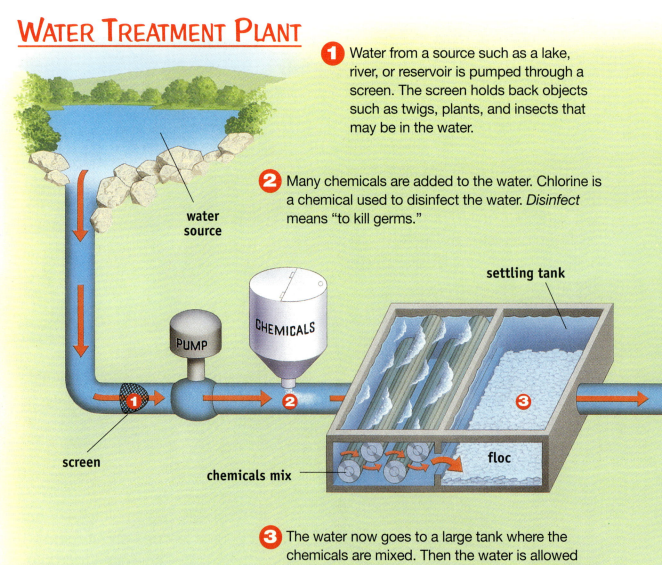

1 Water from a source such as a lake, river, or reservoir is pumped through a screen. The screen holds back objects such as twigs, plants, and insects that may be in the water.

2 Many chemicals are added to the water. Chlorine is a chemical used to disinfect the water. *Disinfect* means "to kill germs."

3 The water now goes to a large tank where the chemicals are mixed. Then the water is allowed to settle. Chemicals, such as alum (al′əm), cause the unwanted particles in the water to stick together, forming larger particles called floc. The floc settles to the bottom and is removed.

We also know that protists and bacteria that live in fresh water can be harmful to people by causing illness.

Other unwanted living things in fresh water include algae (al′jē). In the activity on page D36, fertilizer is added to aquarium water and tap water. Fertilizer is food for algae. With plenty of food, the algae grow and multiply, turning the aquarium water cloudy.

To make fresh water safe for people to use, the water must first be filtered. After filtering, the water must be treated, with chemicals, to kill unwanted, harmful living things. These processes are done in a water treatment plant. Use the drawing below to learn about the steps in the process of water being filtered and disinfected (dis in fek′tid). ■

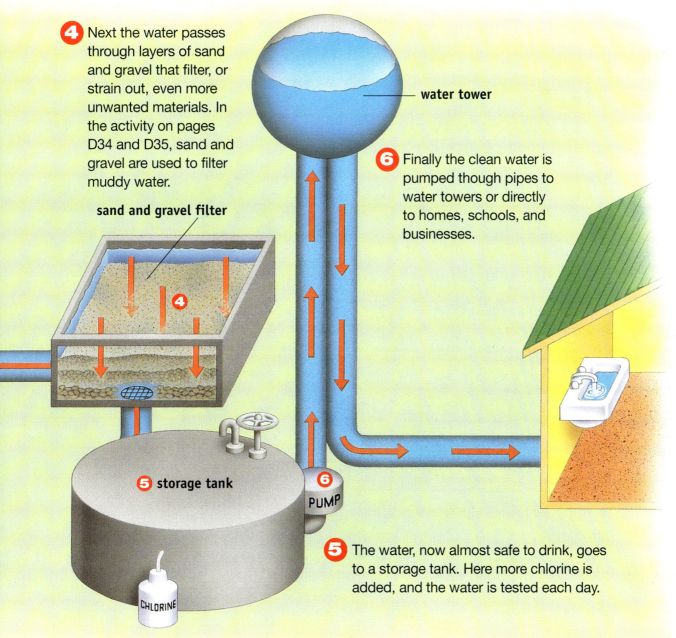

4 Next the water passes through layers of sand and gravel that filter, or strain out, even more unwanted materials. In the activity on pages D34 and D35, sand and gravel are used to filter muddy water.

sand and gravel filter

water tower

6 Finally the clean water is pumped though pipes to water towers or directly to homes, schools, and businesses.

5 storage tank

6 PUMP

5 The water, now almost safe to drink, goes to a storage tank. Here more chlorine is added, and the water is tested each day.

Industrial-Revolution Pollution

Reading Focus How have some inventions led to pollution, and what has been done to stop pollution?

Since people first lived in communities, they have been polluting their environment. But pollution has become more serious in modern times. That's because there are so many more people on Earth today than ever before.

The time line shows some events of the past that have made people's lives easier. It also presents some of the harmful effects that these events have led to, such as pollution. As you read the time line, look for things that people have done to stop pollution.

Industrial Revolution begins in England, moves to America. New machines are invented and many factories are built. The machines burn coal that pollutes the air, changing clean rainwater to acid rain. More people move to cities, so more pollution is released into rivers. **1750**

Thomas A. Edison invents the electric light bulb. Electricity is produced by burning coal and fuel oil. More air pollution and acid rain result. **1879**

First Clean Water Act is passed by Congress. Cleanup of lakes and rivers begins. **1948**

1859 E. L. Drake drills the first oil well in Pennsylvania. Oil is later refined to make products such as gasoline. When burned, gasoline puts pollutants into the air.

D40

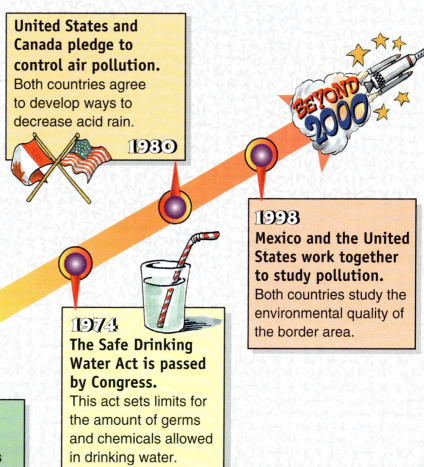

The Environmental Protection Agency (EPA) is formed. This U.S. government agency is given the job of setting standards for air, water, and soil quality. **1971**

United States and Canada pledge to control air pollution. Both countries agree to develop ways to decrease acid rain. **1980**

1998 Mexico and the United States work together to study pollution. Both countries study the environmental quality of the border area.

1974 The Safe Drinking Water Act is passed by Congress. This act sets limits for the amount of germs and chemicals allowed in drinking water.

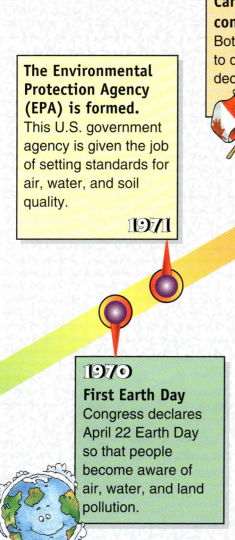

1970 First Earth Day Congress declares April 22 Earth Day so that people become aware of air, water, and land pollution.

You can see that many things have happened to help improve the environment and reduce pollution. More still needs to be done. What wise choices can you make to reduce pollution?

UNIT PROJECT LINK

Continue your plans for an Environmental Fair. With your class, plan and carry out a way that you can help care for Earth's water. Then, with your group, make a poster to show what you did to protect Earth's water.

Technology Link
For more help with your Unit Project, go to **www.eduplace.com**.

Water Worries

Reading Focus What are two ways that fresh water supplies are in danger?

You have been hired to solve the mystery of a polluted (pə lōōt′əd) river. Any part of the environment that is polluted contains unwanted or harmful materials. Look below. How many kinds of harmful materials, called pollutants, are getting into the river? See page D43 for the answers.

Salty-Water Worries

The pollution of rivers is only one of our "water worries." Oceans get polluted, too. People once thought that the oceans were so big that sewage or trash dumped into them wouldn't hurt them. But these things *have* harmed the oceans.

LOOKING FOR POLLUTION

Scientists who studied the oceans found that sewage was the worst pollutant. Next came plastics, oil, and chemicals from factories and farms. These pollutants often flowed into rivers first and then flowed out to the ocean. Often these pollutants wash out to sea and then wash back to shore, making swimming at some beaches dangerous.

Over the years, laws have been passed in the United States to prevent the dumping of pollutants into rivers, lakes, and oceans. These bodies of water are much cleaner today than they were even a few years ago.

INVESTIGATE FURTHER!

RESEARCH

Find out where your water comes from. Is it from a river, a reservoir, or an aquifer? Draw a map showing the location of your water supply. Share your map with your class.

Running Dry

Water pollution isn't the only way that fresh water supplies are in danger. Having enough fresh water for everyone is also a concern.

How many of these causes of river pollution did you find on page D42? What would be your suggestions to help reduce pollution of the river?

LEAKING GAS TANK There's an old gas station, no longer in business, next to the factory. Gasoline is leaking from the underground tank that is cracked. Where will the gasoline go?

TOWN DUMP Look at the dump. Trash from the town is dumped into a hole in the ground. When it rains, the rainwater mixes with substances such as battery acids, paints, and cleaners in the trash. This polluted rainwater also flows into the river.

OIL CHANGE Find the person changing the oil in a truck. If the oil is poured on the ground or down a drain, it will seep into the river.

FARMING CHEMICALS A farmer has been using fertilizers to grow better crops. The farmer has also been using chemicals to kill weeds and insects. When it rains, these materials could be carried by the rain into the river.

LEAKING SEPTIC TANK The school has an old, leaking septic tank buried under the ground. Septic tanks are containers that hold waste water from sinks and toilets. Old septic tanks often crack and leak. When they do, the waste water moves through the soil to the river.

YARD CHEMICALS Find the family doing yardwork. Fertilizers and chemicals used to kill insects and weeds can mix with rainwater and seep into the river. Smoke from the lawn mower also pollutes the air.

FACTORY WASTES What happens to the waste water coming from the factory? Also notice the smoke coming from the chimneys. Smoke from chimneys can have harmful chemicals in them. When they do, the chemicals can combine with water vapor in the air to form **acid rain**. What might happen to plants and animals in the river if acid rain falls into it?

OGALLALA AQUIFER

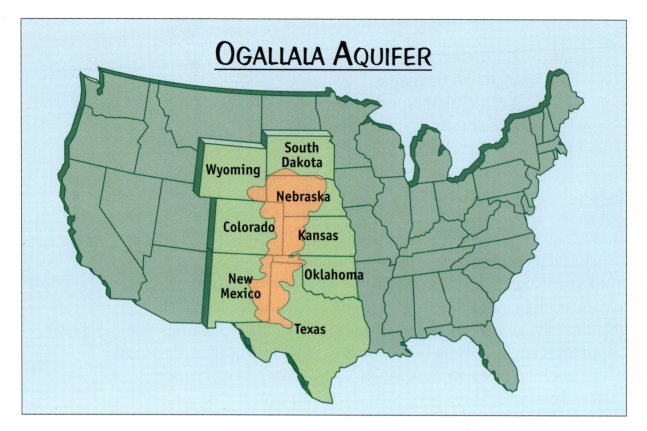

▲ Does the Ogallala Aquifer supply your state with water?

The worry about running out of water is very real in some parts of the United States. People who use water from the Ogallala Aquifer, shown, are especially worried. Scientists estimate that the water remaining in the aquifer will last only about 40 more years. In the southwestern corner of Kansas, the aquifer level has dropped about 60 m (198 ft) in the last 45 years. Plans to save water have been put into place. In fact, the aquifer level has risen in some parts of Texas.

Water should be treated as the valuable natural resource that it is. If we keep water supplies clean and use water wisely, we can have a future that is free from water worries. ■

INVESTIGATION 2 WRAP-UP

REVIEW

1. What are some ways that fresh water becomes polluted?

2. How is water made safe for people to drink?

CRITICAL THINKING

3. You're hiking and you're thirsty. Would you drink water from a stream? Why or why not?

4. Waste water from homes and factories is treated in sewage plants before being released into rivers. How does this help limit pollution?

REFLECT & EVALUATE

Word Power

Write the letter of the term that best matches the definition. *Not all terms will be used.*

1. Area behind a dam that collects and stores water
2. Tiny living thing that can make you sick
3. Change from liquid water to a gas
4. Underground layer of rock where water collects
5. Path that water follows as it changes from a liquid to a gas, back to a liquid, and falls as rain
6. Water that is a gas

a. acid rain
b. aquifer
c. condense
d. evaporate
e. germ
f. reservoir
g. water cycle
h. water vapor

Check What You Know

Write the term in each pair that best completes each sentence.

1. When water vapor changes to a liquid, it is said to (condense, evaporate).
2. Smoke combining with water in the air sometimes forms (water vapor, acid rain).
3. People drill through rock to reach water in the (aquifer, reservoir).
4. Water that exists on land is called (ground water, surface water).

Problem Solving

1. Earth's surface is three-fourths water. Why, then, are people worried about running out of clean drinking water?
2. Suppose you are shipwrecked on an island. You can't find any fresh surface water. What will you do?
3. Pretend you work at a water treatment plant. One day the "cleaned" water looks cloudy. What could have happened? Explain what you might do.

Study the drawing. Then, in your own words, explain what can happen to the river water after a heavy rain.

D45

CHAPTER 3

LAND AS A NATURAL RESOURCE

We live on it. We use it to grow crops. We mine minerals from it. We use it to build things. What is it? It's land! How is the land changing?

PEOPLE USING SCIENCE

Resources Management Specialist

Jordon C. Pope works for the Bureau of Land Management in Washington, D.C. This bureau manages 264 million acres of public lands. Public lands are owned by all Americans.

Jordon Pope's job is to analyze people's ideas on how to best use the public lands. Some public lands are national parks and forests. Other public lands may be used for mining fossil fuels and minerals. Still other public lands are set aside for dinosaur digs, as wildlife refuges, and as historical and cultural sites.

Jordon Pope said the most rewarding part of his job is knowing that he has helped protect and preserve public lands and other resources for future Americans. What are land resources? To find out, read this chapter.

Coming Up

How Do the Forces of Nature Change Earth's Surface?
............D48

Why Are Rocks and Soil Important?
............D54

◀ Jordon Pope studies how to best use public lands.

INVESTIGATION 1

How Do the Forces of Nature Change Earth's Surface?

How can a mountain be changed if it's hard as rock? In this investigation you'll find out how forces of nature can change mountains.

Activity

Hard Rock

How hard are rocks? Find out!

MATERIALS
- goggles
- 2 small rocks
- white paper
- *Science Notebook*

SAFETY
Wear goggles during this activity.

Procedure

With your group, **predict** what will happen if you rub two rocks against each other. **Record** your prediction in your *Science Notebook*. Hold two small rocks over a clean sheet of white paper. Press them together and rub hard. **Record** your observations.

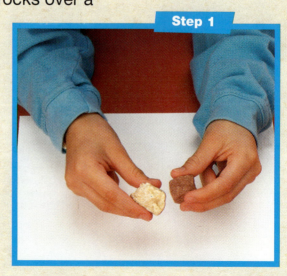

Step 1

Analyze and Conclude

1. What happened to the rocks when they were rubbed together?

2. **Infer** what might happen to large rocks that are struck over and over again by wind-blown sand.

Activity

A Force of Nature

Can we change Earth's surface? Find out!

MATERIALS
- goggles
- small rocks or gravel, sand, water
- small plastic container
- freezer
- ruler
- soil
- rectangular aluminum pan
- paper towel
- *Science Notebook*

SAFETY
Wear goggles during this activity. Clean up spills immediately.

Procedure

1. Make a model of a glacier (glā′shər). A **glacier** is a large mass of slow-moving ice. Place a handful of small rocks in the bottom of a small container. Sprinkle some sand among the rocks. Then fill the container with water and place it in a freezer.

2. With your group **predict** what will happen to the surface of the soil if the glacier is dragged over it. **Record** your predictions in your *Science Notebook*.

3. The next day, put about 3 cm of soil in an aluminum baking pan. Take the model glacier out of the container. Use a paper towel to move the glacier in one direction over the soil in the pan. **Record** your observations.

4. Predict what the soil will look like if the glacier melts. Leave the ice in the pan until it melts. **Record** your observations.

Step 3

Analyze and Conclude

1. What happened to the soil when you moved the glacier over it? What happened to the soil after the glacier melted?

2. Infer what would happen if a glacier the size of a football field slid slowly down a mountain. How would the mountain be affected? How is your model different from a real glacier? How is it like a real glacier?

D49

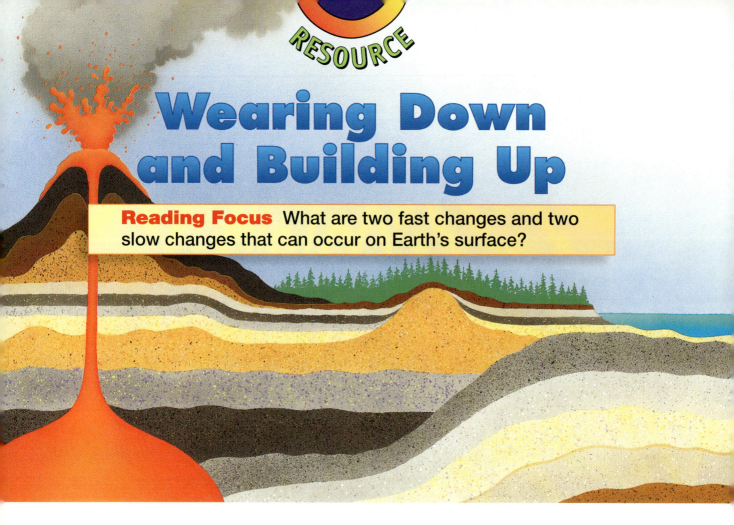

Wearing Down and Building Up

Reading Focus What are two fast changes and two slow changes that can occur on Earth's surface?

Earth's surface is always changing. What causes it to change? The answer lies deep within Earth. Pretend that you could bore a tunnel into Earth. If you could travel safely through the tunnel, what might you see?

It's a Bore

In most places you would pass a layer of soil at the surface of Earth. This soil layer could be anywhere from a few centimeters to about 30 m (100 ft) thick.

As you went farther into Earth, you would begin to see layers of different kinds and colors of rock. These rock layers lie beneath the land. Similar layers of different kinds of rock lie beneath the oceans. As you continued down the tunnel, you'd pass thick layers of solid rock. Farther down, the rock layers change. The great mass of rock in the upper layers weighs heavily on the deeper rock layer. As a result, heat and pressure are very great. The heat causes some of the rock to flow like liquid. This liquid rock inside Earth is called **magma** (mag′mə).

Quick Change

On your return to Earth's surface, you are happy to once again be on solid ground. And yet, Earth's surface is really a lot less solid and unchanging than it might look! Several different forces in nature cause changes to Earth's surface.

Hot Rock

Sometimes the changes that occur to Earth's surface are sudden. In some parts of the world, magma is close to Earth's surface. Sometimes this hot liquid shoots out of an opening in the ground called a **volcano** (väl kā′nō). Once on the surface of Earth, the liquid rock is called **lava** (lä′və).

Hot liquid rock cools and hardens when it reaches the surface. When the lava cools around the opening, it may form a cone-shaped volcano. Lava flowing away from the volcano can burn everything in its path before it cools. When the lava cools, it adds a layer of rock to Earth's surface. So volcanoes are one of the forces of nature that change Earth's surface.

Trembling Earth

Other sudden changes to Earth's surface can result from an earthquake. The solid layers of rock beneath the surface are actually broken up into large sections. Sometimes these sections move suddenly. This sudden movement of large sections of rock beneath Earth's surface causes an **earthquake**.

The energy of an earthquake can cause landscapes to change in a dramatic way. During an earthquake, hills and boulders can appear where none were in sight just moments before. Other times, rocks and hills disappear in an instant. You can see that Earth's surface can change quickly during an earthquake.

Lava can flow far from the volcano as shown in this photo from Hawaii. How is Earth's surface changing? ▼

▲ **An earthquake in Idaho caused a sudden change to Earth's surface. Here, a section of the ground dropped.**

Slow Motion

The changes to Earth's surface caused by volcanoes and earthquakes happen very quickly. But slow changes to the surface are taking place all the time. Sometimes the results of these changes can only be seen after many years. The Grand Canyon is one example.

About 6 million years ago, there was no Grand Canyon. Over time the Colorado River slowly wore away the rock along its banks and carried away the rock materials. Even today the river continues to carve the Grand Canyon deeper and deeper.

The breaking up or wearing away of rocks is called **weathering** (we*th*'ər iŋ). The breaking up and moving of weathered rocks from one place to another is **erosion** (ē rō'-zhən). Rain weathers the cliff walls of the Grand Canyon by wearing away pieces of rock on either side. Then erosion washes the weathered rock material into the Colorado River, which carries it away.

Where does all this weathered rock go? Some is left along the sides of the river, as shown in the photo. The rest is carried to the end, or mouth, of the river. Over time, weathered materials build up Earth's land surface.

Blowing in the Wind

Wind is another force of nature that can cause weathering. Wind can pick up sand and blow it against large rocks. In the activity on page D48, two rocks are rubbed together. This is like the action of sand blowing against large rocks. Windblown sand can act like sandpaper, wearing away the large rocks. Strong winds can carry pieces of weathered rock from one place and deposit them in other places. So wind causes erosion, too.

Using Math The Colorado River carries enough soil out of the Grand Canyon every day to fill 2 million pickup trucks! How much soil is moved by the river in a week?

A Frozen Force

Moving ice can also cause weathering and erosion. A **glacier** (glā′shər) is a large mass of slow-moving ice. As it moves and melts, a glacier changes the surface beneath it as shown in the activity on page D49. A glacier can pick up and move soil and huge rocks great distances.

The changes that are caused by earthquakes and volcanoes occur quickly. Those caused by moving water, wind, and glaciers occur more slowly. But all these forces of nature change Earth's surface through weathering and erosion. ■

▲ This glacier in Alaska is melting. The rocks in the water were pushed there by the glacier.

INVESTIGATE FURTHER!

Use the **Best of the Net—CD-ROM**, Earth Sciences, *Blackcomb Glaciers* site to find out how glaciers form and move. You'll also find out how fast a glacier can move and you'll learn about ice worms.

INVESTIGATION 1 WRAP-UP

REVIEW

1. Identify four forces of nature that change Earth's surface. Describe how each can cause change.

2. How do erosion and weathering differ?

CRITICAL THINKING

3. Explain how gravity and temperature help a glacier change Earth's surface.

4. Describe two ways that Earth's surface can be built up by forces of nature.

Why Are Rocks and Soil Important?

Have you ever heard the phrase "It's dirt cheap"? It seems as though dirt should be cheap. But soil is a very valuable resource. What other valuable resources come from the land? How can these resources be protected?

Activity

Soak It Up

How are soils different? Does water pass through different soils at the same rate?

Procedure

1. Cover your work area with newspaper. Use the top part of a plastic soda bottle as a funnel. Place a piece of cheesecloth over the opening in the neck of the funnel, as shown. Hold the cheesecloth tightly in place with a rubber band.

2. Place the funnel, neck down, in the bottom part of the bottle. Fill the funnel halfway with gravel.

3. Pour 250 mL of water into a measuring cup. Now pour the water into the funnel. Wait one minute.

See **SCIENCE and MATH TOOLBOX** page H7 if you need to review **Measuring Volume**.

MATERIALS
- goggles
- newspaper
- plastic soda bottle, cut in half
- cheesecloth
- rubber band
- gravel, sand, topsoil
- metric measuring cup
- water
- container
- timer
- plastic dish
- Science Notebook

SAFETY
Wear goggles during this activity. Clean up spills immediately.

Step 1

4. After one minute, move the funnel to an empty container. Pour the water from the bottom part of the bottle into the empty measuring cup. **Measure** the amount of water that passed through the gravel.

5. In your *Science Notebook,* **make a chart** like the one shown below.

Step 3

Kind of Soil	Water That Passed Through in One Minute (in mL)
Gravel	
Sand	
Topsoil	

6. In the chart **record** the amount of water that passed through the gravel. Empty the measuring cup and the funnel, and rinse off the cheesecloth.

7. **Talk with your group** and **predict** what will happen if you repeat the activity, first using sand and then using topsoil. **Record** your predictions. Repeat the steps, using sand and then topsoil.

Analyze and Conclude

1. Through which kind of soil did the water pass the fastest? the slowest? **Compare** your predictions with the results.

2. **Describe** the different properties of the three soils. Of the soils tested, which absorbed water the best? How do you know?

3. **Infer** what can happen to rainwater when it falls on different kinds of soil.

UNIT PROJECT LINK

Continue your plans for an Environmental Fair. With your class, plan and carry out a way that you can help care for Earth's land. Then, with your group, make a poster to show what you did to protect Earth's land.

For more help with your Unit Project, go to www.eduplace.com.

On Rocky Ground

Reading Focus Why are rocks and soil called natural resources?

What are some uses of rocks? The photos show two buildings that were built from rock. What other ways do people use rocks where you live?

Rock as a Resource

Rock was the first strong, lasting material that people used for building. Houses, roads, and bridges are made of rock. But what is rock made of?

You learned earlier that a mineral is a solid, found in nature, that has a definite chemical makeup. Rocks are made up of minerals. Some rocks contain just one or two kinds of minerals. Other rocks contain several kinds of minerals. Rocks differ from each other in the kinds of minerals they are made from.

▲ This museum in Albany, New York was built from rock about 25 years ago.

Some rocks are soft and weather easily. But other rocks are very hard and do not weather easily. Rocks of all kinds have been used for building.

The Soil of Life

Which is more valuable, gold or soil? **Soil** is the loose material that covers much of Earth's surface. As attractive as gold is, it can't be used to grow food. If it weren't for soil, gold couldn't even be used to *buy* food. Without soil, there would be no food to buy.

◀ Rocks were used to build the Parthenon in Athens, Greece, nearly 2,500 years ago.

▲ Clay soil in Georgia ▲ Sandy soil in Florida ▲ Topsoil in Texas

The most important role of soil is to support living things. Soil is used to grow food crops for people to eat. Crops are also grown to feed livestock such as cows, sheep, and chickens. So both animals and people depend on plants. And plants depend on soil. In other words, most life on land depends on soil. It seems clear, then, that the answer to the question asked earlier is that soil is much more valuable than gold.

Different Kinds of Soil

As you can see, soil is a valuable resource. But where does soil come from? It comes from rocks. When rocks weather, they break up into smaller pieces and become soil.

Soil used for growing crops is called topsoil. **Topsoil** is a mixture of weathered rock and humus (hyoo′məs). Humus is decayed plant and animal matter that makes topsoil rich in minerals that plants need. Water and air are also in topsoil. Healthy crops get many of the things they need to grow from rich topsoil.

Not all the soil on Earth is topsoil. For example, sandy soils don't have much humus in them. Sandy soils are made up of fairly large grains of weathered rock. Such soils let water pass through them quickly. Clay soil has very small grains of weathered rock. Sometimes water can't flow through clay soils. The speed with which water passes through different kinds of soils is shown in the activity on pages D54 and D55.

It's Nonrenewable

It's unlikely that people will use up Earth's supply of rock. And because it is in such large supply, rock is thought of as an inexhaustible resource.

You've learned that metals and fossil fuels—coal, oil, and natural gas—are nonrenewable resources. The supply of metals is fixed. And it takes nature millions of years to make fossil fuels. So once these resources are used, they are gone.

Topsoil can be thought of as a nonrenewable resource, too. If topsoil is blown away by strong winds or washed away by heavy rains, it won't be replaced by nature for thousands of years.

What can your family do to improve topsoil? If your family has a garden, you can start a compost pile. You make a compost pile by layering grass clippings and kitchen wastes with soil. Kitchen wastes can include potato peelings, egg shells, apple cores, and coffee grounds.

The compost pile must be turned once a week to add oxygen. It also needs to be kept moist and covered with plastic to hold in the heat. After a few months the compost can be added to garden soil.

Composting makes sense. It improves the topsoil and helps feed plants. And it reduces the amount of trash that needs to be thrown away. ■

Internet Field Trip
Visit **www.eduplace.com** to see minerals that make up rocks.

Science in Literature

Plant, Recycle, Conserve!

"There are things we can do to keep Earth clean and less polluted. . . . We can pick up trash that we see in parks, in school yards, or on sidewalks. We can recycle our trash. . . . This will help to take care of the land."

Take Care of Our Earth
by Gare Thompson
Steck-Vaughn Co., 1998

Plant a tree, recycle trash, conserve water! There are many things that we can do to take care of Earth. Find out what children around the world are doing for a cleaner Earth by reading *Take Care of Our Earth* by Gare Thompson. You'll also learn what you can do to keep Earth clean.

Save It From a Rainy Day

Reading Focus How do people around the world protect soil from erosion?

Living things on land depend on soil. It's the most important resource from the Earth. How can soil be protected from erosion?

Causes of Erosion

A major cause of soil erosion worldwide is the loss of plants from an area. The roots of trees, grasses, and other plants hold soil in place. When plants no longer grow in an area, wind and rain are likely to erode the soil.

What are some reasons that plants disappear from an area? One is overgrazing. For example, in some parts of the world, cattle are allowed to eat all the grass in a pasture. Then the soil is left exposed to wind and water, and erosion can occur.

A drought is a long period without rainfall. A drought can cause all the plants in a region to die off. Then the soil of that region, now very dry, lacks plants to hold it in place. Such soil can be easily blown or washed away.

Many thousands of plants may die during a large forest fire. So forest fires too can lead to erosion.

Topsoil erosion is a major concern to people worldwide. Today, many farmers know about the causes of erosion. So they know how to avoid it. Look at the next page to see how people have solved the problems of erosion in different parts of the world.

Plants hold soil in place. Without plants, topsoil is eroded by rain and wind. ▼

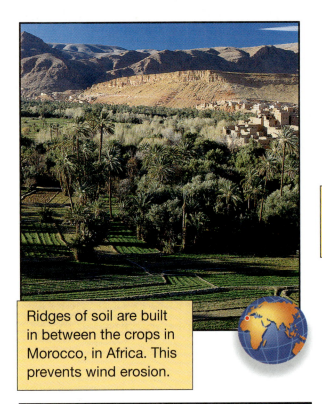

Prickly pear cactus are planted between orange trees in Mexico to prevent soil erosion.

Ridges of soil are built in between the crops in Morocco, in Africa. This prevents wind erosion.

Natural fertilizers are used in China to improve soil. More crops grow in fertile soil, which helps prevent erosion.

A seedling nursery in Brazil grows trees. When they are bigger, the seedlings will be planted where forests have been cut down.

The only way to feed more than 6 billion people on Earth is by farming. So almost nothing people do to save the planet is more important than protecting Earth's rich soil. ∎

INVESTIGATION 2 WRAP-UP

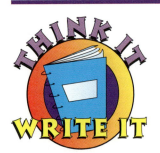

REVIEW

1. Why is rock thought of as an inexhaustible resource?

2. What is soil, and where does it come from?

CRITICAL THINKING

3. Why might plants not grow well in soil that is packed down?

4. Explain why life on Earth depends on soil. Give as many reasons as you can to support your answer.

CHAPTER 3 REVIEW: REFLECT & EVALUATE

Word Power

Write the letter of the term that best matches the definition. *Not all terms will be used.*

1. Hot liquid rock inside Earth
2. Breaking up or wearing away of rocks
3. Opening in the ground through which hot liquid rock shoots out
4. Large mass of slow-moving ice
5. Loose material that covers much of Earth's surface
6. Movement of weathered rocks from one place to another

a. earthquake
b. erosion
c. glacier
d. magma
e. lava
f. soil
g. volcano
h. weathering

Check What You Know

Write the term in each pair that best completes each sentence.

1. Rock is (a nonrenewable, an inexhaustible) resource.
2. Slow changes to Earth's surface are caused by (volcanoes, glaciers).
3. Decayed plant and animal matter is (sand, humus).

Problem Solving

1. Light tan, reddish brown, and dark brown are just a few of the many colors of soils. What causes soils to vary in color?
2. How does weathering help add to Earth's land resources?
3. Why do farmers plow the soil before they plant crops?

Look at the photo. These rock structures are found in the desert. What kind of erosion—wind, water, or ice—do you think formed them? Explain your answer.

UNIT D

Using Reading Skills

Cause and Effect

As you read science, it's important to figure out what happens and why it happens. Why things happen is called the *cause*. What happens is called the *effect*.

Read the paragraphs below. Then complete the exercises that follow.

Use these hints to determine cause and effect.
- Find signal words: *because, and so, as a result.*
- As you read, ask yourself why something is happening.

Hot Rock

In some parts of the world, magma is close to Earth's surface. Sometimes this hot liquid shoots out of an opening in the ground called a **volcano**. Once on the surface of Earth, the liquid rock is called **lava**.

Hot liquid rock cools and hardens when it reaches the surface. When the lava cools around the opening, it may form a cone-shaped volcano. Lava flowing away from the volcano can burn everything in its path before it cools. When the lava cools, it adds a layer of rock to Earth's surface. So volcanoes are one of the forces of nature that change Earth's surface.

Copy each lettered statement. Write *C* in the blank after each cause. Write *E* in the blank after each effect.

1. When the lava cools around the opening ___, it may form a cone-shaped volcano ___.

2. Lava flowing away from the volcano ___ can burn everything in its path before it cools ___.

3. When the lava cools ___, it adds a layer of rock to Earth's surface ___.

4. So volcanoes are one of the forces of nature ___ that change Earth's surface ___.

Using Math Skills

Circle Graph

This circle graph shows how a family of four people uses water. Each section of the circle represents 100 L. Each color represents a different way in which water is used.

Use the circle graph to complete the exercises.

1. How many liters are used for laundry each day?

2. How many liters are used for showering and bathing each day?

3. Is more water used daily for toilet flushing or for showering and bathing? Explain how you know.

4. What fraction of the circle shows the water used daily for toilet flushing? for showering and bathing?

You may wish to use a calculator for Exercises 5 and 6.

5. What is the total number of liters used each day?

6. How much water would this family use in one week? in one year?

D63

UNIT D WRAP-UP!

On your own, use scientific methods to investigate a question about Earth's resources.

THINK LIKE A SCIENTIST

Ask a Question

Pose a question about Earth's resources that you would like to investigate. For example, ask, "How does acid rain affect underground water supplies?"

Make a Hypothesis

Suggest a hypothesis that is a possible answer to the question. One hypothesis is that acid rain has no effect on underground water.

Plan and Do a Test

Plan a controlled experiment to model the effect of acid rain on an underground water supply. You could start with soil, a pan, a fine screen, vinegar, and a watering can. Develop a procedure that uses these materials to test the hypothesis. With permission, carry out your experiment. Follow the safety guidelines on pages S14–S15.

Record and Analyze

Observe carefully and record your data accurately. Make repeated observations.

Draw Conclusions

Look for evidence to support the hypothesis or to show that it is false. Draw conclusions about the hypothesis. Repeat the experiment to verify the results.

WRITING IN SCIENCE
Letter of Request

Write a letter to the people in charge of recycling in your community. Invite them to send a speaker to tell your class about the local recycling program. Use these guidelines.

- Include the parts of a formal letter—heading, inside address, greeting, and closing.
- Briefly state your request and include your school's phone number.

Roles of Living Things

Theme: Constancy and Change

THINK LIKE A SCIENTIST
FIND THAT INSECT E2

CHAPTER 1 **Relationships Among Living Things** E4
Investigation 1   What Do Living Things Need? E6
Investigation 2   How Do Living Things Get the
                            Food They Need? E14
Investigation 3   What Are Food Chains and
                            Food Webs? E22

CHAPTER 2 **Adaptations of Living Things** E36
Investigation 1   How Are Living Things Adapted
                            for Getting Food? E38
Investigation 2   How Are Living Things Adapted
                            for Protection? E46

CHAPTER 3 **Living Things in the Environment** E58
Investigation 1   How Can Living Things Change
                            the Environment? E60
Investigation 2   How Are Living Things Adapted to
                            Their Environments? E68

Using Reading Skills E78
Using Math Skills E79
Unit Wrap-up! E80

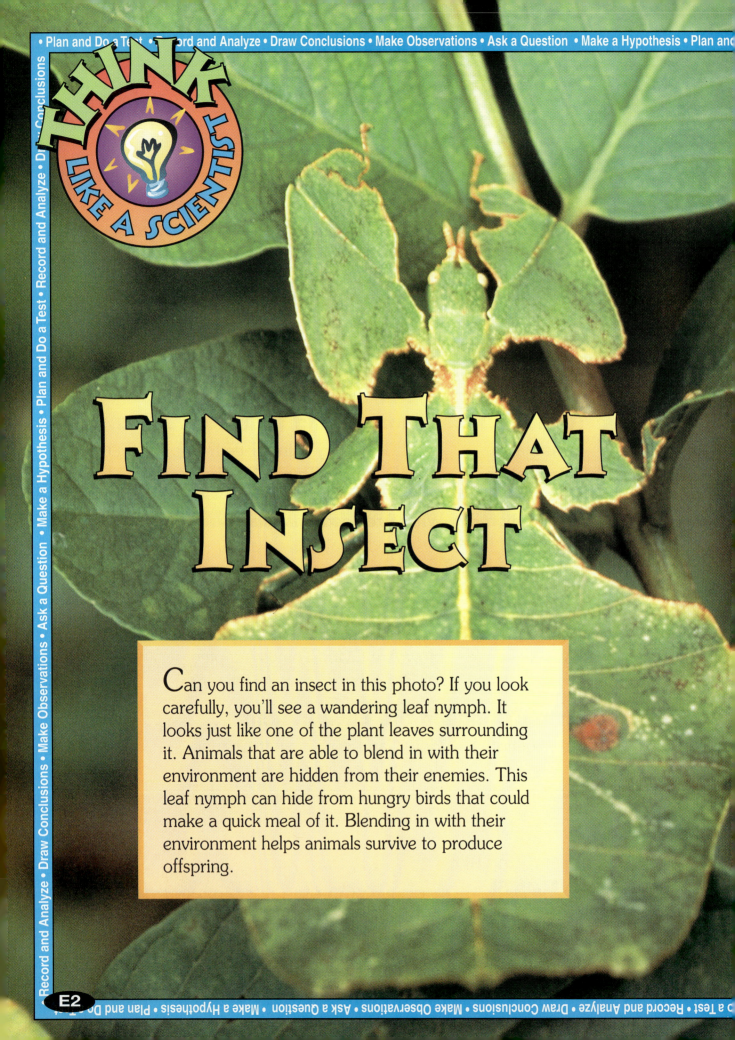

THINK LIKE A SCIENTIST

Find That Insect

Can you find an insect in this photo? If you look carefully, you'll see a wandering leaf nymph. It looks just like one of the plant leaves surrounding it. Animals that are able to blend in with their environment are hidden from their enemies. This leaf nymph can hide from hungry birds that could make a quick meal of it. Blending in with their environment helps animals survive to produce offspring.

THINK LIKE A SCIENTIST

? Questioning In this unit you'll study how living things get what they need to live, and how living things change and adapt to their environment. You'll investigate questions such as these.
- How Do Living Things Get the Food They Need?
- How Are Living Things Adapted for Protection?

Observing, Testing, Hypothesizing In the Activity "Blending In," you'll find out how animals hide from their enemies. You'll also hypothesize why it is hard to find insects that blend in with their environment.

Researching In the Resource "Hiding Out and Other Defenses," you'll find out about many ways that plants and animals protect themselves from their enemies.

Drawing Conclusions After you've completed your investigations, you'll draw conclusions about what you've learned— and get new ideas.

CHAPTER 1

RELATIONSHIPS AMONG LIVING THINGS

Can there ever be too much of a good thing? Unfortunately, the answer is *yes*. Take the fertilizer that helps crops grow. As useful as it is, fertilizer can also cause harm by running off into our water supply and damaging it. Relationships, or how one thing affects another, can be tricky!

PEOPLE USING SCIENCE

National Park Ranger In 1916 the National Park Service was created to preserve national parks. This agency relies on its team of park rangers to protect the wildlife and natural scenery within the parks.

Park rangers do many different jobs. Some rangers patrol the parks to make sure that visitors don't harm or otherwise change the environment. Other park rangers, such as Erin K. Broadbent, work to inform visitors of the history and importance of preserving the parks. As a park ranger in Washington, D.C., Erin Broadbent helps preserve the environments around the national monuments, such as the Washington Monument.

As you read Chapter 1, think about how changes in the environment affect the living things around you.

Coming Up

INVESTIGATION 1
WHAT DO LIVING THINGS NEED?
.... E6

INVESTIGATION 2
HOW DO LIVING THINGS GET THE FOOD THEY NEED?
.... E14

INVESTIGATION 3
WHAT ARE FOOD CHAINS AND FOOD WEBS?
.... E22

◀ Erin Broadbent realized her dream of working for the National Park Service.

What Do Living Things Need?

Imagine that it's a hot day and you're very thirsty. You need to drink a tall glass of water. Water is one of the things you need to live. Other living things need water, too. What else do living things need? In Investigation 1 you'll find out!

Activity

Needs of Plants

Plants seem to grow almost anywhere. What do they need to live?

MATERIALS
- goggles
- marker
- 3 young plants in paper cups
- water
- metric measuring cup
- *Science Notebook*

SAFETY
Wear goggles during this activity.

Procedure

1. With a marker, write *Soil* on a paper cup containing a young plant growing in soil. Label a second such cup *Soil + Water*. Write *Soil + Water + Sunlight* on a third cup. Make a chart like the one shown.

Conditions	Plants After One Week
Soil	
Soil + Water	
Soil + Water + Sunlight	

2. Pour 25 mL of water into the cup labeled *Soil + Water*. Pour another 25 mL of water into the cup labeled *Soil + Water + Sunlight*.

See **SCIENCE and MATH TOOLBOX** page H7 if you need to review **Measuring Volume.**

Step 4

3. Place the cup labeled *Soil* and the cup labeled *Soil + Water* in a place where the plants will get no light. Place the cup labeled *Soil + Water + Sunlight* near a window. **Predict** which conditions will be best for growth. **Record** your prediction in your *Science Notebook*.

4. Every day for one week, check that the soil is moist in the cup labeled *Soil + Water* and in the cup labeled *Soil + Water + Sunlight*. Do not add water to the cup labeled *Soil*.

5. After one week, **observe** the cups to see what the plants look like. **Record** your observations.

Analyze and Conclude

1. Under which conditions did the young plants grow best? What did those plants have that the others did not?

2. How does your prediction compare with your results? From the class results, what can you **conclude** about some of the things plants need to live and grow?

INVESTIGATE FURTHER!

EXPERIMENT

What other questions can you ask about what helps plants to grow? Form a hypothesis and then plan an experiment to test it. After your teacher approves your plan, do the experiment. Share your results with your classmates.

Activity

A Pill Bug's Home

A pill bug's home keeps the pill bug safe and has the things it needs to live. Find out about two conditions that pill bugs need in this activity.

MATERIALS
- goggles
- rectangular baking pan
- paper towels
- tape
- newspaper
- spoon
- pill bugs in a container with a lid
- flashlight
- small cup of water
- *Science Notebook*

SAFETY
Wear goggles during this activity. Wash your hands when you have finished.

Procedure

1. Cover the bottom of a baking pan with paper towels. Tape the edges of the paper towels to the pan. Also seal with tape any places where the paper towels overlap. Place a sheet of newspaper over half of the top of the pan, as shown.

2. Use a spoon to carefully take 3 to 6 pill bugs, one by one, from their container and place them in the middle of the pan.

3. **Predict** whether the pill bugs will move toward light or away from light. **Record** your prediction in your *Science Notebook*. Shine a flashlight on the half of the pan not covered by newspaper. **Observe** where the pill bugs move. **Record** your observations.

Pill bug ▼

Step 1

4. Remove the sheet of newspaper. **Predict** whether pill bugs will move toward a dry area or a wet area. **Record** your prediction. Sprinkle water on the paper towels in half of the pan to make them moist. Leave the other half of the pan dry.

5. **Observe** where the pill bugs move. **Record** your observations. Carefully use a spoon to put the pill bugs back into their container.

Step 4

Analyze and Conclude

1. How did your predictions compare with your results? Which do pill bugs prefer—light or darkness? Do they prefer moist, or dry, places?

2. From your results, what two conditions can you **infer** that pill bugs need in their homes?

3. Pill bugs live in the woods. If you went to the woods to look for them, **predict** where you would most likely find them.

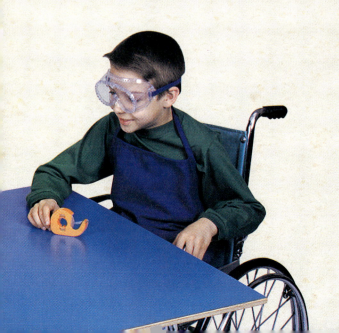

INVESTIGATE FURTHER!

Use the **Best of the Net—Science CD-ROM**, Life Sciences, *The Bear Den and the Cub Den* to find out how bears adapt to their environment. You'll find out where bears live. And you'll learn what some bears do when the weather gets cold.

E9

A Perfect Place to Live

Reading Focus How are the needs of living things alike, and how do their needs differ?

What do you really need? Perhaps you need a haircut. But you have more basic needs than that. Food, water, and air are some of the things you *really* need. Other living things need food, water, and air, too.

Living things also need a place to live. The place where an animal or a plant lives is its **habitat** (hab′i tat). Everything that surrounds and affects a living thing is its **environment** (en vī′rən mənt). All living things need an environment that is suited to their needs.

Salty or Not, Cold or Hot

Living things often have very different needs. So an environment that is good for one living thing may not be good for another. For example, all water animals need a water environment. But most dolphins need to live in salt water. The ocean is a good environment for most dolphins. Other water animals, such as lake trout, small-mouth bass, and minnows, would die in salt water. They need to live in the fresh water of lakes and streams.

This dolphin lives in the ocean. ▼

▲ Life in a freshwater lake

A spotted moray eel ▼

Some water animals need to live near the surface of the water, where light from the Sun keeps the water warm. Others need to live near the bottom. If you've ever gone fishing, you may know that bass need the warm water near the surface. But lake trout need the colder waters that are found at the bottom of a lake.

Many animals share the same habitat. The spotted moray eel lives in the warm, shallow ocean waters around coral reefs. Reef sharks, butterflyfish, batfish, and hogfish live in this habitat, too.

Turn Off the Lights, Please!

Some living things need a lot of sunlight, and some need darkness. The activity on pages E6 and E7 proves that plants need sunlight to live. Without sunlight, plants couldn't make food and would die.

Different kinds of living things need different amounts of sunlight. For example, some kinds of flowers need shade. Other kinds need a lot of bright sunlight.

Pill bugs, which are observed in the activity on pages E8 and E9, need to live in a place that is dark and moist. Pill bugs will dry out in bright sunlight.

▲ A tropical rain forest in Costa Rica

Moles live underground. ▼

Some types of animals dig down into the soil to live in underground habitats. Animals such as earthworms need a dark, moist habitat. These animals would dry up and die in the bright, hot sunlight.

Moles also live underground. A mole is almost blind but has a keen sense of smell. A mole digs until it can smell the tiny insects and worms that are its food.

Very Wet or Very Dry

Some plants need a lot of rain, and others need almost no rain. The plants of the tropical rain forest need to be warm and wet. And they are! It rains almost every day of the year in the rain forest.

▲ Desert plants need very little rain.

Too Tiny to See

All living things need a suitable environment—even living things too small to see with just the eyes. Bacteria (bak tir′ē ə) are living things that can't be seen without a microscope. Bacteria are everywhere. They can be found living in soil, air, water, and even in your body. To survive, bacteria need a warm and wet environment.

From bacteria to whales, living things need an environment that meets their needs. You know that living things need food, water, and air. They also need a way to get rid of wastes. What needs do you have? ■

Bacteria need warmth and moisture. ▼

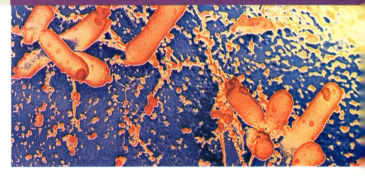

Other plants need a dry place to live. The teddy bear cholla, shown above, is a cactus that grows in the desert. It rains very little in the desert. But that's fine for a cactus. They don't need a lot of water.

INVESTIGATION 1 WRAP-UP

REVIEW

1. Name three basic needs of living things.

2. How does a plant's or animal's environment help it to survive?

CRITICAL THINKING

3. Think about two different animals that have the same needs and live in the same habitat. What things in their environment would they compete for?

4. You plant grass in soil that is shaded by trees. The grass sprouts but turns yellow. What might be causing the problem?

E13

How Do Living Things Get the Food They Need?

When you are very hungry, what are your favorite foods? Living things get food in different ways. Where does your food come from? What are some ways other living things get food? Find out in Investigation 2!

Activity

MATERIALS
- Science Notebook

Meat and Potatoes

Do you eat plants, animals, or both? Find out by doing this activity.

What I Eat	
Food	From Plant or Animal

Procedure

In your *Science Notebook*, **make a chart** like the one shown. **Predict** whether most foods you eat come from plants or animals. For one week, **record** the kinds of foods you eat. List each part of a food and tell where it comes from. At the end of the week, share your observations with your classmates.

Analyze and Conclude

Do most of the foods you eat come from plants or from animals? How does your prediction compare with your findings?

Activity

A Menu for Molds

Do this activity to find out how living things called molds get food.

MATERIALS
- goggles
- bread (1 slice)
- cheese (1 slice)
- sealable plastic bag
- tape
- hand lens
- *Science Notebook*

SAFETY
Wear goggles during this activity. Some molds are harmful. Do not open the bag containing the food.

Procedure

1. Place one slice of moist bread and one slice of cheese in a sandwich bag. Seal the bag and tape it closed. Put the bag in a warm, dark place for one week. **Predict** what will happen to the foods in the bag. **Record** your prediction in your *Science Notebook*.

2. After one week, use a hand lens to **observe** the foods in the bag. Look for mold. *Do not open the bag.*

 See **SCIENCE and MATH TOOLBOX** page H2 if you need to review **Using a Hand Lens**.

3. **Make drawings** of what you see. **Describe** how the food has changed.

4. Put the bag back in the same warm, dark place for another week. Repeat steps 2 and 3 at the end of the second week.

Analyze and Conclude

1. What happened to the food in the bag? **Compare** your prediction with your results.

2. From your results, **infer** what the molds you saw used for food.

3. **Predict** what would happen to the food if you left it in the bag for several months.

Step 1

Step 2

E15

What's for Dinner?

> **Reading Focus** How can you classify living things by what they eat?

Plants make their own food. ▼

Imagine never needing to eat breakfast, lunch, or dinner! If you were a plant, you would never need to eat. You would make your own food.

Food Makers

Plants make their own food inside their leaves. Plants take in water and air from their environment. The leaves soak up sunlight. Plants use the Sun's energy to make food from water and a gas in the air. This food can be stored in roots, leaves, and other plant parts for use later on.

Living things that can make their own food are called **producers** (prō dōōs'ərz). Plants are producers. Producers make up the basic food supply in the environment. Without them, most other kinds of living things would not be able to exist.

May I See a Menu?

Since your body can't produce its own food, as a plant does, you have to get it another way—by eating something else. That means that you are a consumer (kən sōōm'ər).

E16

A **consumer** is a living thing that eats plants, animals, or other living things.

What kinds of things are usually on your dinner plate? Crunchy crickets and other insects? You might eat these animals if you were a praying mantis. A praying mantis is an animal eater. Animals that eat only other animals are called **carnivores** (kär′nə vôrz). Spiders, many insects, and some worms are carnivores. Cats, snakes, wolves, owls, and many fish are carnivores, too.

◀ **A praying mantis is a carnivore.**

Wolves are carnivores. ▼

E17

Brown bears sometimes eat plants. ▼

Prairie dogs do not eat other animals. They crawl out of their underground burrows and feed on plants. Marine iguanas (i gwä′nəz) also eat only plants, enjoying a meal of salty seaweed. Animals such as prairie dogs and marine iguanas are called herbivores (hur′bə vôrz). A **herbivore** is an animal that eats only plants. Elephants and horses are herbivores. So are caterpillars and deer. What other plant-eating animals can you think of?

Many animals are omnivores (äm′ni vôrz). **Omnivores** are animals that eat both plants and animals. Brown bears are omnivores. They eat berries and other fruits, but they also eat small animals, like fish.

Raccoons are also omnivores. So are some types of mice, birds, and turtles. The activity on page E14 investigates whether the food people eat comes from plants, animals, or both. If you eat both plants and animals, you're an omnivore, too!

Breaking It Down

In every environment there is an important group of consumers called decomposers (dē kəm pōz′ərz). **Decomposers** feed on the remains of once-living things. Bacteria, mushrooms, yeast, and molds are decomposers. Molds grow on foods that haven't been stored in the right way. Mold is grown in the activity on page E15. What can you do to prevent molds from growing?

Brown bears eat fish, too. ▼

E18

▲ A raccoon is an omnivore.

Decomposers are important to the environment. They break down materials from once-living things into simpler materials. Decomposers release these simpler materials back into the water, soil, and air, where they can be used again by other living things. Rotting logs and rotting leaves on the forest floor are signs that decomposers have been at work. ■

Mushrooms are decomposers. ▶

Saber Teeth!

Reading Focus How were saber-toothed cats similar to African lions?

The cat watches its prey, waiting for the right moment to attack. Finally, it uses its short but powerful legs to leap onto the grazing animal. The heavy weight of the cat brings down its prey, a bison, in an instant. The cat uses its knifelike 23-cm (9-inch) teeth to slash into the belly of the bison.

This is no ordinary cat. It's a saber-toothed cat. But you won't see any of these cats around today. They became extinct around 11,000 years ago.

This bison, trapped in a tar pit, is about to be attacked by a saber-toothed cat. ▼

Extinction (ek stiŋk′shen) is the dying out of all living things of a certain kind. Can you think of any other animals that are extinct?

Scientists learn about saber-toothed cats by studying their remains, which are mostly preserved bones. Such remains are called fossils. Scientists have found many fossils in a place in California called the La Brea Tar Pits.

The La Brea Tar Pits is a bog, a place where the ground is wet and spongy. Water covers the bog. The tar pits contain a tarlike substance. Scientists have found thousands of bones from extinct animals, including saber-toothed cats, in the tar pits. Why are there so many fossils at La Brea?

▲ **Compare the skull of the extinct saber-toothed cat to that of the modern African lion. What are the differences? What are the similarities?**

Although saber-toothed cats are extinct, there are big cats alive today. These cats are something like those extinct cats. Compare the modern African lion, top right, to the saber-toothed cat, top left. They are both about the same size but the saber-toothed cat had shorter, more powerful legs. It also had a shorter tail and weighed almost twice as much as an African lion.

Scientists think that the saber-toothed cat hunted differently than a lion. It's likely that the saber-toothed cat was not as fast as today's big cats. It probably did not chase its prey. A saber-toothed cat most likely waited and watched for its prey to come close. When that prey came close enough, the big cat would pounce on it. ■

Internet Field Trip
Visit **www.eduplace.com** to learn more about how saber-toothed cats lived.

INVESTIGATION 2 WRAP-UP

REVIEW

1. What is a producer? What is a consumer? Which one are you? Explain your answer.

2. Compare the diets of carnivores, herbivores, and omnivores.

CRITICAL THINKING

3. Could carnivores live if all plants became extinct? Why or why not?

4. If scientists found the skeleton of an unknown animal, what clues would help them find out what kinds of foods the animal ate?

INVESTIGATION 3

WHAT ARE FOOD CHAINS AND FOOD WEBS?

Slurp! The fast tongue of a frog catches a juicy fly. Gulp! A snake eats the frog. Will the snake become a meal for some other animal? In Investigation 3 you'll explore different eating relationships.

Activity

Making a Food-Chain Mobile

Do you eat hamburgers, fruit, and salad? No matter what you eat, you're part of a food chain. Do this activity to find out more about food chains.

MATERIALS
- books about plants and animals
- old magazines
- scissors
- crayons or colored markers
- tape
- yarn or string
- wire coat hanger
- Science Notebook

Procedure

1. In your *Science Notebook,* **make a list** of four living things. First, list one kind of plant. Then, think about the kind of animal that would eat that plant. List that animal. Next, think about an animal that would eat the animal you listed. List the second animal. Now do the same for a third animal. Get ideas by looking through animal books and magazines or from your own observations.

2. Cut out pictures from old magazines or **draw** pictures of the four living things in your food chain. Then tape your pictures to a piece of yarn, as shown. Put the living things in order of who eats whom. Think back to Investigation 2 to help you decide what should be at the bottom of your food chain. Tape the end of the yarn to a wire hanger. You've made a food-chain mobile.

Analyze and Conclude

1. Which living thing is the producer in your food chain?

2. Which living things are consumers?

3. Look at the food-chain mobiles of your classmates. What can you **infer** about the kind of living thing that is at the bottom of a food chain?

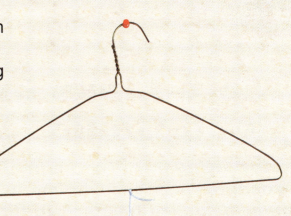

Step 2

Activity

More Links in the Food Chain

MATERIALS
- index cards
- crayons or colored markers
- short lengths of blue yarn and red yarn
- scissors
- *Science Notebook*

Most living things eat more than one kind of food. Because they do, many food chains may be linked together. In this activity you will play a game to see how food chains can link to form food webs.

Procedure

1. Work in a group to **write** the names of the following living things on index cards, one per card: berries, nuts, water plants, mouse, snake, big fish, small fish, crayfish, owl, bear, chipmunk.

2. Place all the cards face up. With your group, arrange some of the cards to form a food chain.

3. Place a piece of blue yarn, about 10 cm long, on top of two cards so that each end is on a card. Use additional lengths of blue yarn to connect the other cards in the food chain.

Step 3

 Math Hint "About 10 cm" is an estimate. The length of yarn does not have to be exactly 10 cm.

4. Use the remaining cards and blue yarn to create two more food chains.

5. Now **look** at the food chains you have made. **Find** a living thing in one food chain that can eat or be eaten by something in another food chain. Use a length of red yarn to connect these two cards.

Step 5

6. You have just linked two food chains together to form a food web. Find all the links between the food chains that you can. Connect the cards with lengths of red yarn. **Make a drawing** of your food web in your *Science Notebook*.

7. Look at the food webs made by other groups in your class. **Compare** these webs to the one your group made.

8. Think about what would happen if there were no producers. Take away the producer cards. **Infer** what would happen to the living things that eat the producers. **Infer** what would happen to the other members of the food web.

Analyze and Conclude

1. Explain how a food chain is different from a food web.

2. Suppose that most of the plants in a certain place die off. **Hypothesize** about what will happen to the animals that eat those plants.

UNIT PROJECT LINK

For this Unit Project you will make a mural of a tropical rain forest. Explore the producers of the different layers of the rain forest—the canopy, the understory, and the forest floor. With your classmates, make a mural showing different rain forest plants.

For more help with your Unit Project, go to **www.eduplace.com**.

Who Eats Whom?

Reading Focus What is the difference between a food chain and a food web?

A Food Chain

Plant

Grasshopper

Lizard

A grasshopper clings to a plant in the bright sunlight and nibbles on a leaf. Suddenly a lizard darts up from behind. It shoots out its tongue and eats the grasshopper. As the lizard slips away through the grass, a snake strikes and swallows the lizard whole. Later, an owl catches the snake and flies off to feed it to her young.

Food Chains

Every living thing needs food because food provides energy. When one animal eats another animal or a plant, they both become part of a food chain. A **food chain** is the path that energy takes as one living thing eats another. In the example above, the plant, grasshopper, lizard, snake, and owl are all connected to one another in a food chain. Cards are connected by yarn to show a food chain in the activity on pages E22 and E23. The plant, grasshopper, lizard, snake, and owl are all part of the same food chain.

Different environments, such as forests, deserts, or lakes, have different food chains. Some food chains are short, and some are long. But all food chains begin with a producer.

Links in the Chain

A plant is a producer and can make its own food. A producer is the first link in all food chains.

A consumer is the next link in a food chain. Animals are consumers. Some animals, such as grasshoppers, feed on plants. Then other animals, such as lizards, eat the animals that ate the plants.

Animals that hunt other animals for food are called **predators** (pred′ə tərz). The animals that are hunted by predators are called **prey**.

An animal can be both predator and prey. For example, a housefly may be eaten by a frog. In this case the frog is a predator. The fly is its prey. But the frog can become prey if a raccoon makes a meal of the frog.

▲ A frog can be predator and prey.

Likewise, the raccoon becomes prey if it's eaten by a predator, such as a cougar.

If no larger animal eats the cougar, does that mean the cougar is the top consumer in the chain? Not really. When the cougar dies, its body will become food for the last of the consumers—the decomposers. Bacteria, molds, and other decomposers feed on the remains of animals and break down these remains.

A Food Web

▲ What animals compete for the same food?

Chains Tangle Into Webs

There are some simple food chains in nature. But usually two or more food chains overlap and link, forming a **food web**. A model of a food web is made in the activity on pages E24 and E25.

A forest food web might include an oak tree. When the oak tree drops its acorns, hungry squirrels may eat the acorns and collect some for winter. Deer, mice, shrews, bears, and raccoons also eat acorns.

But acorns are not the only food these animals eat. Deer also eat grass, leaves, moss, twigs and other plant parts. Mice also nibble on grass and eat insects and spiders.

Raccoons also eat frogs, fish, fruit, crabs, grasshoppers, and sometimes even bird eggs.

You can see that in a large food web, many animals are connected to one another by the kinds of foods that they eat. Food webs show that every kind of living thing depends on other kinds of living things. Wherever you look in nature—in forests, lakes, meadows, oceans, or deserts—plants and animals are connected to one another through a web of life. ■

Internet Field Trip

Visit **www.eduplace.com** to learn about the food webs that spiders depend on for survival.

E29

Cane Toads in Leaping Numbers

Reading Focus How did cane toads change the food chains and food webs in Australia?

Did you ever make a problem worse by trying to fix it? That's what happened in Australia in 1935. At that time, scientists thought they had discovered a way to get rid of the insects that were eating their crops. The result of their action was a country covered with huge toads, called cane toads. Cane toads may be as much as 23 cm (9 in.) long!

Cane toads live in Hawaii and other parts of the tropics. In 1935, scientists brought a group of cane toads to Australia to eat the beetles that were destroying the sugar cane crops. The scientists' idea might have worked except for one problem. The beetles' habitat is inside the sugar cane plants, but the toads' habitat is on the ground. Their paths never crossed, so the toads never ate the beetles.

Using Math: This cane toad shown is life-size. How does the size of this cane toad compare with the size of your hand?

Although the cane toads didn't solve the beetle problem, they did make a difference. The toads changed the natural community (kə myōō'nə tē). A **community** is a group of plants and animals that live in the same area and depend on one another. When an animal is added to or taken away from a community, the food chains and food webs change.

The cane toads became part of the food chains and food webs in their new home. The huge toads gobbled up many of Australia's native lizards, snakes, mice, and birds. Scientists became worried about the possible extinction of these native animals.

The toad problem quickly became worse. Cane toads were laying up to 20,000 eggs at a time. And the toads had no natural predators. That's because the toads can protect themselves from being eaten by releasing poison from their necks. The native animals that tried to eat them were often poisoned to death!

In spite of the trouble they've caused, cane toads have become part of the culture in Australia. Some people consider them a tourist attraction. One politician even suggested putting up a statue to honor the cane toad! What do you think? Is Australia's cane toad a pet or a pest? ■

Science in Literature

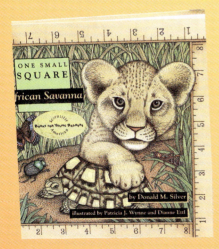

One Small Square: African Savanna
by Donald M. Silver
Illustrated by
Patricia J. Wynne and Dianne Ettl
W. H. Freeman & Co., 1994

Grass Eaters Run For Life!

"The African savanna is home to the biggest, the tallest, and the fastest land animals on earth. It is where killer dogs work together as a team, and tiny termites build nests as high as the ceiling in your room and as hard as cement. One minute all is calm. The next, there is panic as thousands of grass eaters run for their lives."

More interesting facts can be found in the book *One Small Square: African Savanna* by Donald M. Silver. Enjoy fun activities while you explore life in the dangerous savanna.

Deadly Links

> **Reading Focus** What caused the brown pelican to become endangered?

Suppose insects were destroying tomato plants you were growing. What would you do? You might spray an insecticide (in sek'tə sīd) on the plants to kill the insects. Insecticides are chemicals used to destroy insects that harm plants or carry diseases.

Killing Pests

Insecticides have been used widely throughout the world. Insecticides can help farmers keep crops growing healthy and strong. But these chemicals may remain in the soil for years. Some insecticides sprayed before you were born may still be in the soil today!

Through research, scientists found out that insecticides can harm more than the pests they were made to kill. The poisonous chemicals can be carried off by wind and moving water to new places. Once in these new places, the chemicals can harm wildlife. This was the case with DDT, an insecticide. DDT can kill many kinds of flies and mosquitoes that carry diseases. Even though DDT was useful for killing pests, it had harmful effects on other animals, such as the bald eagle and the brown pelican.

▲ Insecticides can help crops grow.

Follow the path of chemicals through this food chain. The addition of chemicals can cause changes in food chains, too. ▼

Pelican Problems

In California, DDT came close to killing all of the state's brown pelicans during the 1960s and 1970s. Scientists found that DDT from a factory was carried off in the waste water from the plant. Some of this waste water ended up in ocean waters. There the DDT was taken in by fish. When the brown pelicans ate these fish, the birds took DDT into their own bodies.

As DDT moves along a food chain, it is stored in the bodies of animals for a long time. When the brown pelicans laid their eggs, the DDT stored in the parent birds' bodies caused most eggs to have very thin shells. Most shells broke before the baby pelicans could grow. Because of DDT, there were hardly any new baby brown pelicans during those years. So the number of brown pelicans greatly decreased.

Brown pelicans on the East Coast and in Louisiana were also being harmed by DDT. In Louisiana the brown pelican had been named the state bird back when there were close to 100,000 pelicans in the state. Because of DDT, pelicans in Louisiana disappeared completely!

▲ DDT caused brown pelicans to lay eggs with very thin shells.

The Start of a Solution

In 1970 the pelican was listed as endangered. Something had to be done, or there would be no brown pelicans left. Finally, DDT was banned in the United States in 1972. Since then the number of pelicans has been on the rise.

Pelicans were not the only birds that were harmed by DDT. Bald eagles and peregrine falcons also laid eggs with thin shells because of the DDT stored in their bodies.

The law preventing the use of DDT has helped each of these great birds recover from the harmful chemical. But other countries still use DDT.

Although the use of DDT has been banned in the United States, there is still a need for insecticides. Today farmers use safer chemicals in smaller amounts. This means there is far less harm to the environment than with the use of DDT. ■

INVESTIGATION 3 WRAP-UP

REVIEW

1. What is the difference between a food chain and a food web?

2. Can an animal be a predator and also prey? Explain your answer.

CRITICAL THINKING

3. Think about the different things you eat and where they come from. Draw a diagram that shows you as part of a food web.

4. You see a sign that says, "Our new insecticide kills all bugs!" Do you think buying this product is a good idea or a bad idea? Explain your answer.

REFLECT & EVALUATE

Word Power

Write the letter of the term that best matches the definition. *Not all terms will be used.*

a. carnivore
b. environment
c. food chain
d. food web
e. habitat
f. omnivore
g. predator
h. producers

1. Path that energy takes as one thing eats another
2. Animal that eats plants and other animals
3. Living things that make their own food
4. Everything that surrounds and affects a living thing
5. Animal that hunts another animal for food
6. Place where an animal lives

Check What You Know

Write the term in each pair that best completes each sentence.

1. Bacteria, mushrooms, and molds are (producers, decomposers).
2. Two food chains that overlap form (a food web, an environment).
3. A living thing that eats plants, animals, or other living things is (a consumer, a predator).
4. Animals that are hunted are (predators, prey).

Problem Solving

1. Some animals are herbivores, others are carnivores, and still others are omnivores. Which are you? How do you know? Use the definitions of all three terms in your answer.
2. Suppose a tree near your home dies. Explain how this may cause changes in a food chain.

Study the drawings. Explain how a frog can be both predator and prey.

CHAPTER 2

ADAPTATIONS OF LIVING THINGS

To survive, or stay alive, plants and animals need to have food. They need to protect themselves from danger, too. How could a good sense of hearing help an animal get food? What part of a plant could stop a hungry animal from eating it?

PEOPLE USING SCIENCE

Aquarium Curator Would you like to give a 200-pound harbor seal a dental exam? That's one of the jobs that Rhona St. Clair-Moore did while working at the Thomas H. Kean New Jersey State Aquarium where she headed the marine mammal program. She was also the first woman to be named curator (kyōō rāt′ər) at the aquarium. A curator is a person in charge of a section of a museum, library, or aquarium.

Rhona St. Clair-Moore says she has always liked animals. "When I was young, I watched nature shows with my father. I asked questions about animals." Her interest led her to follow a career at the aquarium.

In this chapter you'll read how many kinds of living things survive in their environment.

Coming Up

INVESTIGATION 1
HOW ARE LIVING THINGS ADAPTED FOR GETTING FOOD?
.... E38

INVESTIGATION 2
HOW ARE LIVING THINGS ADAPTED FOR PROTECTION?
.... E46

Rhona St. Clair-Moore blows a whistle when a seal is rewarded with food for good behavior. ▼

E37

How Are Living Things Adapted for Getting Food?

A big eagle swoops down from the sky. It grabs a fish out of the water and flies away. How are eagles adapted to catch, carry, and eat fish? In Investigation 1 you'll explore many adaptations living things have for getting food.

Activity

The Right Beak for the Job

Why do birds have different kinds of beaks? How does a beak's shape help birds get food?

MATERIALS
- goggles
- rectangular pan
- sand
- water
- raisins
- uncooked rice
- plastic straw
- scissors
- toothpick
- plastic fork with tape on tines
- plastic soup spoon
- Science Notebook

SAFETY
Do not eat any raisins or rice. Wear goggles during this activity.

Procedure

1. Set up a pan with sand, as shown. Add water to the pan until it is two-thirds full.

2. Bury six to ten raisins in the sand. Sprinkle rice in the shallow water where the sand begins to slope upward.

3. Cut a plastic straw into five pieces. Place the pieces in the water so that they float.

Step 1

E38

4. The raisins are models of small animals that live buried in the sand. The rice grains are small plants and animals that live in shallow water. The pieces of straw are models for fish. A toothpick, a plastic fork with taped tines, and a plastic soup spoon represent different kinds of bird beaks. In your *Science Notebook,* **predict** which beak is best for getting each kind of food.

5. **Make a chart** like the one shown. Use the toothpick to find and pick up raisins in the sand. **Count** the number of raisins you pick up in ten tries. **Record** this number in your chart. Now use the toothpick to pick up rice and then pieces of the straw. **Record** all your results in your chart.

Step 5

Kind of "Beak"	Number of Raisins	Number of Rice Grains	Number of Straw Pieces
toothpick			
fork			
spoon			

6. Replace the raisins, rice, and straw pieces. Repeat step 5, using the fork and then the spoon. **Describe** the methods you used with the different beaks and the different kinds of foods.

Analyze and Conclude

1. Which beak was best for collecting which food?

2. Think about the birds that would catch the plants and animals described in step 4. **Hypothesize** what each one's beak would look like. How is each bird's beak better than the models that you made?

3. **Infer** what birds with similar kinds of beaks have in common.

Technology Link CD-ROM

INVESTIGATE FURTHER!

Use the **Best of the Net—Science CD-ROM**, Life Sciences, *Miocene Sharks' Teeth of Calvert County* to learn more interesting facts about sharks. You'll find out about the many shark fossils dating back millions of years that geologists have found. And you'll learn how well sharks are adapted to their watery environment.

E39

Catching Lunch

Reading Focus How do adaptations help living things get food?

When you say "I'm starved!" does someone make you a sandwich or snack? Animals in nature must find food in order to get a meal. Their task is made a little easier by the adaptations (ad əp tā′shənz) they have. **Adaptations** are behaviors or parts of living things that help the living things survive in a certain environment. Animals have adaptations for getting food. And so do some unusual plants.

It Makes Good Sense

Animals have special body parts that help them get food. Many animals have extraordinary vision, a super sense of hearing, or a sharp sense of smell that helps them get food. Hunting birds, such as eagles and hawks, have very good eyes. They can spot prey from over a kilometer (half a mile) away! A dog's keen sense of smell can help uncover a tasty bone buried last year. The dog follows a scent trail that you couldn't smell at all! An owl, hunting at night, is able to swoop down on a mouse it can see running in the dark.

Deadly Weapons

Animals often have body parts that they can use as deadly weapons. A praying mantis clamps its front legs around butterflies, grasshoppers, and other insects before it eats them. Many snakes have fangs that can inject poison that can paralyze and kill their victims. A chameleon (kə mēl′ē ən) has a sticky lump on the end of its tongue that insects get trapped on. A brown bear uses sharp claws and teeth to catch and eat large fish.

This snake injects poison. ▼

A Handy Tool!

The activity about bird beaks on pages E38 and E39 shows that some beaks are better for catching certain kinds of foods than other beaks. Woodpeckers use their pointed beaks to drill into trees so that they can catch insects.

An owl catches a deer mouse. ▼

Hummingbirds have long beaks and tongues that they use for sipping nectar from flowers.

Using Math *You can make your own nectar for hummingbirds by mixing 1 part sugar to 4 parts water. How many cups of sugar would you use with 8 cups of water?*

The flamingo uses its bill as a strainer to trap tiny plants, shrimp, and snails found in shallow muddy waters. In the tropical rain forest, parrots and cockatoos use their strong beaks to crack nuts and seeds or to tear open fruit.

Mealtime Manners

You've seen how some body parts are adaptations for getting food. The behavior of an animal can also be an adaptation for getting food. **Behavior** is the way an animal typically acts in certain situations.

Electric eels, a kind of fish, have a really shocking way of getting food. They catch fish by stunning them with an electric shock! An archerfish catches an insect on a nearby water plant by using its long, tubelike mouthparts to shoot out water drops

An archerfish shoots water at an insect. ▼

that knock the insect into the water. Grasshoppers are able to hop more than a meter (about 3 ft) to search for a meal. That's 20 times the length of a grasshopper's body. If you had the muscle power of a grasshopper, you could jump about 24 m (80 ft)!

Some animals use tools from the environment to gather or eat food. While swimming on its back, the sea otter holds a rock on its belly and uses the rock to break open shells. Chimpanzees eat termites from a stick much the way you eat with a fork.

▲ A Venus' flytrap catches an insect for lunch.

◀ A chimpanzee uses a stick to dig for termites and then eats the insects as they crawl along the stick.

They peel the bark from a stick and poke it into a termite mound. When they pull out the stick, it is covered with tasty termite treats!

Other animals stalk, or secretly follow, their food. Have you ever watched a neighborhood cat sneak up on a bird? This method is the same one a leopard uses when it stalks a young gazelle on the African plain.

Plants That Trap Insects

Plants need certain nutrients (n$\overline{oo}$′trē ənts). **Nutrients** are substances that provide materials needed for growth. Most plants absorb these nutrients from soil.

Plants have different adaptations to get these nutrients. The Venus' flytrap, sundew, and pitcher plants are known for "eating" insects. By trapping and digesting insects, these plants get nutrients that are missing from the soil in which they grow.

All living things need nutrients that food provides. You can see that plants and animals have many adaptations that help them get food. ■

A Quick Tongue

Reading Focus How is a chameleon adapted to its environment?

In the trees of a tropical forest, a chameleon walks along the branches in search of prey. The chameleon seems to be moving in slow motion. How can such a slow animal ever catch a fast-moving insect? The chameleon has some unusual adaptations for getting its food. Find out about them on these pages.

ODD EYES The chameleon's eyes look odd because each eye can move separately. With this adaptation, the chameleon can keep one eye on its prey while the other eye looks for predators.

WHAT A TAIL! A chameleon moves high up in the trees. If it loses its balance, it can curl its strong tail around a branch to keep from falling.

NEAT FEET The chameleon's foot has three toes joined on one side and two toes joined on the other side. The V-shaped foot is good for grabbing onto branches.

A TALENTED TONGUE The chameleon's tongue is very long—sometimes as long as its entire body. At the end of its tongue is a sticky patch that prey can get stuck on. When inside the chameleon's mouth, the tongue is folded much like an accordion. When prey comes within range, the chameleon shoots out its tongue. Its tongue moves so fast that it would be hard for you to see it move.

Difficult to Spot

The chameleon has a good chance of surprising its prey. That's because of **camouflage** (kam′ə-fläzh)—the ability to blend in with the surroundings. Besides helping the chameleon sneak up on its prey, camouflage makes it hard for predators to spot the chameleon.

INVESTIGATE FURTHER!

RESEARCH

Plants and animals have adaptations that help them survive. With a group, choose an animal from your community. What kinds of adaptations does it have? Create a poster of your animal describing its adaptations and show the poster to your classmates.

INVESTIGATION 1 WRAP-UP

REVIEW

1. Describe how body parts help living things get food.

2. Describe how behaviors help living things get food.

CRITICAL THINKING

3. Are humans the only living things that use tools? Argue for or against this theory based on the behaviors of sea otters and chimpanzees.

4. Invent an animal. Draw your animal, showing the kinds of adaptations it would have for getting food. Explain your animal's behavior for getting food.

How Are Living Things Adapted for Protection?

Danger! What do you do? Do you run or hide? Do you stand as still as you can? Living things have different adaptations to protect themselves. Find out about these adaptations in Investigation 2.

Activity

Blending In

Frogs, spiders, and birds are just a few of the predators that eat insects. How do insects protect themselves? This activity will help you find out.

MATERIALS
- colored paper
- colored markers, colored pencils, or crayons
- scissors
- tape
- *Science Notebook*

Procedure

1. Your job is to **design** and **draw** a new kind of insect—one that could hide from predators in your classroom. Look around your classroom for different colors, shapes, and patterns that your insect could blend with and not be easily seen.

2. To draw your insect, use any or all of the drawing materials listed. Remember, your insect must have camouflage so that it blends in and is hard to find.

Step 3

3. When you have finished drawing your insect, cut it out. Your teacher will tell you when to "hide" your insect. **Predict** where your insect will be hardest to find. Then put your insect in that place. If your insect hides on the wall, use a very small piece of tape to attach it. See if others can find it.

4. In your *Science Notebook,* **describe** what your insect looks like in its hiding place.

Analyze and Conclude

1. Which insect in your class was the hardest to find? **Hypothesize** why it was hard to find that insect.

2. Infer how the color, shape, or size of your insect helped it hide. **Explain** your answer.

3. Predict what would happen to an insect that didn't have any way to hide from predators. How might such an insect be able to survive?

UNIT PROJECT LINK

Research how animals of the tropical rain forest are adapted to their environment. Construct some rain forest animals and attach them to your mural. Make some camouflaged animals and "hide" them among the plants. Also attach predators and their prey to show a food web.

Technology Link
For more help with your Unit Project, go to **www.eduplace.com**.

Hiding Out and Other Defenses

Reading Focus What are some adaptations that help plants and animals protect themselves?

▲ Crab spider on flower

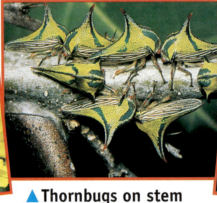
▲ Thornbugs on stem

▲ Tulip tree beauty moth on tree bark

You Can't See Me

Hide-and-seek is fun. But animals in nature must stay safe from enemies and catch food to eat. How they play the game can be a matter of life or death! The activity on pages E46 and E47 shows how camouflage is an important adaptation for defense for many animals. When a young spotted fawn is left alone, it can keep very still and blend in with the forest floor. This keeps predators from seeing the fawn.

An insect called a katydid has wings that look like the leaves of the trees it lives on. Its wings even have brown spots that look like spots found on real leaves. In the photos above, how does camouflage help the animals hide?

The thorns on a rose are a sharp defense. ▼

Don't Come Too Close!

Some plants have sharp thorns or bristles that help protect them from being eaten. An animal that has nibbled on a sweet-smelling rose and gotten pricked by a thorn, for example, is not likely to make that mistake again.

Some plants contain poisonous or irritating chemicals that keep many animals away. Have you ever touched poison ivy or poison sumac? If so, you know that days of skin sores and itching can result. Because of these effects, many people have learned to stay away from these plants.

Sometimes a plant's defense is its bitter taste. For this reason, some people plant marigold plants around their vegetable gardens. Rabbits are often attracted to the bright orange and yellow colors of these flowers.

◀ **A katydid stays safe because predators mistake it for a leaf.**

A marigold's bitter taste keeps it safe from hungry animals. ▶

E49

But after tasting the marigolds, the rabbits usually go elsewhere in search of more pleasant-tasting plants to nibble.

Animals that are covered with quills or spines have a defense against being eaten. No animal wants to eat quills or spines. The quills of porcupines and spines of hedgehogs provide prickly protection.

Most of the time a puffer fish does not look prickly. But when it is attacked, or when it fears attack, it can suck in water and blow itself up into a spine-covered ball. Its shape, size, and spines make it impossible for even a large fish to eat the puffer fish!

You're Copying Me!

Some animals are protected from enemies because they look like other, more dangerous, animals. Most wasps and hornets have black and yellow stripes. Animals that have been stung by these dangerous insects learn to avoid them. Some harmless beetles also have black and yellow stripes. These beetles may not be attacked by predators because they look like the more dangerous hornets and wasps.

Using Math Do you think a porcupine is more likely to have 30 quills or 30,000 quills? Explain your answer.

A relaxed puffer fish ▼   An alarmed puffer fish under attack ▼

Other copycats include the harmless kingsnake, which looks like the poisonous coral snake. Both snakes have red, yellow, and black stripes, but the colors are arranged differently. Although the creature on the right looks like a snake, it's actually a caterpillar from a Costa Rican rain forest. Some butterflies and moths fool predators because of two bright spots on their wings. The spots look like the eyes of large owls.

Tricked You, Didn't I?

The opossum is famous for tricking predators into thinking it's dead. The trick works because the opossum's enemies eat only freshly killed meat. The squid also tricks its enemy. It sprays an inklike substance in its enemy's face. This inky cloud prevents the enemy from seeing the squid. While the enemy is blinded, the squid swims away.

This caterpillar *(left)* and butterfly *(right)* scare away predators by looking like other animals.

The kingsnake *(right)* is a copycat of the poisonous coral snake *(left)*.

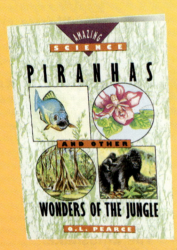

▲ An ostrich protecting its young

pounces on the tail and eats it while the rest of the lizard escapes!

Many birds pretend to be hurt to protect their chicks. The African ostrich flaps its wings and cries out when a predator heads toward its young. This gets the attention of the predator, which goes after the adult bird instead of the chicks.

Going My Way?

Some animal behaviors are adaptations for protection against parasites (par′ə sīts). **Parasites** are creatures that live on or in other living things and harm them. Adaptations that protect against parasites have led to some very unusual friendships.

Some lizards have a last-chance defense against predators by losing their tails! The tail continues to twitch after it has dropped off the lizard. This tricks the predator, which

Science in Literature

RIVER SHARK EATS COW!

"If you saw a list of the world's most dangerous fish, you would likely find the piranha near the top. . . . This fish is equipped with an arsenal of stabbing, cutting teeth. . . . An animal as large as a cow can be devoured in just a few minutes, leaving nothing but bare bones."

Piranhas and Other Wonders of the Jungle
by Q. L. Pearce
Illustrated by Mary Ann Fraser
Julian Messner, 1990

Discover more interesting facts about rain forest life in the book *Piranhas and Other Wonders of the Jungle* by Q. L. Pearce. Learn how different jungle creatures survive and protect themselves by adapting to their environment.

Birds called oxpeckers eat a meal off the hide of a rhinoceros. ▶

Oxpeckers, or tickbirds, are small African songbirds. These birds eat ticks and other annoying parasites off the tough skin of the rhinoceros, buffalo, and elephant. By allowing the birds to remain on them, these large animals protect themselves from parasites. In exchange, the birds are protected from predators as they dine. Few animals would attack a bird sitting on a fierce rhino.

Another unusual friendship occurs in coral reefs under the sea. A small fish called the cleaner fish removes parasites from the skin, gills, and mouth of many other reef fish. The coral reef fish are protected from parasites, and the cleaner fish has an easily found meal.

As you can see, plants and animals have many defenses. All are a matter of survival. ■

◀ **The arrows point to two cleaner fish eating parasites from a coral reef fish.**

Medicines From Nature

Reading Focus How is nature like a drugstore?

When you're sick, a family member probably gets you medicine from the drugstore. In some places, though, you might just be told, "Take a hike!"

Hitting the Nature Trail

People all over the world hike along woodland paths to find healing plants. They rely on nature's drugstore for relief. If you live in the Ozark Mountains of Missouri, your family might brew spicebush tea to bring down your fever. If you live in the Appalachian Mountains and have a stomachache, someone might serve you a gentle drink of slippery elm bark tea. This treatment was used by pioneers over 200 years ago.

Plants produce chemicals that help in their protection and survival. The chemicals are in leaves, bark, roots, blossoms, and seeds. The use of these chemicals as medicine goes back thousands of years.

Medicines From Living Things

Many plant parts and chemicals, as well as animal parts, have been used as medicines. The ancient Greeks used a powder made from substances in the bark of the willow tree to treat pain and reduce fever.

The main ingredient in aspirin is similar to a substance in the bark of the willow tree. ▶

In the 1890s a German chemist studied the substances in willow bark. In a laboratory, he developed a similar substance, aspirin. Today aspirin is probably the most-widely-used medicine in the world.

Early settlers in America often relied on medicines used by Native Americans. The Cherokees used the bark of the sassafras tree to treat sores. They then applied a soothing paste of powdered maize, or corn, and soft turkey down feathers!

Navajo (nav'ə hō) healers still use the root of the strong-smelling osha plant. Not only does osha root help treat colds, but it also has been found to keep snakes away.

▲ The Ohlone people in California use the roots of the horsetail plant to make a syrup for coughs.

A Cherokee helps heal an early settler with bark and powdered maize. ▶

In some places, people use snakes as part of a cure. Some shops in China offer medicines made from snake blood, venom, and skin to improve vision.

Natural First-Aid Kit

Some people keep an aloe plant in the kitchen. Burns from cooking can be soothed by breaking off a fleshy aloe leaf and squeezing its clear liquid onto the burns.

Today nearly half of all prescribed drugs contain at least one chemical from nature. Scientists have climbed mountains and crossed deserts in their search for plants that can be used to produce new medicines.

Scientists are hopeful that many discoveries will be made in tropical rain forests. Most plants in the rain forests haven't yet been identified. The search for medicines from nature continues. ■

Plants and animals of the rain forest may hold new cures. ▶

An aloe plant ▼

INVESTIGATION 2 WRAP-UP

REVIEW

1. Describe two protective adaptations found in plants.

2. How does camouflage protect an animal?

CRITICAL THINKING

3. Is an animal's ability to learn an adaptation? Explain your answer.

4. Imagine you are walking through a forest to observe the animals that live there. Describe some of the adaptations the animals might have to protect themselves.

CHAPTER 2 REVIEW

REFLECT & EVALUATE

Word Power

Write the letter of the term that best matches the definition. *Not all terms will be used.*

1. The way an animal acts
2. Creatures that live on or in other living things and harm them
3. Behaviors or parts of living things that help them survive
4. Ability to blend in with the surroundings

a. adaptations
b. behavior
c. camouflage
d. nutrients
e. parasites

Check What You Know

Write the term in each pair that best completes each sentence.

1. The shape of a bird's beak is an adaptation for (getting food, protection).
2. By digesting an insect, a Venus' flytrap gets (parasites, nutrients).
3. An opossum pretending to be dead is an example of an adaptive (behavior, body part).
4. An adaptation that helps protect a rose plant is its (leaves, thorns).
5. A cleaner fish eats (predators, parasites) from coral reef fish.

Problem Solving

1. A rabbit begins to eat a plant. But after one bite, the rabbit won't ever eat that plant again. Explain an adaptation the plant might have that protects it from being eaten by the rabbit.

2. Some animals hunt food only at night. The darkness may protect them from predators, but how do they find their food in the dark? Explain how certain senses might be adaptations that help these animals find food in the dark.

Study the photograph of the lobster. What adaptations does the lobster have for catching food or for protecting itself?

E57

CHAPTER 3

LIVING THINGS IN THE ENVIRONMENT

What living things change the environment the most? If you guessed humans, you're right. And right now people are very quickly changing the country of Brazil. Some of those changes are destroying the environments of plants and animals.

PEOPLE USING SCIENCE

Wildlife Photographer Luiz Claudio Marigo is a Brazilian wildlife photographer. Many of the animals and plants in his photographs no longer exist. His pictures are all that are left of them.

But Luiz Marigo is doing more than recording vanishing animals and their forest homes. He is trying to show his country's wonderful wildlife. Luiz Marigo wants people to save Brazil's forests.

Luiz Marigo's interest in photography began as a child on his first trip to a wildlife area. He knew at once that he would devote himself to capturing nature with his camera.

As you read this chapter, think about the living things that share your environment. How do changes affect the plants, animals, and people around you?

Coming Up

▲ Luiz Claudio Marigo

 **INVESTIGATION 1**
How Can Living Things Change the Environment? **E60**

 **INVESTIGATION 2**
How Are Living Things Adapted to Their Environments? **E68**

◀ A photo by Luiz Marigo of two Brazilian jaguars

INVESTIGATION 1

How Can Living Things Change the Environment?

Have you ever seen a house being built? Big machines are used to move dirt and cut down trees. In Investigation 1, find out how people and other living things change their environments.

Activity

My Neighborhood Keeps Changing!

Think about an old photograph that shows your home or neighborhood. Then think about your home or neighborhood as it is today. What changes have taken place? How do people make changes to their environments?

MATERIALS
• Science Notebook

Dallas, Texas in 1908 ▼

Procedure

1. Observe the two pictures on page E61. The neighborhood shown has changed in many ways over the years. In your *Science Notebook*, **make a list** of all the changes you can find. **Compare** your list with those of other group members to see if there is anything that you missed.

Step 1

2. Look at your list. **Infer** who made the changes. **Talk with your group** and **hypothesize** how the changes affected living things in the area.

Analyze and Conclude

1. What caused the changes in this neighborhood? **Explain** how these changes affected the environment.

2. Think about the neighborhood that you live in. **Predict** what your neighborhood will look like when you grow up. How might people and other living things change your neighborhood?

INVESTIGATE FURTHER!

RESEARCH

Tape-record sounds from your neighborhood. Then bring the tape to school. Have your classmates identify which sounds are made by nature and which are made by people. Hypothesize what your neighborhood may have sounded like 100 years ago.

Busy Beaver Construction Co.

Reading Focus How do beavers change the environment, and how do the changes affect other living things?

People build dams to control the flow of water from rivers and streams. The beavers of North America, without any training in construction, or building, do the same thing. These hard-working animals build dams and keep them in repair.

Timber!

Beavers do a lot of work to build a dam. They use their sharp teeth to chew away at the trunks of trees. Beavers can chomp through a tree trunk 1 m (3 ft) thick! The trees come crashing down. Then the beavers cut the trunks and branches into logs, again using their sharp teeth. They float the logs into position in the stream. Then they cement the logs together with mud, stones, and leaves.

A Warm, Dry Lodge

Beavers build dams across the moving waters of streams and rivers. The dams create ponds. In the still water of the ponds, beavers build their habitat—a lodge. A lodge is a small living area made of tree parts and mud. The lodge rises up from the pond. The lodge protects a group of beavers from cold weather and from predators.

A Home for Others

The ponds created by dams become homes for other animals, too. Many kinds of fish as well as insects, spiders, frogs, and salamanders live in the quiet ponds. Water birds build nests near the ponds. Many of these animals would not be able to make their homes in streams that lacked dams.

dam

A Changed Place

Beavers cut down many trees along the shore to build their dams and lodges. When the beavers have cut down most of the trees near the pond, they move. They leave behind the results of their hard work and start all over again.

Over time, the ponds created by beaver dams fill with rich soil. They become beautiful meadows. Plants such as grasses and wildflowers grow in the meadows. By cutting down trees, building dams, creating ponds, and making lodges, beavers greatly change the environment. ◾

The beavers enter their lodge through an underwater tunnel. ▼

lodge

People Change the Environment

Reading Focus How can changes people make to the wetlands be helpful and harmful?

What would the world look like without the changes people have made? There would be no buildings, no streets, and no highways. What else would be different?

The activity on pages E60 and E61 shows old and new pictures of a neighborhood. The changes were caused by the activities of people.

Too Wet

A place where living and nonliving things interact is called an **ecosystem**. Sometimes people change an ecosystem because they want to use land for farming or to build on. But not all land is suitable for these purposes. For example, some land may be too wet.

Science in Literature

KILLER ANTS MARCH!

"One of the most frightful creatures in Central Africa is less than one inch long. Feared by humans and animals alike, it is the driver ant. In a single colony, there may be up to 20 million biting ants, and once they have begun their march, nothing in their path is safe."

Read about how these dreaded ants are used to help people in the book *Piranhas and Other Wonders of the Jungle* by Q. L. Pearce.

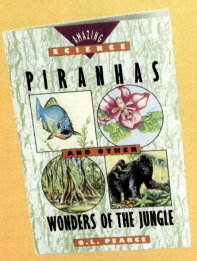

Piranhas and Other Wonders of the Jungle
by Q. L. Pearce
Illustrated by Mary Ann Fraser
Julian Messner, 1990

Building on wetlands is an example of a change that people have made to an ecosystem. **Wetlands** include swamps, marshes, and bogs. People drain the water from wetlands to use the land for farming, housing, and industry. Today, less than half the wetlands in the United States remain.

The wetlands are home to birds, insects, fish, snakes, beavers, and a large variety of plants. When people change wetland environments, many living things may lose their homes.

Making Things Better

People also make changes that improve their environments. Many people are working together to protect the world's wetlands. Some people even fill wetlands with water during long periods of dry weather.

People create new parks in which animals and plants are protected. They plant trees and gardens that become new homes for many different living things. In many ways, people are always changing the natural environment.

Giants Stadium in New Jersey (left) was built on wetlands. The Everglades are wetlands in Florida (right). The original 48 states contained a total of 215 million acres of wetlands. Only 95 million acres remain. How many acres of wetlands have been lost?

Bringing Back the Buffaloes

Reading Focus What caused buffaloes to nearly disappear, and why have their numbers increased?

Long ago the Great Plains of the United States and Canada were covered with large roaming herds of American bison, also called buffaloes. But the large herds of buffaloes began to disappear. And so did the prairies, or grasslands, they once roamed.

People changed much of the prairie land to make it suitable for building and farming.

But today, even without their old prairie land, the buffaloes are back in growing numbers. Take a trip back in time to find out why the buffaloes almost disappeared and how they've come back.

The horse arrives in North America, brought by Spanish explorers. By using horses, the people of the Great Plains learn how to ride and hunt, making it easier to kill buffaloes.
1600

All buffaloes east of the Mississippi River have been killed.
1800

1880
Hundreds of hunters wipe out the buffaloes of the Canadian plains.

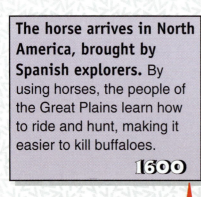

E66

Several thousand buffaloes are moved to Wood Buffalo National Park in Alberta, Canada.
1920

1990s
Because they are protected, buffaloes are no longer in danger of becoming extinct.

1894
The buffalo is nearly extinct. Theodore Roosevelt, who would later become President of the United States, wants to protect the buffalo. Congress passes a law against killing buffaloes. The herds slowly begin to grow again.

According to the National Bison Association, there are over 200,000 buffaloes in the United States. In Canada, the total number of buffaloes is expected to reach 120,000 by the year 2000.

Today, most buffaloes are in parks because the prairie land they once roamed has been changed. Farmland, factories, towns, and roads have replaced much of the old prairies. ■

INVESTIGATION 1 WRAP-UP

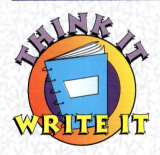

REVIEW

1. Explain how an animal can change its environment. Explain how people change their environments.

2. Give three examples of wetlands.

CRITICAL THINKING

3. You observe that a large part of a tropical rain forest has been cut down. How might such a change affect the living things in that area? Explain your answer.

4. Give an example of two living things that have different habitats but live in the same ecosystem.

E67

INVESTIGATION 2

How Are Living Things Adapted to Their Environments?

Why do you sweat when your environment is hot and shiver when it's cold? These are examples of adaptations. In Investigation 2, discover other ways living things are adapted to their environments.

Activity

Keeping Heat In

Adaptations help living things survive. In this activity find out how some animals are adapted to cold weather.

MATERIALS
- 2 large plastic jars
- 2 small plastic jars
- down feathers
- hot tap water
- 2 thermometers
- timer
- *Science Notebook*

SAFETY
Clean up spills immediately.

Procedure

1. In this activity, you'll **make models** of two animals. One has feathers. The other one does not. **Talk with your group** and **predict** which animal model will lose more heat in 30 minutes. **Record** your prediction in your *Science Notebook*.

2. Make a chart like the one shown.

Time (in min)	Temperature (°C) Model With Feathers	Temperature (°C) Model Without Feathers
0		
15		
30		

3. To make your models, place a small jar in a larger jar. Place down feathers around the small jar. Cover the sides of the small jar completely with feathers but don't pack the feathers tightly.

4. Place another small jar in a different larger jar. Don't put anything around this small jar.

5. Fill each small jar halfway with hot tap water. Take care not to wet the feathers. Put a thermometer in each small jar. **Measure the temperature** of the water in each jar. **Record** your readings under the correct heading on the first line in your chart.

Step 5

 See **SCIENCE and MATH TOOLBOX** page H8 if you need to review **Using a Thermometer.**

6. After 15 minutes, **record** the temperature of the water in each jar. Wait another 15 minutes. Then **record** both temperatures again.

Analyze and Conclude

1. By how many degrees did the temperature in each jar change?

2. Which animal model lost more heat? How does this result compare with your prediction?

3. Study your models. **Hypothesize** about how down feathers help a bird stay warm.

INVESTIGATE FURTHER!

Use the **Best of the Net—Science CD-ROM**, Life Sciences, *Bristlecone Pine* to find out about the discovery of ancient bristlecone pine trees, the oldest living things on Earth. Find out how growth rings reveal changes in Earth's environment.

Beating the Heat

Reading Focus How are different plants and animals adapted to desert environments?

Both animals and plants have adaptations that protect them from extreme heat. On a blazing hot day in summer, what do you do to stay cool? To protect your skin from burning in the sunlight and your body from overheating, you'd likely head for a shady spot.

Your body has a built-in way of cooling down. In hot weather your skin becomes covered with tiny droplets of perspiration, or sweat. The ability to sweat is an adaptation that helps prevent overheating. When sweat dries up, the drying process cools your skin.

Although sweating is an important adaptation to humans, few other animals sweat. In a desert, if an animal did sweat, it would quickly become dried out. There is little water available in the desert to replace the body's lost moisture.

Life in the Desert

How does a desert animal, which lives where the Sun scorches the sand all day, survive? There are no tall leafy trees for shade. In some deserts, daytime air temperatures can reach 55°C (131°F). Rain is scarce, and there are few water holes to drink from. Deserts may seem to be impossible places to live in. But, amazingly, the world's deserts are home to thousands of kinds of plants and animals. All have adaptations to "beat the heat."

Using Math *In the Namib Desert in Africa, shown here, surface temperatures can reach as high as 77°C (170°F). Compare this temperature to the daytime air temperature in the desert, given in the text above.*

Insects Keep Cool

Some desert insects have body designs that keep them cool. One little beetle that lives in the Namib Desert of southwestern Africa survives by keeping its body away from the hot sand. How does it do this? Nicknamed the stilt beetle, this insect "tiptoes" over sun-baked sand dunes on long stiltlike legs.

The black color of some beetles can be a problem in the desert. This is because dark-colored material heats faster than does light-colored material. Many desert beetles have white or yellow wax covering their dark bodies. The light-colored wax reflects sunlight, keeping the insect's body cool. Because wax is waterproof, the waxy covering also helps hold in moisture, keeping the beetle from drying out.

What characteristics of a stilt beetle help it survive in the desert?

Never Thirsty

The behaviors of desert animals are also adaptations to the hot, dry environment. Kangaroo rats have some unusual adaptations for conserving water. A kangaroo rat may go its entire life without ever taking a drink of water! Kangaroo rats get moisture from the food they eat—seeds, juicy grasses, and the pulp of cactus plants. These animals don't sweat, and they are active only at night.

Internet Field Trip
Visit **www.eduplace.com** to find out how desert animals have adapted to their dry environments.

▲ **A kangaroo rat burrows in the sand to stay cool during the day.**

The saguaro cactus grows in deserts of the southwestern U.S. and northern Mexico. ▼

During the day, kangaroo rats sleep sealed inside their "cool" burrows. Their burrows are about 0.3 m (1 ft) below the desert sand. Since the Sun doesn't heat this sand directly, the temperature in the burrow is a cool 30°C (86°F).

Hidden Water

Plants also have adaptations to the hot, dry desert environment. Cactus plants hold a lot of water inside. They have thick stems and slender, spiny leaves that keep in moisture. Cactus roots are widespread just beneath the desert's surface. These shallow roots can rapidly take in water from a rare desert rainfall before the sunlight causes the water to dry up. Then the water is stored for weeks inside the cactus.

The largest kind of cactus is the saguaro (sə gwär′ō). After years of growing slowly, a saguaro can reach 15 m (50 ft) in height and can store hundreds of liters of water.

A flowering saguaro cactus ▼

UNIT PROJECT LINK

Another environment that you have read about in this unit is the tropical rain forest. Tropical rain forests have many important resources. Find out why tropical rain forests are disappearing. Make a poster that lists things you and your friends can do to help save the rain forests.

Technology Link

For more help with your Unit Project, go to **www.eduplace.com**.

When the Going Gets Tough...

Reading Focus What adaptations do some plants and animals have to survive cold winters?

Maple trees drop their leaves, robins fly south, and woodchucks curl up in dens and go into a deep sleep. These things all happen as the cold of winter approaches. Why?

In nature there are many cycles— summer and winter, rainy season and dry season, and others. These natural cycles happen in different places around the world. Sometimes a cycle creates big changes in the environment. Then plants and animals have to change in some way, too, in order to survive.

Winter Travel

How can an animal survive through a cold, snowy winter if it can't find enough food to eat? One way is for the animal to **migrate** (mī′grāt), or travel to a warmer place where it can find food.

Many kinds of birds migrate. It's not the cold weather that makes them leave. The activity on pages E68 and E69 shows that feathers help birds stay warm. Some birds can survive cold weather if they can find enough food.

The lesser golden plover and the Arctic tern are two kinds of birds that migrate. ▼

▲ Lesser golden plover

Some seed-eating birds, such as blue jays and cardinals, don't migrate.

But insect-eating birds and birds whose food is often covered by snow or ice usually migrate before winter comes. Some fly long distances. The lesser golden plover migrates over 3,200 km (2,000 mi)—from Alaska to Hawaii. And the Arctic tern migrates about 20,000 km (12,000 mi)—from the Arctic in the north to the Antarctic in the south!

▲ A chipmunk hibernates through most of the winter but may wake up on warmer days to eat.

◀ Arctic tern

Winter Sleep

How else do animals survive a cold winter without food? Some animals go into a deep sleep, called **hibernation** (hī bər nā′shən). Bears, ground squirrels, woodchucks, snakes, and bats all may hibernate during winter.

While an animal is in this deep sleep, its body temperature usually drops. Its heartbeat rate slows, and it breathes less. All these changes mean that an animal uses up less energy. Therefore, it can survive a long time without eating.

When warmer weather returns, the animal begins to warm up, too. Its heart starts beating faster, and soon it wakes up—to spring and a new supply of food!

Plants in Winter

Plants are rooted to one spot, so they can't migrate. But their activities can slow, as if they were going into a deep sleep. This decrease in plant activity is called **dormancy** (dôr′mən sē). Plants become dormant during the winter.

As winter approaches, many trees—such as maples, oaks, poplars, elms, and chestnuts—lose their leaves. Without leaves, a tree can't make food. So, during dormancy the tree lives off food that is stored elsewhere in the plant—for example, in the roots.

Some plants, such as ferns, die above ground. But their roots survive underground through winter. When the weather warms up, the plants begin to grow again. ■

▲ Each autumn, trees like this maple lose their leaves.

INVESTIGATION 2 WRAP-UP

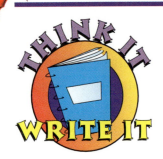

REVIEW

1. Describe one adaptation of an animal and one adaptation of a plant for survival in the desert.

2. Compare hibernation and dormancy.

CRITICAL THINKING

3. There is snow on the ground and on tree branches and bushes. You see only one or two kinds of birds. What adaptation do the birds have for keeping warm? Why did other kinds of birds leave?

4. What adaptation do you have to beat the heat? Do most desert animals have the same adaptation? Explain your answer.

Chapter 3 Review: REFLECT & EVALUATE

Word Power

Write the letter of the term that best completes each sentence.

a. dormancy
b. hibernation
c. migrate
d. wetlands

1. Environments that include swamps, marshes, and bogs are ___.
2. To travel to a warmer place to find food is to ___.
3. A decrease in activity in plants during winter is called ___.
4. Some animals go into a deep winter sleep called ___.

Check What You Know

Write the term in each pair that best completes each sentence.

1. When people change environments, many living things may lose their (adaptations, homes).
2. Sweating is an adaptation for keeping (wet, cool).
3. When food is scarce, some birds (migrate, hibernate).
4. While an animal hibernates, its heartbeat rate (slows down, speeds up).

Problem Solving

1. A family on vacation decides to go scuba diving. The group leader tells the family not to take any of the plants and animals from their underwater environment. Why is it important for the divers not to change the underwater environment?

2. Brown bears build up fat in their bodies before hibernating. How is this an adaptation?

Study the drawing. List all the ways that the beavers changed their environment. How did these changes affect other animals?

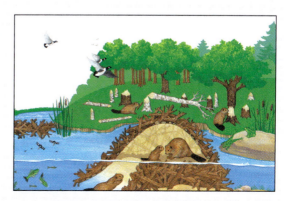

E77

Compare and Contrast

When you read, ask if two or more things, events, or ideas are being compared. Look for signal words that tell how things are alike and how they are different.

Read the paragraphs below. Then complete the exercise that follows.

Look for these signal words to help you compare and contrast.

- To show similar things: *like, the same as*
- To show different things: *different from, by contrast*

What's for Dinner?

Plants make their own food inside their leaves. Plants take in water and air from their environment. The leaves soak up sunlight. Plants use the Sun's energy to make food from water and a gas in the air. This food can be stored in roots, leaves, and other plant parts for use later on. . . . Living things that can make their own food are called **producers**. Plants are producers.

Since your body can't produce its own food, as a plant does, you have to get it another way—by eating something else. That means that you are a consumer. A **consumer** is a living thing that eats plants, animals, or other living things.

Make a chart like the one shown. Compare and contrast producers and consumers by completing your chart.

Producers	Consumers

Using Math Skills

Analyze Data

Some birds migrate very long distances. This table shows distances, in kilometers, that some birds migrate.

Migration Distances of Selected Birds	
Bird	**One-way Distance (km)**
Arctic tern	17,600
Atlantic brant	1,400
Barn swallow	9,600
Long-tailed jaeger	11,200
Pacific brant	4,000
Pacific golden plover	3,200
Snow goose	4,000
Whooping crane	4,800

Use the data in the table to complete the exercises.

1. Write the migration distances for these birds in order from shortest to longest.

2. Which of the birds listed migrates the longest distance? the shortest distance?

3. The arctic tern migrates for eight months each year. How many months is this bird not migrating?

4. How far does the whooping crane travel on a round-trip migration?

You may wish to use a calculator for Exercises 5 and 6.

5. How much longer is the round trip of the snow goose than the round trip of the Atlantic brant?

6. The Pacific brant migrates 4,000 km in three days. If the bird were to fly the same distance each day, how many kilometers would it fly in a day?

UNIT E WRAP-UP!

On your own, use scientific methods to investigate a question about roles of living things.

THINK LIKE A SCIENTIST

Ask a Question

Pose a question about roles of living things that you would like to investigate. For example, ask, "How does temperature affect the activity of decomposers?"

Make a Hypothesis

Suggest a hypothesis that is a possible answer to the question. One hypothesis is that a low temperature slows the activity of decomposers.

Plan and Do a Test

Plan a controlled experiment to compare the action of decomposers at different temperatures. You could start with two samples of moldy bread, self-sealing sandwich bags, and a refrigerator. Develop a procedure that uses these materials to test the hypothesis. With permission, carry out your experiment. Follow the safety guidelines on pages S14–S15.

Record and Analyze

Observe carefully and record your data accurately. Make repeated observations.

Draw Conclusions

Look for evidence to support the hypothesis or to show that it is false. Draw conclusions about the hypothesis. Repeat the experiment to verify the results.

WRITING IN SCIENCE
Outline

Write an outline for a report on animal or plant adaptations. Research the information for your outline. Follow these guidelines for your outline.

- Write a title for your outline.
- Put Roman numerals (I, II, III) next to main ideas.
- Put capital letters (A, B) next to supporting details.
- Include three main heads with two details for each.

E80

Science and Math Toolbox

Using a Hand Lens..H2

Making a Bar Graph.....................................H3

Using a Calculator.......................................H4

Making a Tally Chart...................................H5

Using a Tape Measure or Ruler....................H6

Measuring Volume......................................H7

Using a Thermometer.................................H8

Using a Balance..H9

Making a Chart to Organize Data..............H10

Reading a Circle Graph.............................H11

Measuring Elapsed Time...........................H12

Measurements...H14

Using a Hand Lens

A hand lens is a tool that magnifies objects, or makes objects appear larger. This makes it possible for you to see details of an object that would be hard to see without the hand lens.

Look at a Coin or a Stamp

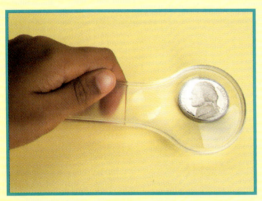

▲ Place the lens above the object.

1. Place an object such as a coin or a stamp on a table or other flat surface.

2. Hold the hand lens just above the object. As you look through the lens, slowly move the lens away from the object. Notice that the object appears to get larger.

3. Keep moving the lens until the object begins to look a little blurry. Then move the hand lens a little closer to the object until the object is once again in sharp focus.

▲ Move the lens slowly toward you.

If the object starts to look blurry, move the lens toward the object. ▶

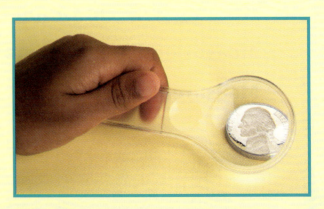

Making a Bar Graph

A bar graph helps you organize and compare data.

Make a Bar Graph of Animal Heights

Animals come in all different shapes and sizes. You can use the information in the table to make a bar graph of animal heights.

Heights of Animals	
Animal	Height (cm)
Bear	240
Elephant	315
Cow	150
Giraffe	570
Camel	210
Horse	165

1. Draw the side and the bottom of the graph. Label the side of the graph as shown. The numbers will show the height of the animals in centimeters.

2. Label the bottom of the graph. Write the names of the animals at the bottom so that there is room to draw the bars.

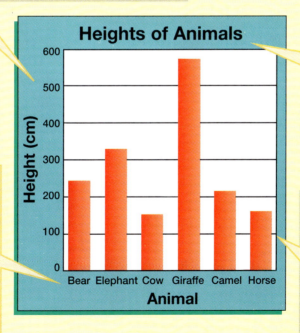

3. Choose a title for your graph. Your title should describe the subject of the graph.

4. Draw bars to show the height of each animal. Some heights are between two numbers.

H3

Using a Calculator

After you've made measurements, a calculator can help you analyze your data.

Add and Multiply Decimals

Suppose you're an astronaut. You may take 8 pounds of Moon rocks back to Earth. The table shows the weights of the rocks. Can you take them all? Use a calculator to find out.

Weight of Moon Rocks	
Moon Rock	Weight of Rock on Moon (lb)
Rock 1	1.7
Rock 2	1.8
Rock 3	2.6
Rock 4	1.5

1. To add, press:

1 . 7 + 1 . 8 +

2 . 6 + 1 . 5 =

Display: 7.6

2. If you make a mistake, press the clear entry key (CE/C) once. Enter the number again. Then continue adding. (Note: If you press CE/C twice, it will clear all.)

3. Your total is 7.6 pounds. You can take the four Moon rocks back to Earth.

4. How much do the Moon rocks weigh on Earth? Objects weigh six times as much on Earth as they do on the Moon. You can use a calculator to multiply.

Press: 7 . 6 × 6 =

Display: 45.6

5. The rocks weigh 45.6 pounds on Earth.

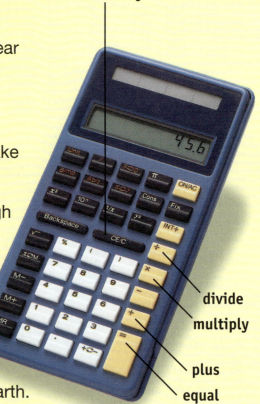

clear entry

divide

multiply

plus

equal

Making a Tally Chart

A tally chart can help you keep track of items you are counting. Sometimes you need to count many different items. It may be hard to count all of the items of the same type as a group. That's when a tally chart can be helpful.

Make a Tally Chart of Birds Seen

These students are bird watchers. They're making a tally chart to record how many birds of each type they see.

Here are the tallies they have made so far.

Type of Bird	Tally
Cardinal	||
Blue jay	|||| |||| ||||
Mockingbird	||||
Hummingbird	|||| ||
House sparrow	|||| |||| |||| |||| |
Robin	|||| |||| ||

Every time you count one item, you make one tally.

When you reach five, draw the fifth tally as a line through the other four.

To find the total number of robins, count by fives and then ones.

You can use your tally chart to make a chart with numbers.

Type of Bird	Tally
Cardinal	2
Blue jay	15
Mockingbird	4
Hummingbird	7
House sparrow	21
Robin	12

What kind of bird was seen most often?

Now use a tally chart to record how many cars of different colors pass your school.

Using a Tape Measure or Ruler

Tape measures and rulers are tools for measuring the length of objects and distances. Scientists most often use units such as meters, centimeters, and millimeters when making length measurements.

Use a Tape Measure

1. Measure the distance around a jar. Wrap the tape around the jar.

2. Find the line where the tape begins to wrap over itself.

3. Record the distance around the jar to the nearest centimeter.

Use a Metric Ruler

1. Measure the length of your shoe. Place the ruler or the meterstick on the floor. Line up the end of the ruler with the heel of your shoe.

2. Notice where the other end of your shoe lines up with the ruler.

3. Look at the scale on the ruler. Record the length of your shoe to the nearest centimeter and to the nearest millimeter.

Measuring Volume

A graduated cylinder, a measuring cup, and a beaker are used to measure volume. Volume is the amount of space something takes up. Most of the containers that scientists use to measure volume have a scale marked in milliliters (mL).

Measure the Volume of a Liquid

1. Measure the volume of juice. Pour some juice into a measuring container.

2. Move your head so that your eyes are level with the top of the juice. Read the scale line that is closest to the surface of the juice. If the surface of the juice is curved up on the sides, look at the lowest point of the curve.

3. Read the measurement on the scale. You can estimate the value between two lines on the scale.

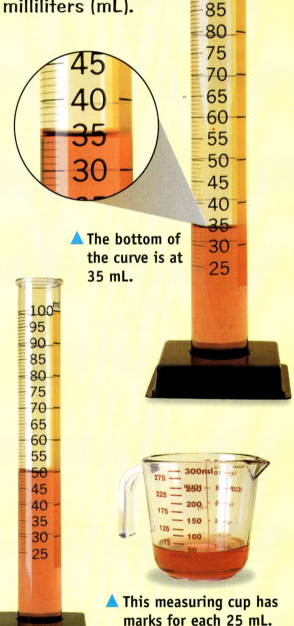

▲ The bottom of the curve is at 35 mL.

This beaker has marks for each 25 mL. ▶

This graduated cylinder has marks for every 1 mL. ▶

▲ **This measuring cup has marks for each 25 mL.**

H7

Using a Thermometer

A thermometer is used to measure temperature. When the liquid in the tube of a thermometer gets warmer, it expands and moves farther up the tube. Different scales can be used to measure temperature, but scientists usually use the Celsius scale.

Measure the Temperature of a Cold Liquid

1. Take a chilled liquid out of the refrigerator. Half fill a cup with the liquid.

2. Hold the thermometer so that the bulb is in the center of the liquid. Be sure that there are no bright lights or direct sunlight shining on the bulb.

3. Wait a few minutes until you see the liquid in the tube of the thermometer stop moving. Read the scale line that is closest to the top of the liquid in the tube. The thermometer shown reads 21°C (about 70°F).

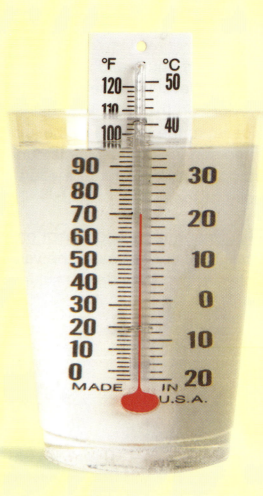

Using a Balance

A balance is used to measure mass. Mass is the amount of matter in an object. To find the mass of an object, place it in the left pan of the balance. Place standard masses in the right pan.

Measure the Mass of a Ball

1. Check that the empty pans are balanced, or level with each other. When balanced, the pointer on the base should be at the middle mark. If it needs to be adjusted, move the slider on the back of the balance a little to the left or right.

2. Place a ball on the left pan. Then add standard masses, one at a time, to the right pan. When the pointer is at the middle mark again, each pan holds the same amount of matter and has the same mass.

3. Add the numbers marked on the masses in the pan. The total is the mass of the ball in grams.

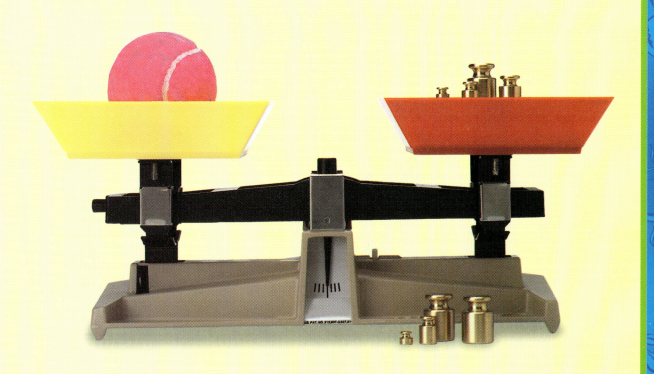

Making a Chart to Organize Data

A chart can help you keep track of information. When you organize information, or data, it is easier to read, compare, or classify it.

Classifying Animals

Suppose you are studying characteristics of different animals. You want to organize the data that you collect.

Look at the data below. To put this data in a chart, you could base the chart on the two characteristics listed—the number of wings and the number of legs.

My Data

Fleas have no wings. Fleas have six legs.

Snakes have no wings or legs.

A bee has four wings. It has six legs.

Spiders never have wings. They have eight legs.

A dog has no wings. It has four legs.

Birds have two wings and two legs.

A cow has no wings. It has four legs.

A butterfly has four wings. It has six legs.

Give the chart a title that describes the data in it.

Name categories, or groups, that describe the data you have collected.

Make sure the information is recorded correctly in each column.

Animals—Number of Wings and Legs

Animal	Number of Wings	Number of Legs
Flea	0	6
Snake	0	0
Bee	4	6
Spider	0	8
Dog	0	4
Bird	2	2
Cow	0	4
Butterfly	4	6

Next, you could make another chart to show animal classification based on number of legs only.

Reading a Circle Graph

A circle graph shows a whole divided into parts. You can use a circle graph to compare the parts to each other. You can also use it to compare the parts to the whole.

A Circle Graph of Fuel Use

This circle graph shows fuel use in the United States. The graph has 10 equal parts, or sections. Each section equals $\frac{1}{10}$ of the whole. One whole equals $\frac{10}{10}$.

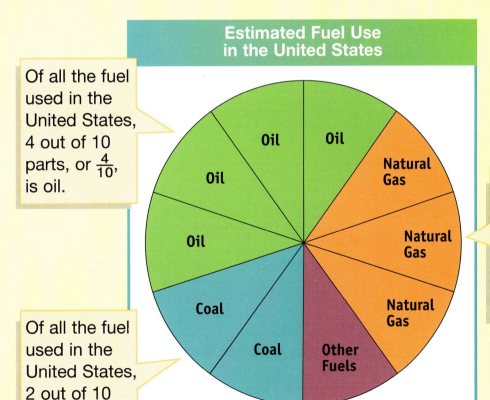

Of all the fuel used in the United States, 4 out of 10 parts, or $\frac{4}{10}$, is oil.

Of all the fuel used in the United States, 3 out of 10 parts, or $\frac{3}{10}$, is natural gas.

Of all the fuel used in the United States, 2 out of 10 parts, or $\frac{2}{10}$, is coal.

Measuring Elapsed Time

A calendar can help you find out how much time has passed, or elapsed, in days or weeks. A clock can help you see how much time has elapsed in hours and minutes. A clock with a second hand or a stopwatch can help you find out how many seconds have elapsed.

Using a Calendar to Find Elapsed Days

This is a calendar for the month of October. October has 31 days. Suppose it is October 22 and you begin an experiment. You need to check the experiment two days from the start date and one week from the start date. That means you would check it on Wednesday, October 24, and again on Monday, October 29. October 29 is 7 days after October 22.

Monday, Tuesday, Wednesday, Thursday, and Friday are weekdays. Saturday and Sunday are weekends.

Last month ended on Sunday, September 30.

October

Sunday	Monday	Tuesday	Wednesday	Thursday	Friday	Saturday
	1	2	3	4	5	6
7	8	9	10	11	12	13
14	15	16	17	18	19	20
21	22	23	24	25	26	27
28	29	30	31			

Next month begins on Thursday, November 1.

Using a Clock or a Stopwatch to Find Elapsed Time

You need to time an experiment for 20 minutes.

It is 1:30 P.M.

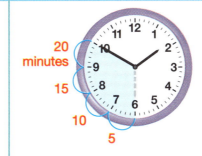
Stop at 1:50 P.M.

You need to time an experiment for 15 seconds. You can use the second hand of a clock or watch.

60 seconds = 1 minute

Start the experiment when the second hand is on number 6.

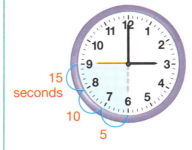
Stop when 15 seconds have passed and the second hand is on the 9.

You can use a stopwatch.

Press the reset button on a stopwatch so that you see 0:00₀₀.

Press the start button. When you see 0:15₀₀, press the stop button.

H13

MEASUREMENTS

Volume
1 L of sports drink is a little more than 1 qt.

Area
A basketball court covers about 4,700 ft^2. It covers about 435 m^2.

Mass and Weight
A basketball has a mass of about 650 g. It weighs about $1\frac{1}{2}$ lb.

Metric Measures

Temperature
Ice melts at 0 degrees Celsius (°C)
Water freezes at 0°C
Water boils at 100°C

Length and Distance
1,000 meters (m) = 1 kilometer (km)
100 centimeters (cm) = 1 m
10 millimeters (mm) = 1 cm

Force
1 newton (N) =
   1 kilogram x meter/second/second
   (kg x m/s^2)

Volume
1 cubic meter (m^3) = 1 m x 1 m x 1 m
1 cubic centimeter (cm^3) =
   1 cm x 1 cm x 1 cm
1 liter (L) = 1,000 milliliters (mL)
1 cm^3 = 1 mL

Area
1 square kilometer (km^2) = 1 km x 1 km
1 hectare = 10,000 m^2

Mass
1,000 grams (g) = 1 kilogram (kg)
1,000 milligrams (mg) = 1 g

Temperature
The temperature at an indoor basketball game might be 25°C, which is 77°F.

Length/Distance
A basketball rim is about 10 ft high, or a little more than 3 m from the floor.

Customary Measures

Temperature
Ice melts at 32 degrees Fahrenheit (°F)
Water freezes at 32°F
Water boils at 212°F

Length and Distance
12 inches (in.) = 1 foot (ft)
3 ft = 1 yard (yd)
5,280 ft = 1 mile (mi)

Weight
16 ounces (oz) = 1 pound (lb)
2,000 pounds = 1 ton (T)

Volume of Fluids
8 fluid ounces (fl oz) = 1 cup (c)
2 c = 1 pint (pt)
2 pt = 1 quart (qt)
4 qt = 1 gallon (gal)

Metric and Customary Rates
km/h = kilometers per hour
m/s = meters per second
mph = miles per hour

GLOSSARY

Pronunciation Key

Symbol	Key Words
a	cat
ā	ape
ä	cot, car
e	ten, berry
ē	me
i	fit, here
ī	ice, fire
ō	go
ô	fall, for
oi	oil
o͝o	look, pull
o͞o	tool, rule
ou	out, crowd
u	up
ʉ	fur, shirt
ə	a in ago
	e in agent
	i in pencil
	o in atom
	u in circus
b	bed
d	dog
f	fall

Symbol	Key Words
g	get
h	help
j	jump
k	kiss, call
l	leg
m	meat
n	nose
p	put
r	red
s	see
t	top
v	vat
w	wish
y	yard
z	zebra
ch	chin, arch
ŋ	ring, drink
sh	she, push
th	thin, truth
th	then, father
zh	measure

A heavy stress mark (′) is placed after a syllable that gets a heavy, or primary, stress, as in **picture** (pik′chər).

acid rain (as'id rān) Rain that contains a large amount of acids, and that results from the burning of fossil fuels. (D43) *Acid rain* can harm living things.

adaptation (ad əp tā'shən) Behavior or part of a living thing that helps it survive in a certain environment. (A28, E40) A rose's thorns and a camel's hump are *adaptations*.

adult (ə dult') The last stage of a life cycle. (A23) The butterfly is the *adult* stage of a caterpillar.

air pollution (er pə lōō'shən) Any harmful or unclean materials in the air. (D17) Burning fuels can cause *air pollution*.

aquifer (ak'wə fər) An underground layer of rock where ground water collects. (D31) The water in a well usually comes from an *aquifer*.

astronomer (ə strän'ə mər) A scientist who studies the origin, features, and motion of objects in space. (B14) *Astronomers* use telescopes, cameras, and space probes to study the stars.

atmosphere (at'məs fir) The layer of gases surrounding Earth or another planet. (B12, D8) Earth's *atmosphere* is made up of gases such as oxygen, nitrogen, and carbon dioxide.

atom (at'əm) The smallest particle of matter. (C20) Water is made up of the *atoms* of two different substances—hydrogen and oxygen.

axis (ak'sis) The imaginary line on which an object rotates. (B38) Earth's *axis* runs between the North Pole and the South Pole.

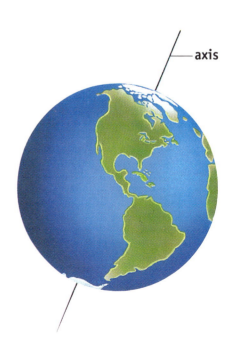

H17

B

behavior (bē hāv′yər) The way an animal typically acts in a certain situation. (E42) One *behavior* of pill bugs is to move toward moist, dark places.

C

camouflage (kam′ə fläzh) The ability to blend in with the surroundings. (E45) An animal's fur or skin can be *camouflage*, helping the animal hunt or avoid hunters.

carnivore (kär′nə vôr) An animal that eats only other animals. (E17) Wolves, cougars, lions, hawks, and owls are *carnivores*.

chemical change (kem′i kəl chānj) A change in matter in which different kinds of matter are formed. (C23) A *chemical change* occurs when wood burns and becomes gases and ash.

chemical property (kem′i kəl präp′ər tē) A description of how matter can change into another kind of matter. (C14) A *chemical property* of paper is its ability to burn.

community (kə myōō′nə tē) A group of plants and animals that live in a certain area and depend on one another. (E31) A pond's plants and animals form a *community*.

complete metamorphosis (kəm plēt′ met ə môr′fə sis) The four-stage life cycle of many insects. (A23) A life cycle that goes from egg to larva to pupa to adult is described as a *complete metamorphosis*.

compound machine (kam-pound mə shēn′) A machine that is made up of two or more simple machines. (C76) A pair of scissors is a *compound machine* because it contains two kinds of simple machines—a lever and a wedge.

condense (kən dens′) To change form from a gas to a liquid. (C55, D29) When water vapor in the air cools, it *condenses* into tiny droplets of liquid water.

conduction (kən duk′shən) The movement of heat by direct contact between particles of matter. (C47) Heat moves by *conduction* from warmer matter with faster-moving particles to cooler matter with slower-moving particles.

conductor (kən duk′tər) A material that transfers heat or electricity easily. (C48) Metals are good *conductors* of heat.

cone (kōn) The part of a conifer that produces pollen or seeds. (A50) Each *cone* is a woody stalk covered with stiff scales.

constellation (kän stə lā′shən) A group of stars that form a pattern that looks like a person, animal, or object. (B46) Different *constellations* are visible from Earth at different times of year.

consumer (kən soōm′ər) A living thing that eats other living things to survive. (E17) Animals are *consumers*.

controlled experiment (kən-trōld′ ek sper′ə mənt) A test of a hypothesis in which the setups are identical in all ways except one. (S7) In the *controlled experiment*, one beaker of water contained salt; all the other beakers contained only water.

convection (kən vek′shən) The circulation of heat through a liquid or gas (fluid) by the movements of particles from one part of the matter to another. (C48) *Convection* takes place in a room with a heater: As hot air rises from the heater, cool air flows down to take its place.

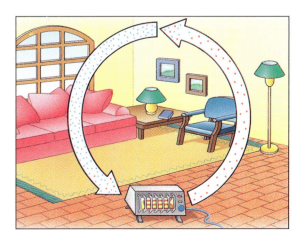

crater (krāt′ər) A bowl-shaped pit. (B11) *Craters* on the Moon and on Earth were formed by meteorites striking the surface.

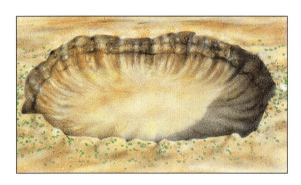

decomposer (dē kəm pōz′ər) A living thing that breaks down and feeds on the remains of once-living things. (E18) *Decomposers* such as mushrooms recycle the remains of once-living things.

dormancy (dôr′mən sē) A decrease in plant activity during the winter. (E76) Sap flows in maple trees in the spring after the tree's *dormancy* during winter.

earthquake (ʉrth′kwāk) A sudden movement of large sections of rock beneath Earth's surface. (D51) Books tumbled from shelves during the *earthquake*.

ecosystem (ek′ō sis təm) A place where living and nonliving things interact. (E64) The animals, plants, and insects in the tops of trees in a rain forest have their own *ecosystem*.

egg (eg) The first stage in the life cycle of almost all animals. (A14) Birds hatch from *eggs* outside the mother bird's body.

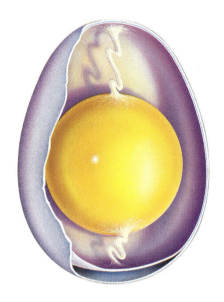

embryo (em′brē ō) An animal or plant in the earliest stages of its development. (A15, A39) A plant *embryo* is the tiny plant that is found inside a seed.

energy (en′ər jē) The ability to cause a change in matter. (C31) A car uses *energy* from gasoline or diesel fuel to run.

energy of motion (en′ər jē uv mō′shən) The energy that moving matter has. (C31) Sliding downhill on a sled, tossing a basketball into the air, and flying a kite in the wind are examples of *energy of motion*.

environment (en vī′rən mənt) All the surrounding living and nonliving things that affect a living thing. (E10) A drop of water, a rotting log, a desert, an ocean, and a rain forest are examples of different *environments*.

equator (ē kwāt′ər) An imaginary line that circles Earth halfway between the two poles. (B64) If you live near the *equator*, you live in a hot climate because your region receives direct sunlight most of the time.

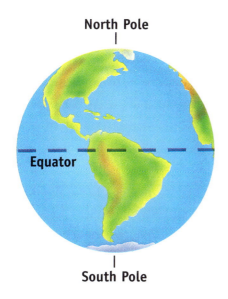

erosion (ē rō′zhən) The breaking up and moving of weathered rocks from one place to another. (D52) The Grand Canyon was formed by millions of years of *erosion*.

evaporate (ē vap′ə rāt) To change form from a liquid to a gas. (C54, D29) On a warm dry day, puddles on the sidewalk *evaporate* quickly.

extinction (ek stiŋk′shən) The permanent disappearance of all living things of a certain kind. (E20) The *extinction* of the saber-toothed cat is a mystery that some scientists are working to solve.

flare (fler) A bright area on the surface of the Sun caused by a solar storm. (B27) A solar *flare* is hotter than surrounding areas of the Sun and so is brighter.

food chain (fo͞od chān) The path that energy takes through a community as one living thing eats another. (E26) The first link in a *food chain* is usually a plant.

food web (fo͞od web) Two or more food chains that overlap and link. (E28) A *food web* connects animals through the plants and animals that they eat.

force (fôrs) A push or a pull. (C64) When you open a door, you apply a *force*.

fossil fuel (fäs′əl fyo͞o′əl) A fuel formed over time from the remains of plants or animals. (D10) *Fossil fuels* such as oil, coal, and natural gas are found underground.

freeze (frēz) To change form from a liquid to a solid. (C55) The loss of heat causes a liquid to *freeze*.

friction (frik′shən) A force that makes it hard for two objects to move past one another easily when the objects touch. (C46) *Friction* causes your hands to get warm when you rub them together.

fruit (fro͞ot) The part of a flower that forms around a seed. (A45) Cucumbers, tomatoes, oranges, peaches, and pears are *fruits*.

fulcrum (ful′krəm) The fixed point around which a lever turns. (C73) If you use a lever to lift an object, the *fulcrum* is located between you and the object you are lifting.

gas (gas) A state of matter that has no definite shape and does not take up a definite amount of space. (C20) A *gas* spreads out evenly to fill whatever space it is in.

germ (jʉrm) A tiny organism that can cause disease. (D37) Chlorine kills some of the *germs* in water.

germinate (jur′mə nāt) To sprout and begin to develop into a seedling. (A40) Most kinds of seeds need moisture, air, and warmth to *germinate*.

glacier (glā′shər) A large mass of slow-moving ice. (D53) When a *glacier* meets the sea, large chunks of ice fall off, forming icebergs.

gravity (grav′i tē) A force that pulls two or more objects toward each other. (B22, C65) To fly into space, a rocket must overcome Earth's *gravity*.

ground water (ground wôt′ər) The water found beneath Earth's surface. (D31) In some areas, *ground water* fills the small spaces that are between underground rocks, soil, and sand.

habitat (hab′i tat) The place where an animal or a plant lives. (E10) Deer live in a woodland *habitat*.

heat (hēt) The energy of moving particles of matter. (C32) Adding *heat* to matter causes its particles to move faster.

herbivore (hur′bə vôr) An animal that eats only plants. (E18) Cows and rabbits are *herbivores*.

hibernation (hī bər nā′shən) A deep sleep that helps some animals survive the winter. (E75) An animal that is in *hibernation* breathes slowly, has a slow heartbeat, and has a low body temperature.

hypothesis (hī päth′ə sis) An idea about or explanation of how or why something happens. (S6) The *hypothesis* that the Earth revolves around the Sun has been supported by evidence gathered by astronomers.

inclined plane (in klīnd′ plān) A simple machine with a slanted surface. It allows objects to be raised or lowered from one level to another without lifting them. (C74) A ramp is a kind of *inclined plane*.

incomplete metamorphosis
(in kəm plēt′ met ə môr′fə sis)
The three-stage life cycle of some insects. (A24) A life cycle that goes from egg to nymph to adult is called *incomplete metamorphosis*.

inexhaustible resource (in eg-zôs′tə bəl rē′sôrs) A natural resource that does not decrease, or become used up, as people use it. (D11) Wind can't be used up so it is an *inexhaustible resource*.

insulator (in′sə lāt ər) A poor conductor of heat or electricity. (C48) Air that is trapped in the small spaces between fibers of clothing acts as an *insulator*.

larva (lär′və) The second stage in the life cycle of an insect that undergoes complete metamorphosis. (A23) A butterfly *larva* is called a caterpillar.

lava (lä′və) Liquid rock flowing on the surface. (D51) Fires broke out when *lava* reached the wooden frames of houses.

lever (lev′ər) A simple machine made up of a bar that turns, or rotates, around a fixed point. (C73) A *lever* helps to lift a heavy object or a tight lid with less effort.

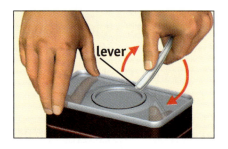

life cycle (līf sī′kəl) The ordered changes that occur during the lifetime of a living thing. (A9) An insect goes through three or four stages in its *life cycle*.

liquid (lik′wid) A state of matter that has no definite shape but takes up a definite amount of space. (C20) At room temperature, water is a *liquid*.

lunar eclipse (lōō′nər i klips′) The darkening of the Moon when it moves into Earth's shadow. (B76) During a *lunar eclipse*, Earth blocks the Sun's light from reaching the Moon directly.

machine (mə shēn′) Something that makes a task easy to do by reducing the amount of force needed to do a job. (C72) A *machine* can make it easier to move, lift, carry, or cut something.

magma (mag′mə) Liquid rock deep inside Earth. (D50) After *magma* flows out of a volcano the magma is called lava.

mass (mas) The amount of matter that something contains. (C10) An elephant has more *mass* than an insect.

matter (mat′ər) Anything that has mass and takes up space. (C10) Every living and nonliving thing around you is made of *matter*.

melt (melt) To change form from a solid to a liquid. (C54) Ice *melts* at 0°C (32°F) and iron melts at 1,530°C (2,786°F).

meteorite (mēt′ē ər īt) A chunk of rock or metal that has fallen from space. (B11) A *meteorite* may be as small as a grain of sand or as large as a house.

migrate (mī′grāt) To move to another region as the seasons change. (E74) Many northern birds and butterflies *migrate* south during the winter.

minerals (min′ər əlz) Solids found in nature that have a definite chemical makeup. (D10) Calcium is a *mineral* found in milk and cheese.

natural resource (nach′ər əl rē′sôrs) A material found in or on Earth that people use. (D9) *Natural resources* include water, minerals, fossil fuels, soil, plants, and animals.

nonrenewable resource (nän ri noo′ə bəl rē′sôrs) A natural resource that cannot be replaced within a person's lifetime. (D11) Diamonds are *nonrenewable resources* because it will take nature millions of years to make more.

H25

nutrient (no͞o′trē ənt) Any substance used by living things for energy, growth, repair, or other life processes. (E43) Proteins, carbohydrates, and fats are *nutrients* found in food.

nymph (nimf) The second stage in the life cycle of an insect undergoing incomplete metamorphosis. (A24) A grasshopper *nymph* looks similar to a small adult.

omnivore (äm′ni vôr) An animal that eats both plants and animals. (E18) Because bears will eat both berries and fish, bears are classified as *omnivores*.

opaque (ō pāk′) Materials that block light. (C35) *Opaque* curtains are used in theaters to block the light from windows.

orbit (ôr′bit) The path a planet, moon, or other object takes around another. (B46) The Moon is seen in different phases as it moves through its *orbit* around Earth.

parasite (par′ə sīt) A living thing that, at some point in its life, lives on or in another living thing and harms it. (E52) Fleas, lice, and some kinds of worms are *parasites*.

petal (pet′′l) The brightly colored part of a flower that helps attract birds, bees, and other insects to the flower. (A44) A *petal* is one of the three main parts of a flower.

phase (fāz) Any stage in the series of changes in the apparent shape of the Moon. (B53) The Moon's shape appears to change with each *phase*.

physical change (fiz′i kəl chānj) A change in the size, shape, or state of matter. (C23) When water freezes, it undergoes a *physical change* from a liquid to a solid.

physical property (fiz′i kəl präp′ ər tē) A quality of matter that can be measured or observed with the senses without changing the matter into another kind of matter. (C14) A *physical property* of ice is its hardness.

pistil (pis′til) The central part in a flower where seeds form. (A44) For seeds to form in a plant, the pollen must travel to the *pistil*.

planet (plan′it) A large body that orbits a star and does not produce light of its own. (B47) Earth is a *planet*.

pollen (päl′ən) The powdery grains in a flower; they must be carried from a stamen to a pistil in order for seeds to form. (A44) Bees move *pollen* from one flower to another.

pollination (päl ə nā′shən) The process by which pollen reaches a pistil. (A44) After *pollination*, a flower can produce seeds.

pollution (pə lōō′shən) Any unwanted or harmful material found in the environment. (D17) Air *pollution* can cause damage to your lungs.

precipitation (prē sip ə tā′shən) The liquid or solid forms of water that fall to Earth. (D31) Rain, sleet, hail, and snow are different kinds of *precipitation*.

predator (pred′ə tər) An animal that hunts other animals for food. (E27) Hawks, cougars, and sharks are *predators*.

prey (prā) An animal hunted for food by another animal. (E27) Rabbits, mice, small fish, and insects are often *prey* for larger animals.

producer (prō dōōs′ər) A living thing that can make its own food. (E16) Plants, such as trees and grass, are *producers*.

prominence (präm′ə nəns) A huge loop of gas that appears on the edge of the Sun. (B27) *Prominences* are caused by magnetic storms on the Sun.

property (präp'ər tē) Something that describes matter. (C12) A *property* of water in its liquid form is its ability to flow.

pulley (pool'ē) A wheel around which a rope or chain is passed. (C75) A *pulley* helps lift objects that would be too heavy to lift directly.

pupa (pyoo'pə) The third stage in the life cycle of an insect undergoing complete metamorphosis. (A23) As a *pupa*, an insect is enclosed in a cocoon, or case.

radiation (rā dē ā'shən) The movement of heat energy in the form of waves. (C49) Heat from a campfire reaches you through *radiation*.

renewable resource (ri noo'ə-bəl rē'sôrs) A natural resource that can be replaced within a person's lifetime. (D11) Lumber is a *renewable resource* if new trees are planted to replace cut trees.

reservoir (rez'ər vwär) The body of water that is stored behind a dam. (D31) A *reservoir* stores fresh water for a town or city.

revolve (ri välv') To move in a circle or orbit. (B46) Earth *revolves* around the Sun.

rotation (rō tā'shən) The spinning motion around an axis. (B38) Earth takes 24 hours to complete one *rotation*.

scale (skāl) A cone's woody part on which seeds grow. (A51) A pine cone's *scales* protect its seeds.

season (sē'zən) Any of the four parts of the year. (B65) The four *seasons* are spring, summer, fall, and winter.

seed coat (sēd kōt) The part of a seed that protects the plant embryo. (A39) The *seed coat* of a coconut is hard, thick, and brown.

seedling (sēd'liŋ) The new plant that develops from an embryo and has roots, a stem, and leaves. (A41) A tomato *seedling* can be started indoors in early spring and planted outside in May.

simple machine (sim′pəl mə shēn′) A device that changes the size or direction of a force. (C73) A lever is a *simple machine*.

soil The loose material that covers much of Earth's surface. (D56) As they grow, most plants extend their roots into *soil*.

solar eclipse (sō′lər i klips′) The blocking of light from the Sun when the Moon moves between it and Earth. (B75) During a *solar eclipse*, the Sun's light is blocked by the Moon.

solar energy (sō′lər en′ər jē) Energy produced by the Sun. (C36) *Solar energy* can be used to produce electricity.

solar system (sō′lər sis′təm) The Sun and all the planets and other objects that orbit it. (B47) Earth is one of nine planets in the *solar system*.

solid (säl′id) A state of matter that has a definite shape and takes up a definite amount of space. (C19, D14) A rock, a piece of ice, and a chair are all examples of *solids*.

species (spē′shēz) A group of living things that can produce living things of the same kind. (A10) The lion *species* cannot produce young of the gorilla *species*.

stamen (stā′mən) The part of a flower that produces pollen, which is needed to form seeds. (A44) *Stamens* are often long and have a fuzzy end.

star (stär) A ball of very hot gases that gives off light and other energy. (B27) The Sun is a *star*.

states of matter (stāts uv mat′r.) The three forms that matter takes—solid, liquid, and gas. (C19) Water exists naturally in all three *states of matter*.

stored energy (stôrd en′ər jē) Energy in matter that can cause matter to move or change. (C31) Fuels have *stored energy* from the Sun.

sunspot (sun′spöt) A dark area on the surface of the Sun, caused by a solar storm. (B27) A *sunspot* appears darker because it is cooler than surrounding areas of the Sun.

surface water (sur′fis wôt′ər) Fresh water in lakes, streams, and rivers. (D30) People often pipe *surface water* to nearby cities.

T

telescope (tel′ə skōp) A device that makes distant objects appear larger and brighter. (B15) A *telescope* is used to study stars and other planets.

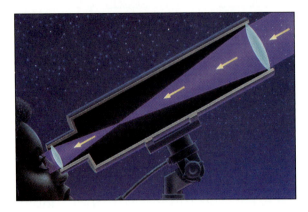

temperature (tem′pər ə chər) A measure of how hot or cold something is. (C45) *Temperature* is measured with a thermometer.

theory (thē′ə rē) A hypothesis that is supported by a lot of evidence and is widely accepted by scientists. (S9) The big-bang *theory* offers an explanation for the origin of the universe.

topsoil (täp′ soil) A mixture of weathered rock and humus (decayed plant and animal matter). (D57) *Topsoil* contains nutrients that help plants to grow.

V

variable (ver′ē ə bəl) The one difference in the setups of a controlled experiment; provides a comparison for testing a hypothesis. (S7) The *variable* in an experiment with plants was the amount of water given each plant.

volcano (väl kā′nō) An opening in the ground through which hot ash, gases, and lava move from inside Earth to the surface, sometimes forming a cone-shaped hill or mountain. (D51) Lava poured out of the *volcano,* adding a new layer of rock to the land.

volume (väl yōōm) The amount of space that matter takes up. (C11) A *volume* of water that measures a pint weighs about a pound.

water cycle (wôt′ər sī′kəl) The path that water follows as it evaporates into the air, condenses into clouds, and returns to Earth as rain, snow, sleet, or hail. (D30) In the *water cycle*, water evaporates from lakes and oceans into the air, and then condenses and falls back to Earth as rain or snow.

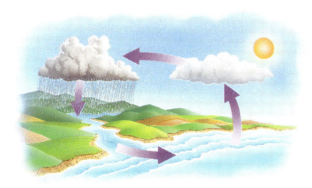

water vapor (wôt′ər vā′pər) Water that is in the form of a gas. (D29) Steam, which is invisible, is *water vapor*.

weathering (weth′ər iŋ) The breaking up or wearing away of rocks. (D52) Rock formations in Arches National Park have been formed by the *weathering* action of wind and rain.

wetlands (wet′landz) Swamps, marshes, and bogs that are home to many kinds of animals and plants. (E65) *Wetlands* are low-lying areas where water is absorbed into underground aquifers.

wheel and axle (hwēl ənd ak′səl) A simple machine that is made up of two wheels that turn together. (C75) A doorknob, along with its shaft, is an example of a *wheel and axle*.

H31

INDEX

A
Adaptations
  body parts as weapons, E40–E41
  cactus, A59
  to cold winters, E74–E76
  defined, A28, E40
  hiding eggs, A29
  laying many eggs, A29
  by living things, E36–E56
  plant, A60
  of the senses, E40
African lion, E21
Air
  natural resource, D8–D9
  trapping for warmth, C50–C51
Air pollution, D17–D18
Alaska, B71
Aldrin, Edwin "Buzz," B23
Algae, D39
Almanacs, B69
Aloe plant, E56
Alum, D38
Amaryllis, A58
Ancient machines, C58
Animals
  and competition for food, E28–E29
  defenses, E48–E53
  life cycles of, A4–A33
Anise (spice), E55
Antarctic, A19
Aquifer, D31
Archerfish, E42
Arctic tern, E75
Armstrong, Neil, B23
Aryabhata I, B48
Aspirin, E55
Atmosphere, B12, D8, D14–D16
Atoms, defined, C20
Axis, of Earth, B38–B39
Axle, C75

B
Babies, animal
  bears, A19
  born alive, A18–A19
  crocodile, A18
  elephant, A18
  hatched, A18–A19
  owl, A19
  penguin, A19
  wallaby, A18
Bacteria, D37, D39
Balance, C8–C9*, C13
Baleen, A31
al-Battani, B49
Beaks, E38–E39*, E41
Beavers, environment of, E62–E63
Beetles, A21, A24
Behavior, animal, E42
Big Dipper, B36–B37, B40
Bill, E42
Birds, scattering seeds, A45
Bison, American, E66–E67
Blue spruce, A51
Blue whales, A30
Breaching (of a whale), A32
Broadbent, Erin K., E4
Brown bears, E18
Brown pelican, E33–E34
Bulbs, plant, A41
Bureau of Land Management, D46
Butterfly, E51
  life cycle of, A23

C
Cactus, adaptation of, to desert, A59
Caesar, Julius, B68–B69
Calcium, A15
Calendars, B67–B69
Calf
  blue whale, A30
  elephant, A18
Camouflage, E45
Cape Verde Islands, D32
Carbon dioxide, D8, D15–D16
  and bird egg, A14
Caring for young animals, A26–A27*
Carnivores, E17
Cassiopeia, B36–B37*
Caterpillar, E51
Cane toads, E30–E31
Chameleon, adaptation of, to environment, E44–E45
Changes, in living things (chart), A6–A7*
Chemical change, C23
Chemical energy, C33
Cherokees, E55
Chimpanzee, E43
Chinese calendar, B68
Chlorine, D38–D39
Cicada, A24
City life, A8–A9
Claudio, Dr. Corazon, D4

*Activity

Clay, D57
Cleaner fish, E53
Clocks, Czech and American, B41
Colors, C35
Community, E31
Compost pile, D58
Compound machines, C76
Condensation, C55, D29, D30
Conduction, C47*, C48
Cones, A48–A49*, A50
Conifer, A48
  life cycle of, A51–A52
Constellations, B44–B45*, B46–B47
Contraction, C56
Convection, C48–C49
Copernicus, Nicolaus, B49
Coral reef fish, E53
Coral snake, E51
Corn, use of (time line), A38
Cowbirds, and their young, A28
Crab spider, E48
Craters, moon, B11–B12
Crescent, B53
Crocodiles, A18
Cuttings, plants, A41

D
Dams, beaver, E62–E63
DDT, E32–E34
Dear Benjamin Banneker (Pinkney), B69
Decomposers, E18
Desalination, D32–D33
  process, D33
Desert environment, E13
DiLabio, Michael, C26
Directions, from Sun's shadow, B35
Dormancy, E76
Douglas fir, A50
Drake, E. L., D40
Drip Drop: Water's Journey (Stwertka), D29

Driver ants, E64
Drought, D59

E
Earth
  axis of, B38–B39, B65
  basic materials of, D8–D9
  early scientists' view of, B48–B49
  and moon measurements, B6–B7*
  as planet, B47
  revolution of, B46–B47
  roundness of, B64
  surface of, D50–D53
  tilt of, B62–B63*
Earth Day, D41
Earthquakes, D51
Eclipse, B72–B73*, B74–B76
Ecosystems, E64
Edison, Thomas, C38, D40
Eggs
  bird, A14–A16
  chicken, A12–A13*
  coverings of, A15
  described, A14–A16
  insect, A22–A23
  parts of, A14, A15
Electrical energy, C32
Embryo
  of bird egg, A15
  seed, A39
Energy
  defined, C31
  and force, C64–C65
  forms of, C32–C33, C37–C39
  and motion, C28–C29*, C31
  from stars, B27
Environment, E10–E13, E60–E61*
Environmental Protection Agency (EPA), D41
Equator, B60–B61*
  defined, B64

  living near, B70
Erosion, D52
  protecting soil from, D59–D60
Evaporation, C54, D30
  defined, D29
Evergreens, A50–A53
Expansion, C56
Extinction, E20

F
Fangs, E40
Flare (of the Sun), B27
Flexibility, C7
Floc, D38
Flowering plants, life cycle of, A44–A47
Flowers
  as "parents" of plants, A44
  parts of, A42–A43*
Fluorescent screen, C38
"Follow the Drinking Gourd," B32
Food
  consumers, E16–E17
  producers, E16
  source, E14*, E15*
Food chain, E22–E23*, E26–E29
  chemicals in, E32–E34
Food web, E24–E25*
  defined, E28–E29
Force, C64
  and change in direction, C64–C65
Forest fires, A52–A53
Fossil fuels, D10
Four-stage life cycle, A22–A24
Freezing, C55
Fresh water, E10–E11
Friction, C46, C65
Frog, A29, E27
Fruit, A45
Fulcrum, C68*, C73

* Activity

H33

G

Gases, defined, C20
Germination, A40–A41, A47
Germs, D37
Giants Stadium, NJ, E65
Glacier, D49*, D53
Grand Canyon, D52
Grasshopper, life cycle of, A25
Gravity, C62–C63*, C65
  and atmosphere, D14
  defined, B22
  zero, B53
Greenhouse gases, D12–D13*, D15
Ground water, D31
Growth
  of mealworms, A20–A21*
  of plants, A47
  of trees, A54–A55*
Grub, A24

H

Habitat, E10
Hammond, Jay, A4
Hatching, A17
Heat
  adding and subtracting, C54–C56
  and conifers, A52–A53
  and energy forms, C38–C39
  and matter, C44–C45
  and temperature, C45
Heat energy, C32
Heat, and waves, C49
Hemlock, A50
Herbivores, E18
Hibernation, E75
H_2O, D26
Hubble Space Telescope, B15
Hummingbirds, E41
Humpback whales, A31–A32
Humus, D57
Hydrogen, D26
Hypothesis, S6

I

Ice, freezing under pressure, C9
Inclined plane, C74
Incubator, A17
Indoor Science (Ganeri), C9, C73
Industrial Revolution, and pollution, D40–D41
Inexhaustible resource, D11
Insect(s)
  adult, A22–A23
  in Namib Desert, E71
  and pollination, A45
Insect camouflage, E46–E47*
Insecticides, E32–E34
Insect Metamorphosis: From Egg to Adult (Goor), A24
Insulators, C48
Inuit people, B70

J

Joeys, A18
Jupiter, B47

K

Kangaroo rats, E72
Katydid, E48
Kenya, living in, B70
Killer whales, A31
Kingsnake, E51

L

La Brea Tar Pits, E20
Land of the Midnight Sun, B71
Larva (insect), A22, A23
Lava, D51
Laying eggs, A16
Leap seconds, B69
Leap year, B68
Learning and inheritance, A10–A11
Leeuwenhoek, Anton van, D38
Leo (constellation), B44–B45
Lesser golden plover, E74
Lever, C73
Life cycle(s)
  animal, A4–A33
  conifer, A52
  dog, A8–A9
  flowering plant, A44–A47
  grasshopper, A25
  human, A22
  insect, A22–A23
  plants, A36–A60
  similarity in animals and plants, A8–A9
  three-stage, A24
Life spans, of different animals, A11
Light
  absorption of, C35
  effects of, C34–C35
Light energy, C33
Lima bean, A36–A37*
Liquids, defined, C20
Little Dipper, B36–B37*, B40
Live birth, of whale, A30–A32
Lobster, E57
Lodge, beaver, E62–E63
Longest day of the year, B58
Luna (moon), and lunacy, B55
Lunar eclipse, B76
Lunar surface, B16

M

Machine
  defined, C72
  simple machine, C73
Magma, D50
Magnetic storms, B29
Maize, powdered, E55
  See also Corn.
Marigo, Luiz Claudio, E58–E59
Marigold, E49
Mars, B47
Mass
  defined, B22
  and gravity, C65

*Activity

measuring, C8*
Mating
  birds, A16
  insects, A23
Matter
  changes in, C14–C15, C22–C24
  defined, C10
  kinds of, C10
  motion in, C21
  nature of, C19–C21
  properties of, C12–C15
Mayan calendar, B67
Mealworms, A20–A21*
Mechanical energy, C32
Medicines, from nature, E54–E56
Melting, C54
Mercury, B47
Metamorphosis
  complete, A23
  incomplete, A24
Meteorites, B11
Microscope, D38
Microwaves, C46
Migration, E74–E75
Millimeters, C13
Mixing, with heat energy, C55
Molds, E18
Monte Albán, B74
Moon
  described, B10
  and Earth's gravity, B22
  and Earth's tides, B56
  gravity of, B55
  imaginary pictures in, B55
  movement on, B22–B23
  no atmosphere on, B13
  phases of, B52–B54
  reflected light of, B54
  rotation of, B52
  surface of, B11
"Moon craters," creating, B8–B9*
Moonwalkers, B23

Motion, and energy, C28–C29*
Mushrooms, E19
Mysterious Rays of Dr. Röntgen, The (Gherman), C38

N
Namib Desert, E70–E71
Native Americans
  medicines of, E54–E55
  observation of Sun by, B46
Natural resources, D9
  mineral, D10
Navaho, medicine of, E55
Needs for living, E10–E13
Neptune, B47
"New" Moon, B54
Nonrenewable resource, D11
Northern hemisphere, B64–B65
Northern lights, B29
North Star (Polaris), B39, B40
Nurse logs, A51
Nutrients, E43
Nymph, A24

O
Ocampo, Adriana, B5
Offspring
  animal, A10–A11
  plant, A46
Ogallala Aquifer, D44
Ohlone people, medicine of, E55
Omnivores, E18
One Small Square: African Savanna (Silver), E31
Opacity, C35
"Open Hydrant" (Ridlon), D20
Orbits, B46–B47
Orion (constellation), B44–B45*
Osha root, E55
Ostrich, E52

Overgrazing, D59
Owl, E27, E41
  babies, A19
Oxygen, D8, D15, D26
  and bird eggs, A14, A15

P
Parasites, E52
Parent plant, A46
Particles (matter), C21
  and heat, C45
  moving, C44–C45
Pegasus (constellation), B44–B45*
Peg Leg Joe, B32
Penguin babies, A19
Perspiration, E70
Petals, A42–A44*
Phases, of Moon, B52–B54
Physical change, C23
Piranhas and Other Wonders of the Jungle (Pearce), E64
Pistil, A43*, A44
Planets, B47
Plant protection, A60
Plants
  and clean air, D18
  into foods, A41
  and gravity, A59
  life cycles of, A34–A61
  medicinal, E54–E55
  response to light, A58
  response to water, A58–A59
  in winter, E76
Pluto, B47
Pods, A31
Poison ivy, A60
Polaris, B36–B37*, B62
Poles of Earth, B39, B60–B61*
Pollen, A43*, A44
Pollen cones, A50
Pollination, A44, A47
  of conifer, A52
  methods of, A45–A46

*Activity

H35

Pollution, D16, D17–D18
  industrial, D40–D41
  preventing, D40–D41
Pope, Jordon C., D46
Porcupine, E50
Pores, of egg shells, A15
Prairies, E66–E67
Praying mantis, E17
Precipitation, D31
Predators, E27
Prey, E27
Prism, C35
Prominences of Sun, B27
  during solar eclipse, B75
Properties
  chemical, C14
  measuring, C13
  physical, C14
Proteins, C24
Protists, D37–D39
Ptolemy, B48
Puffer fish, E50
Pulley, C75
Pupa (insect), A22, A23

R
Raccoon, E19
Radiant energy, C49
Radiation, C49
Rain forests, medicines from, E56
Ramp, C62–C63*
Regrowth, forest, A53
Renewable resource, D11
Reproduction, A10–A11
Reservoir, D31
Revolution, Earth's, B46–B47
Rhinoceros, E53
Right angle, C74
Rigidity, C7*
Rocks
  makeup of, D56
  as natural resource, D56–D58
Rotation, of Earth, B38–B41

Runners (plant), A41
Rust, C24

S
Saber-toothed cat, E20–E21
Saguaro cactus, E72–E73
St. Clair-Moore, Rhona, E36
Saltwater environment, E10
Sassafras tree, E55
Saturn, B47
Scales (cone), A49, A51
Scientific methods ("Think Like a Scientist"), S2–S11
  controlled experiment, S7
  hypothesis, S6
  theory, S9
  variable, S7
Scorpius (constellation), B44–B45*
Screw, C74
Sea of Tranquillity, B11
Seasonal affective disorder, B71
Seasons, B64–B66
Sea turtle, A29
Seed(s)
  adaptations, A39–A40
  analyzing, A36–A37*
  coat, A39
  cones, A50
  formation, A47
  kinds of, A39
  needs of, A40–A41
  parts of, A39
  protection, A45
  scattering of, A39–A40
Seedling, A41, A51
Setter (incubator), A17
Shadows, C35
Shells, of eggs, A15
"Shooting stars," B11
Shortest night of the year, B58
Slippery elm bark tea, E54
Snake, E27
Soil
  importance of, D56–D57

  kinds of, D57
  as natural resource, D56–D58
Soil erosion, preventing, D60
Solar, defined, B29
Solar eclipse, B74–B75
Solar energy, C26, C36
Solar storms, B29–B30
Solar system, B47
Solids, defined, C19
Sound energy, C33
Southern hemisphere, B64–B65
Southern lights, B29
Space
  learning about, B14–B17
  and matter, C11
Space probe, B16
Space station, B17
Spacesuits, B21
Species, A10–A11
  protection of, A60
Spicebush tea, E54
Stamen, A43*, A44
Star
  defined, B27
  used to find direction, B32
States of matter, C19–C21
Stilt beetle, E71
Stored energy, C31–C32, C64
Stored food (seed), A39
Sun
  apparent path of, B66
  compared to Earth, B24–B25*
  early scientists' view of, B48–B49
  as Earth's star, B27
  features of, B28
  as food source, B28
  studying, B17
Sundials, B40–B41
Sunlight, B28
  angle of, reaching Earth, B64

*Activity

color of, C35
Sunspots, B27, B30
Sweating, E70

T
Take Care of Our Earth (Thompson), D58
Taproots, A41
Telescopes, B14–B15
Temperature, defined, C45
Theory, S9
Thornbugs, E48
Thorns, A60
Three-stage life cycle, A24
Tides, B56
Tomato, A45
"Tommy" (Brooks), A34
Topsoil, D57
   as nonrenewable resource, D58
Traits
   defined, A10
   and plant reproduction, A46
Tree in the Forest, A (Thornhill), A59
Tropical forest environment, E12
Tubers (plant), A41
Tulip tree, E48
Tundra, A19
Twisted strands, of a bird egg, A15

U
Underground environment, E12
Uranus, B47

V
Vacuum, C49
Venus, B47
Venus' flytrap, E43
Vibration, C44
Volcano, D17, D51
Volume, C11

W
Wallaby babies, A18
Water
   age of, D28
   changing the state of, D28–D29
   dangers to, D42–D44
   observing clarity of, D36*
   as part of living things, D26
   on planet Earth, D22–D33
   ratio of salt to fresh, D25
   recycled, D28–D29
   surface, D30
   uses of, in U.S., D27
Water cycle, D30
Water pollutants, D42–D43
Water treatment, D37–D39
Water vapor, D15–D16
   defined, D29
Waves, and heat, C49
Weathering, D52
Wedge, C74
Wells, D31
Wetlands, changes to, E64–E65
Wheel
   and axle, C75
   development of, C66–C67
White pine, A51
Willow plant, E55
Wolves, E17

X
X-ray, C38

Y
"Year of confusion," B68
Yolks, A15

Z
Zero Gravity (Skurzynski), B16, B53

* Activity

CREDITS

ILLUSTRATORS
Cover: Garry Colby.

Think Like a Scientist: 4–6, 8–9: Garry Colby. 14: Laurie Hamilton. *Borders:* Garry Colby.

Unit A: 8–9: Kathy Rusynyk. 10–11: Steve McInterf. 14–15: A.J. Miller. 22: Doreen Gay Kasssel. 28–29: Adam Mathews. 38: Eldon Doty. 39: *t.* Ka Botzis, *b.* Rebeca Mereles. 44–45: Lori Anzalone. 47, 50, 52: Dan McGowan. 54: Paul Blakey. 58: Julie Carpenter. 61: Lori Anzalone.

Unit B: 7: Richard Courtney. 10: Randy Hamblin. 12–13: Richard Courtney. 14: Stephen Wagner. 20: Jenny Campbell. 21: A.J. Miller. 22: Jenny Campbell. 22: Robert Roper. 23: Jenny Campbell. 27: Richard Courtney. 28: David Barber. 29–31: Richard Courtney. 37: Tom Powers. 39: Verlin Miller. 40: Tom Powers. 42–43: Skip Baker. 44–45: Tom Powers. 46–47: Dennis Davidson. 48–49: Eldon Doty. 51–52, 54: Tim Blough. 55–56: Susan Simon. 57: Tom Powers. 64–65: Liz Conrad. 64–66: Uldis Klavins. 68–69: Jean and Mou-Sien Tseng. 70: Eureka Cartography. 70–71: Traci Harmon. 74–75: Jean and Mou-Sien Tseng. 76: Dennis Davidson. 77: Uldis Klavins.

Unit C: 15, 19–21: Andrew Shiff. 20, 25: Patrick Gnan. 26–27: Susan Simon. 28: Scott Luke. 30–33: Larry Jost. 34–35: Garry Colby. 36: Leslie Wolf. 44–46: Akio Matsuyoshi. 47: A.J. Miller. 49: Robert Roper. 50–51: Randy Hamblin. 54–56: Jim Turgeon. 57: Patrick Gnan. 64–65: Stephen Peringer. 66–67: Eldon Doty. 72: Patrick Gnan. 74: Jeff Stock. 75, 77: Patrick Gnan.

Unit D: 11: Eldon Doty. 14–15: Tim Blough. 16: Mike Kline. 17–18: Tim Blough. 25–27: Bob Brugger. 28: Mike Meaker. 30–31: Stephen Wagner. 31: Dan Clyne. 32–33: Robert Roper. 37: Stephen Bauer. 40–41: Eldon Doty. 42–43: Tom Pansini. 44: Robert Schuster. 45: Tom Pansini. 50: John Youssi. 59: Jeannie Winston. 60: Don Baker.

Unit E: 11–12: Higgins Bond. 16–19: Jim Owens. 20–21: Jeffrey Terreson. 26–27: Jenny Campbell. 27: Jackie Geyer. 28–29: Jenny Campbell. 30: Sarah Jane English. 32–33: Jim Salvati. 35: Jackie Geyer. 44–45: Phil Wilson. 48–53: Jenny Campbell. 54–56: Sarah Jane English. 55: Susan Melrath. 61: Jackie Geyer. 62–63: Deborah Pinkney. 64: Jackie Geyer. 66–67: Eldon Doty. 70–71: Tina Fong. 74–75: Robert Schuster. 77: Deborah Pinkney.

Math and Science Toolbox: *Logos:* Nancy Tobin. 14–15: Andrew Shiff. *Borders:* Garry Colby.

Glossary: 17–18: Richard Courtney. 19: *b.l.* Dan McGowan. *b.r.* Robert Roper. 20: *t.l.* Richard Courtney. *m.r.* A.J. Miller. 21: *m.l.* Liz Conrad. *m.r.* Jeffrey Terreson. 22–23: Stephen Wagoner. 24: Patrick Gnan. 25: Scott Ross. 26: Denise Davidson. 27: Stephen Wagoner. 28: Pat Gnan. 29 Denise Davidson. 30: *t.l.* Stephen Wagoner. *b.r.* Brad Gaber. 31: Stephen Wagoner.

PHOTOGRAPHS
All photographs by Houghton Mifflin Co. (HMCo.) unless otherwise noted.

Front Cover: *t.* Randy Ury/The Stock Market; *m.l.* A & L Sinbaldi/Tony Stone Images; *b.l.* Gary Vestal/Tony Stone Images; *b.r.* Superstock.

Think Like A Scientist: 4–5: Luiz Claudio Marigo/Peter Arnold, Inc.

Table of Contents: xiv: *l.* © James Steinberg/Photo Researchers, Inc.; *m.* © Gary Retherford/Photo Researchers, Inc.; *r.* Zig Leszczynski/Animals Animals/Earth Scenes.

Unit A 1: © Fletcher & Baylis/Photo Researchers, Inc. 2–3: *bkgd* © Fletcher & Baylis/Photo Researchers, Inc.; *inset* © J. Zerschling/Photo Researchers, Inc. 4–5: *bkgd.* Fred Hirschmann; *inset* Erik Hill/Anchorage Daily News. 8: *l.* Dwight R. Kuhn; *r.* Dwight R. Kuhn. 14: E.R. Degginger/Color-Pic, Inc. 16: *t.* E.R. Degginger/Color-Pic, Inc.; *b.* Frans Lanting/Minden Pictures. 17: *l.* Chick Master Incubator Company; *r.* Gil Taylor/Chick Master Incubator Company. 18: *t.* Hans & Judy Beste/Animals Animals/Earth Scenes; *b.r.* © M. Reardon/Photo Researchers, Inc.

19: *t.* Miriam Austerman/Animals Animals/Earth Scenes; *b.l.* Michio Hoshino/Minden Pictures; *b.r.* Frans Lanting/Minden Pictures. 22: *t.l.* Courtesy, Evelyn O'Shea; *t.r.* Courtesy, Evelyn O'Shea; *b.l.* Courtesy, Evelyn O'Shea; *b.r.* Courtesy, Evelyn O'Shea. 23: *t.l.* E.R. Degginger/Animals Animals/Earth Scenes; *t.r.* Patti Murray/Animals Animals/Earth Scenes; *b.l.* Patti Murray/Animals Animals/Earth Scenes; *b.r.* Patti Murray/Animals Animals/Earth Scenes. 25: *t.l.* Raymond A. Mendez/Animals Animals/Earth Scenes; *t.r.* John Pontier/Animals Animals/Earth Scenes; *b.* © David & Hayes Norris/Photo Researchers, Inc. 28: *l.* Anne Heimann; *r.* Anne Heimann. 29: *l.* Anne Heimann; *r.* Trevor Barrett/Animals Animals/Earth Scenes. 30–31: Flip Nicklin/Minden Pictures. 31: Jeff Foott/DRK Photo. 32: *l.* Michio Hoshino/Minden Pictures; *r.* Michio Hoshino/Minden Pictures. 34: © 1994 Jill Krementz. 34–35: *bkgd.* Antonio M. Rosario/The Image Bank. 40: *t.* S. Nielsen/Imagery; *m.* Runk/Schoenberger/Grant Heilman Photography, Inc.; *b.* E.R. Degginger/Color-Pic, Inc. 41: Dwight R. Kuhn. 46: *l.* Superstock; *r.* Superstock. 48: *t.* Grant Huntington for HMCo.; *m.* Grant Huntington for HMCo.; *b.* Grant Huntington for HMCo. 49: *t.r.* E.R. Degginger/Color-Pic, Inc.; *m.* E.R. Degginger/Color-Pic, Inc.; *b.l.* Grant Huntington for HMCo.; *b.r.* E.R. Degginger/Color-Pic, Inc. 53: *t.l.* David Austen/Tony Stone Images; *t.r.* David Austen/Animals Animals/Earth Scenes; *b.* Don Pitcher/Stock Boston. 55: Grant Huntington for HMCo. 56: Grant Huntington for HMCo. 57: *t.* Grant Huntington for HMCo.; *b.* Grant Huntington for HMCo. 58–59: Barry L. Runk/Grant Heilman Photography, Inc. 59: *t.* Runk/Schoenberger/Grant Heilman Photography, Inc. 60: *l.* Runk/Schoenberger/Grant Heilman Photography, Inc.; *r.* Jim Strauser/Grant Heilman Photography, Inc.

Unit B 1: UPI/Corbis Corporation. 2–3: UPI/Corbis Corporation. 4–5: *inset* Victor Aleman/2 Mun-Dos Communications. 11: *l.* NASA; *r.* H.R. Bramaz/Peter Arnold, Inc. 12: NASA/The Stock Market. 13: NASA. 15: *bkgd.* Corbis Corporation; *inset* Frank Rossotto/The Stock Market. 16: *t.* Photri, Inc. 17: NASA. 18: Grant Huntington for HMCo. 19: Grant Huntington for HMCo. 23: *l.* NASA; *r.* © NASA/Science Source/Photo Researchers, Inc. 24: Grant Huntington for HMCo. 25: Grant Huntington for HMCo. 26: Grant Huntington for HMCo. 29: *t.* Photri, Inc.; *b.* © Pekka Parviainen/Science Photo Library/Photo Researchers, Inc. 30: *l.* National Solar Observatory/Sacramento Peak; *r.* NASA/Frank P. Rossotto/Stocktrek. 32–33: E.R. Degginger/Color-Pic, Inc. 34: Grant Huntington for HMCo. 35: *t.* Grant Huntington for HMCo.; *b.* E.R. Degginger/Color-Pic, Inc. 37: *l.* Grant Huntington for HMCo.; *m.* Grant Huntington for HMCo. 38: © Sylvain Grandadam/Photo Researchers, Inc. 40: Dennis Cox/ChinaStock. 40–41: Oddo & Sinibaldi/The Stock Market. 41: *l.* Robert Holmes; *m.* D & J McClurg/Bruce Coleman Incorporated; *r.* Norman Owen Tomalin/Bruce Coleman Incorporated. 52: NASA. 58–59: *bkgd.* John Gerlach/Tom Stack & Associates; *inset* Doranne Jacobson. 62: *t.* Ken Karp for HMCo.; *b.* Ken Karp for HMCo. 63: Ken Karp for HMCo. 67: *bkgd.* Tibor Bognar/The Stock Market; *l. inset* Robert Frerck/Odyssey Productions; *r. inset* D. Donne Bryant. 68: Superstock. 69: *t.* Courtesy, National Maritime Museum. 70: *r.* Superstock. 71: Brian Stablyk/Tony Stone Images. 72: *t.* Ken Karp for HMCo.; *b.* George Post. 73: *t.* Ken Karp for HMCo.; *b.* S.Nielsen/Imagery. 74: Sen Sakamonto/Black Star.

Unit C 1: Adam Woolfitt/Corbis Corporation; 4–5: *bkgd.* G. Bliss/Masterfile Corporation; *inset* Stewart Cohen/Tony Stone Images. 23: *t.* Joyce Design; *b.* Joyce Design. 24: Joyce Design. 29: Grant Huntington for HMCo. 31: PhotoEdit. 32: *t.l.* Grant Huntington for HMCo.; *t.r.* Grant Huntington for HMCo. 33: *t.* Grant Huntington for HMCo.; *m.* Grant Huntington for HMCo.; *b.* Grant Huntington for HMCo. 35: *l.* Uniphoto Picture Agency; *r.* G.K. & Vikki Hart/The Image Bank. 37: David Phillips for HMCo. 38: *t.l.* The Image Bank; *t.r.* Bob Krist/Tony Stone Images. 39: *t.l.* Joe Cornish/Tony Stone Images; *t.r.* Phill Degginger/Color-Pic, Inc.; *b.* Superstock. 48: *l.* Richard Hutchings for HMCo.; *r.* Isaac Geib/Grant Heilman Photography, Inc. 50: *t.* Barry L. Runk/Grant Heilman Photography, Inc. 50–51: John Shaw/Tom Stack & Associates. 51: *b.* Climb High. 54: *t.* Richard Hutchings for HMCo. 55: *t.* Arthur D'Arazien/The Image Bank. 56: *t.* David R. Frazier Photography. 58–59: *bkgd.* Paul Trummer/The Image Bank; *inset* Michael Hampshirengs/National Geographic Society Image Collection.

Unit D 1: John M. Roberts/The Stock Market. 2–3: John M. Roberts/The Stock Market. 4–5: *bkgd.* Bruno P. Zehnder/Peter Arnold, Inc.; *inset* Corazon Claudio. 6: Elliott Smith for HMCo. 8: Frank Rossotto/The Stock Market. 9: *t.l.* Boyd Norton Worldwide Stock Photographs; *b.l.* Steve Wilkings/The Stock Market; *r.* E.R. Degginger/Color-Pic, Inc. 10: Larry Lefever/Grant Heilman Photography, Inc. 17: © John Meehan/Photo Researchers, Inc.; *r.* © Kent & Donna Dennen/Photo Researchers, Inc. 18: © Dingo Agence Vandystadt/Photo Researchers, Inc. 20: Chris Cone for HMCo. 20–21: John David Fleck/The Gamma Liaison Network. 21: © David M. Grossman/Photo Researchers, Inc. 27: *t.l.* Jeff Smith/The Image Bank; *t.r.* © 2000 Jim Richardson/Woodfin Camp & Associates; *b.l.* Lawrence Migdale Photography; *b.r.* Comstock. 36: Ken Karp for HMCo. 37: *t.l.* E.R. Degginger/Color-Pic, Inc.; *t.r.* © London School of Hygiene and Tropical Medicine/Science Photo Library/Photo Researchers, Inc.; *m.* © Moredon Animal Health, Ltd./Science Photo Library/Photo Researchers, Inc.; *b.l.* Brian Parker/Tom Stack & Associates; *b.r.* © Moredon Animal Health, Ltd./Science Photo Library/Photo Researchers, Inc. 46–47: *bkgd.* PhotoDisc, Inc; *inset* Richard Nowitz Photography. 51: *l.* © Francois Gohier/Photo Researchers, Inc.; *r.* David Stoecklein/The Stock Market. 52: © Douglas Faulkner/Photo Researchers, Inc. 53: © 2000 Leo Touchet/Woodfin Camp & Associates. 56: *t.* E.R. Degginger/Color-Pic, Inc.; *b.* © 2000 William Hubbell/Woodfin Camp & Associates. 56–58: *border* © 2000 Mike Yamashita/Woodfin Camp & Associates. 57: *t.l.* © 2000 G. Fokkema/Woodfin Camp & Associates; *t.m.* Tom Stack for HMCo.; *t.r.* E.R. Degginger/Color-Pic, Inc. 59: © 2000 Robert Frerck/Woodfin Camp & Associates. 60: *t.l.* The Stock Market; *t.r.* © 2000 Robert Frerck/Woodfin Camp & Associates; *b.l.* Carlos Humberto/The Stock Market; *b.r.* Dilip Mehta/The Stock Market. 61: © 2000 Robert Frerck/Woodfin Camp & Associates.

H39

Unit E 1: Art Wolfe/Tony Stone Images. 2–3: Art Wolfe/Tony Stone Images. 4–5: Jeff Greenberg/Omni Photo Communications, Inc. 5: Courtesy, Department of the Interior. 7: Grant Huntington for HMCo. 8: Donald Specker/Animals Animals/Earth Scenes. 8–9: Grant Huntington for HMCo. 9: Grant Huntington for HMCo. 10: Doug Perrine/DRK Photo. 11: Al Grotell Underwater Photography. 12: Michael Fogden/DRK Photo. 13: *l.* Stephen J. Krasemann/Peter Arnold, Inc.; *r.* © Dr. Jeremy Burgess/Science Photo Library/Photo Researchers, Inc. 14: Grant Huntington for HMCo. 15: *t.* Grant Huntington for HMCo.; *b.* Grant Huntington for HMCo. 16: *l.* D. Cavagnaro/DRK Photo; *m.* © Farrell Grehan/Photo Researchers, Inc.; *r.* N.H. Cheatham/DRK Photo. 17: *t.* Hans Pfletschinger/Peter Arnold, Inc.; *b.* Jim Brandenburg/Minden Pictures. 18: *t.* © Tim Davis/Photo Researcher, Inc.; *b.* © Tom Bledsoe/Photo Researcher, Inc. 19: *t.* Breck P. Kent/Animals Animals/Earth Scenes; *b.* S. Nielsen/Imagery. 21: *l.* Courtesy, George C. Page Museum; *r.* © Mark Boulton/Photo Researchers, Inc. 22–23: Grant Huntington for HMCo. 23: Grant Huntington for HMCo. 24: Grant Huntington for HMCo. 25: Grant Huntington for HMCo. 26: *l.* © James Steinberg/Photo Researchers, Inc.; *m.* © Gary Retherford/Photo Researchers, Inc.; *r.* Zig Leszczynski/Animals Animals/Earth Scenes. 27: *l.* Ted Levin/Animals Animals/Earth Scenes; *r.* Joe McDonald/Animals Animals/Earth Scenes. 28: *t.l.* Stephen J. Krasemann/DRK Photo; *t.r.* M.P. Kahl/DRK Photo; *b.l.* Stephen Dalton/Animals Animals/Earth Scenes; *b.r.* John Gerlach/Visuals Unlimited. 29: *t.l.* Doug Wechsler/Animals Animals/Earth Scenes; *t.r.* Stephen J. Krasemann/DRK Photo; *m.* Stephen J. Krasemann/DRK Photo; *b.l.* Patrice Ceisel/Visuals Unlimited; *b.r.* Roger Cole/Visuals Unlimited. 30: Australian Picture Library/Leo Meier/Corbis Corporation. 32: © Garry D. McMichael/Photo Researchers, Inc. 34: *l.* © Tim Davis/Photo Researchers, Inc.; *r.* Frans Lanting/Minden Pictures. 36–37: *bkgd.* Kathy Tyrrell/Oxford Scientific Films/Animals Animals/Earth Scenes. 37: *t.* Rhona St.Clair-Moore; *b.* Joe McDonald/Corbis Corporation. 38: Ken Karp for HMCo. 39: Ken Karp for HMCo. 40: © Tom McHugh/Photo Researchers, Inc. 40–41: Dwight Kuhn/DRK Photo. 41: © Anthony Mercieca/Photo Researchers, Inc. 42: © Stephen Dalton/Photo Researchers, Inc. 42–43: Gerry Ellis Nature Photography. 43: © Jeff Lepore/Photo Researchers, Inc. 44–45: © Stephen Dalton/Photo Researchers, Inc. 47: *l.* Ken Karp for HMCo.; *r.* Ken Karp for HMCo. 48: *l.* Hans Pfletschinger/Peter Arnold, Inc.; *m.* John Cancalosi/DRK Photo; *r.* John R. MacGregor/Peter Arnold, Inc. 48–49: Stephen J. Krasemann/Peter Arnold, Inc. 49: *t.* Grant Huntington for HMCo.; *b.* © John Kaprielian/Photo Researchers, Inc. 50: *t.* © Alan Carey/Photo Researchers, Inc.; *b.l.* Marty Snyderman Productions; *b.r.* Marty Snyderman Productions. 51: *t.l.* J. Krasemann/DRK Photo; *t.r.* © Kjell B. Sandved/Photo Researchers, Inc.; *b.l.* © Gregory G. Dimijian M.D./Photo Researchers, Inc.; *b.r.* © S.L. & J.T. Collins/Photo Researchers, Inc. 52: *t.* © William & Marcia Levy/Photo Researchers, Inc. 53: *t.* Stephen J. Krasemann/DRK Photo; *b.* Larry Tackett/Tom Stack & Associates. 54: *r.* Don & Pat Valenti/DRK Photo. 55: Lois Robin. 56: *r.* Gunter Ziesler/Peter Arnold, Inc. 57: Zig Leszczynski/Animals Animals/Earth Scenes. 58–59: *bkgd.* Michael Fogden/DRK Photo; *inset* Luiz Claudio Marigo. 59: Luiz Claudio Marigo. 60: Library of Congress/Corbis Corporation. 65: *l.* Mike Medici/Sonlight Images; *r.* Mark Wilson/Wildshot. 69: Grant Huntington for HMCo. 70–71: Jim Brandenburg/Minden Pictures. 71: William E. Ferguson. 72: John Gerlach/Visuals Unlimited. 72–73: Tom Till/The Wildlife Collection. 73: © Karl H. Switak/Photo Researchers, Inc. 74: John Gerlach/Visuals Unlimited. 75: *t.* Breck P. Kent Photography; *b.* © Mark Rollo/Photo Researchers, Inc. 76: *t.* John Shaw/Tom Stack & Associates; *b.* Joe Devenney/The Image Bank. 79: © Mark Rollo/Photo Researchers, Inc.

Extra Practice

On the following pages are questions about each of the Investigations in your book. Use these questions to help you review some of the terms and ideas that you studied. Each review section gives you the page numbers in the book where you can check your answers. Write your answers on a separate sheet of paper.

Contents

Unit A Life Cycles.................................... R2

Unit B Sun, Moon, and Earth R6

Unit C Matter, Energy, and Forces................ R10

Unit D Earth's Resources........................ R14

Unit E Roles of Living Things R17

R1

Unit A Extra Practice

Investigation 1 pages A6–A11

Use the terms below to solve each riddle.

| death | life cycle | species |

1. I am the ordered stages that occur in a plant's or an animal's lifetime.
2. I am a group of living things that can produce living things of the same kind.
3. I mark the end of each plant's or animal's lifetime.

Complete the following exercises.

4. In an animal's or a plant's life cycle, what does the term *development* refer to?
5. What is an example of a trait that a human being might inherit?
6. What would happen to a species if its members stopped reproducing?

Investigation 2 pages A12–A19

Write the term that best completes each sentence.

| embryo | egg | yolk |

7. A developing chick is called a/an ___.
8. The first stage in the life cycle of almost all animals is called the ___.
9. The stored food for a developing chick is the ___.

Complete the following exercises.

10. What are incubators on chicken farms used for?
11. Name two animals that are born live and two that hatch.
12. Explain why the shell is an important part of an egg.

R2

Unit A Extra Practice

Investigation 3 pages A20–A25

Write the term in each pair that correctly completes each sentence.

13. The last stage in the life cycle of an insect is called the (larva, adult).

14. The wormlike stage in an insect's life cycle is called the (larva, pupa).

15. The third stage in a four-stage life cycle of an insect is called the (adult, pupa).

Complete the following exercises.

16. What are the three stages in the life cycle of an insect that goes through incomplete metamorphosis?

17. Give examples of insects that have a four-stage life cycle.

18. How are the life cycles of a butterfly and a grasshopper the same? How are they different?

Investigation 4 pages A26–A32

Use the terms below to solve each riddle.

baleen	adaptation	calf

19. I am a behavior or part of a living thing that helps it survive.

20. I am bony plates in the mouth of a humpback whale.

21. I am a baby whale.

Complete the following exercises.

22. Give an example of an adaptation that helps frogs survive as a species.

23. Describe some ways that a mother whale takes care of her young.

24. If female sea turtles lay only one egg, why might sea turtles as a species disappear?

R3

Unit A Extra Practice

Investigation 1   pages A36–A41

Write the term in each pair that correctly completes each sentence.

1. A seedling is a (tuber, new plant).
2. To germinate is to (sprout, reproduce).
3. In a seed, the embryo is the (stored food, developing plant).

Complete the following exercises.

4. Describe three ways that seeds are scattered.
5. What does a seed need in order to germinate?
6. Describe one way that seed plants can grow, other than from seed.

Investigation 2   pages A42–A47

Write the term in each pair that correctly completes each sentence.

7. The part of a flower that forms around a seed is called the (stamen, fruit).
8. The powdery material needed to make seeds form is called (pollen, nectar).
9. The brightly colored parts of a flower are called (pistils, petals).

Complete the following exercises.

10. Describe two ways that plants are pollinated.
11. What role do fruits play in scattering seeds?
12. Give two examples of traits that plants inherit.

Unit A Extra Practice

Investigation 3 pages A48–A53

Write the term in each pair that correctly completes each sentence.

13. The parts of an evergreen tree that produce seeds or pollen are the (conifers, cones).

14. Evergreen trees that produce cones are called (scales, conifers).

15. The seeds on a cone are protected by the (scales, pollen).

Complete the following exercises.

16. Describe the life cycle of a conifer.

17. How can fire be helpful to some conifers?

18. How might moisture be harmful to some conifers?

Investigation 4 pages A54–A60

Write the term in each pair that correctly completes each sentence.

19. Plants respond to light by growing (toward, away from) it.

20. Plants take in water through their (leaves, roots).

21. In response to gravity, roots grow (down, up).

Complete the following exercises.

22. Describe two ways in which plants grow.

23. How do quills and thorns protect plants and animals?

24. What adaptations help a cactus survive in the desert?

Unit B Extra Practice

Investigation 1 pages B6–B17

Write the term that best completes each sentence.

| astronomer | meteorite | telescope |

1. A chunk of rock or metal from space that lands on the Moon or Earth is called a/an ___.
2. A device that makes faraway objects look larger is called a/an ___.
3. A scientist who studies objects in space is called a/an ___.

Complete the following exercises.

4. Describe the surface of the Moon.
5. What are some effects of the Moon having no atmosphere?
6. What tools would you use to study the Moon? Explain.

Investigation 2 pages B18–B23

Write the term that best completes each sentence.

| astronaut | gravity | spacesuit |

7. A pull that every object has on every other object is called ___.
8. A set of clothing worn in space to protect the person who wears it is called a/an ___.
9. A person trained to go into space is called a/an ___.

Complete the following exercises.

10. Why do objects weigh less on the Moon than on Earth?
11. How does a spacesuit help someone survive in space? Give as many examples as you can.
12. How is being on the Moon unlike being on Earth?

R6

Unit B Extra Practice

Investigation 3 pages B24–B30

Use the terms below to solve each riddle.

| flare | star | sunspot |

13. I am a bright area on the surface of the Sun.
14. I am a ball of hot gases that gives off energy.
15. I am a dark spot on the surface of the Sun.

Complete the following exercises.

16. Why does the Sun look bigger from Earth than other stars do?
17. Describe a solar storm.
18. Explain why life on Earth could not exist without the Sun.

Investigation 1 pages B34–B41

Write the term that best completes each sentence.

| axis | Polaris | rotation |

1. The spinning motion of Earth is called ___.
2. The make-believe line that runs through Earth is a/an ___.
3. The star that lies almost exactly over Earth's North Pole is called ___.

Complete the following exercises.

4. How does the rotation of Earth cause day and night?
5. How can Polaris help you tell direction?
6. How are sundials and clocks similar? How are they different?

R7

Unit B Extra Practice

Investigation 2 pages B42–B49

Write the term in each pair that correctly completes each sentence.

7. Earth (rotates, revolves) around the Sun.

8. Earth travels in a path called (a rotation, an orbit).

9. Nighttime star patterns are called (solar systems, constellations).

Complete the following exercises.

10. Name the planets in our solar system in order, starting with the planet closest to the Sun.

11. What important ideas put forth by Ptolemy and Copernicus have been shown to be true?

12. How have theories about our solar system changed over time?

Investigation 3 pages B50–B56

Write the term in each pair that correctly completes each sentence.

13. When the side of the Moon facing Earth receives no sunlight at all, a (new Moon, full Moon) occurs.

14. The rising and falling of ocean water along coastlines is called the (phases, tides).

15. When you see the entire daylit half of the Moon, it is called a (new Moon, full Moon).

Complete the following exercises.

16. Explain why the same side of the Moon always faces Earth.

17. When you look at the Moon, where is the light really coming from?

18. Does the Moon have day and night? Explain your answer.

Unit B Extra Practice

Chapter 3

Investigation 1 pages B60–B71

Write the term in each pair that correctly completes each sentence.

1. During winter in your hemisphere, the Sun appears (highest, lowest) in the sky.
2. The imaginary line that circles Earth is called the (axis, equator).
3. The more direct the Sun's rays that strike a place, the (warmer, colder) is that place.

Complete the following exercises.

4. Is it warmer near the equator or the North Pole? Why?
5. Why did the Roman calendar include a leap year? How often does a leap year occur?
6. If you could choose to live near the North Pole or near the equator, which would you choose and why?

Investigation 2 pages B72–B76

Write the term that best completes each sentence.

| full Moon | lunar eclipse | solar eclipse |

7. When the Moon moves directly between the Sun and Earth, a ___ occurs.
8. When the Moon moves into Earth's shadow, a ___ occurs.
9. When the entire daylit half of the Moon can be seen, a ___ occurs.

Complete the following exercises.

10. How do a solar eclipse and a lunar eclipse differ?
11. What does the Moon look like during a lunar eclipse?
12. Which are you less likely to see, a total solar eclipse or a total lunar eclipse? Explain your answer.

Unit C Extra Practice

Investigation 1 pages C6–C15

Write the term that best completes each sentence.

| matter | property | volume |

1. Anything that has mass and takes up space is ___.
2. Color and shape are each examples of a ___.
3. The amount of space an object takes up is its ___.

Complete the following exercises.

4. How do physical properties differ from chemical properties?
5. What are some tools you can use to measure an object's properties?
6. Describe a banana, using its physical properties.

Investigation 2 pages C16–C24

Write the term in each pair that correctly completes each sentence.

7. Matter that has a definite volume and definite shape is a (liquid, solid).
8. The smallest particles of matter are called (atoms, gases).
9. Ice melting is an example of a (physical, chemical) change.

Complete the following exercises.

10. Compare and contrast matter in the liquid state and in the gas state.
11. Explain the difference between a physical change and a chemical change.
12. Is burning paper an example of a physical change or a chemical change? How do you know?

Unit C Extra Practice

Investigation 1 pages C28–C39

Use the terms below to solve each riddle.

| energy | opaque | solar energy |

1. I am able to cause a change in matter.
2. Shadows form behind me because I am a kind of material that blocks light.
3. I am energy from the Sun.

Complete the following exercises.

4. How does light differ from other forms of energy?
5. How is energy changed by a light bulb?
6. Name some ways that you use energy every day.

Investigation 2 pages C40–C51

Write the term that best completes each sentence.

| conductor | temperature | insulator |

7. Heat travels easily through a material that is a/an ___.
8. A measure of the hotness or coldness of a material is its ___.
9. Heat does not travel easily through a material that is a/an ___.

Complete the following exercises.

10. Explain why friction produces heat.
11. Compare and contrast conduction and convection.
12. Would you use a wooden spoon or a metal spoon to stir a pot of hot soup? Explain your answer.

R11

Unit C Extra Practice

Investigation 3 pages C52–C56

Write the term in each pair that correctly completes each sentence.

13. Adding heat to a solid can cause the solid to change to a liquid, or to (freeze, melt).

14. Taking heat away from a gas can cause the gas to change to a liquid, or to (condense, evaporate).

15. Taking heat away from a liquid can cause the liquid to change to a solid, or to (condense, freeze).

Complete the following exercises.

16. How does taking heat away from a solid cause the solid to change state? What state does it change into?

17. Why does liquid water form on the outside of a cold object on a warm day?

18. If you want to freeze water in a container, why is it not a good idea to fill the container all the way to the top?

Investigation 1 pages C58–C67

Use the terms below to solve each riddle.

| force | friction | gravity |

1. I am a force that causes objects to move toward each other.
2. I am a push or a pull.
3. I am a force that makes it hard for two objects that are touching to slide past each other.

Complete the following exercises.

4. Give an example of a force changing an object's motion.
5. Why is gravity considered to be a force?
6. How would life on Earth be different if there were little or no gravity?

Unit C Extra Practice

Investigation 2 pages C68–C76

Use the terms below to solve each riddle.

| fulcrum | inclined plane | pulley |

7. I am a simple machine with a slanted surface.
8. I am the fixed point around which a lever turns.
9. I am a wheel around which a rope or chain is passed.

Complete the following exercises.

10. How would you use a lever to move a heavy rock?
11. What is a compound machine?
12. Tell how a pulley can change the direction of a force.

Unit D Extra Practice

Investigation 1 pages D6–D11

Use the terms below to solve each riddle.

> natural resource   nonrenewable resource   atmosphere

1. I am the blanket of air that surrounds Earth.
2. I am any material found on Earth that is used by people.
3. I am a resource that cannot be replaced within a person's lifetime.

Complete the following exercises.

4. How is Earth's atmosphere important to living things?
5. What are Earth's basic natural resources?
6. Explain the difference between the three types of natural resources.

Investigation 2 pages D12–D18

Write the term in each pair that correctly completes each sentence.

7. Gases that absorb energy released by Earth's surface, helping to warm the atmosphere, are called (inexhaustible resources, greenhouse gases).
8. Unwanted or harmful material in the environment is an example of (pollution, natural resources).
9. Unwanted or harmful material found in the air is called (air pollution, nonrenewable resources).

Complete the following exercises.

10. How do plants and animals renew and recycle air?
11. How do natural causes and the activities of people cause air pollution?
12. What are some ways that people are trying to prevent air pollution?

Unit D Extra Practice

Investigation 1 pages D22–D33

Write the term that best completes each sentence.

| water vapor | ground water | water cycle |

1. Water in the form of a gas is called ___.
2. The path that water follows as it evaporates into the air and then falls as rain or snow is called the ___.
3. Water that fills spaces between rocks and soil is called ___.

Complete the following exercises.

4. How does the amount of fresh water on Earth compare to the amount of salt water?
5. Describe how heat energy is involved when water changes from a solid to a liquid and then to a gas.
6. What are some sources of water that people use?

Investigation 2 pages D34–D44

Write the term in each pair that correctly completes each sentence.

7. Chemicals can combine with water vapor in the air to form (alum, acid rain).
8. Oil and fertilizer that enter fresh water are examples of (protists, pollutants).
9. At water treatment plants, water is treated to kill (pollution, germs).

Complete the following exercises.

10. Why is it important for fresh water to be filtered and treated with chemicals before people use it?
11. Name some ways that water becomes polluted.
12. Why is it important to conserve water?

Unit D Extra Practice

Investigation 1   pages D48–D53

Write the term that best completes each sentence.

| magma | glacier | erosion |

1. Liquid rock inside Earth is called ___.
2. The moving of rock material from one place to another is called ___.
3. A large mass of slow-moving ice is called a ___.

Complete the following exercises.

4. How do volcanoes and earthquakes change Earth's surface?
5. Describe how the Grand Canyon was formed.
6. Distinguish between weathering and erosion.

Investigation 2   pages D54–D60

Write the term that best completes each sentence.

7. The loose material that covers much of Earth's surface is called (soil, lava).
8. A mixture of weathered rock and humus is called (fertilizer, topsoil).
9. A long period without rainfall is (a drought, an aquifer).

Complete the following exercises.

10. Why is soil important to people?
11. How does composting help the environment?
12. What are some properties of topsoil?

R16

Unit E Extra Practice

Investigation 1 pages E6–E13

Write the term in each pair that correctly completes each sentence.

1. The place where an animal or a plant lives is its (habitat, environment).
2. Everything that surrounds and affects a living thing is its (environment, habitat).
3. The ocean is a large body of (fresh water, salt water).

Complete the following exercises.

4. Explain the difference between habitat and environment.
5. Choose a plant or an animal and tell how its habitat helps it meet its needs.
6. Give examples of how different living things can have different needs.

Investigation 2 pages E14–E21

Write the term that best completes each sentence.

| decomposers | consumers | producers |

7. Living things that can make their own food are called ___.
8. Living things that eat plants, animals, or other living things are called ___.
9. Living things that feed on the remains of once-living things are called ___.

Complete the following exercises.

10. How do producers obtain food?
11. How do scientists learn about extinct animals?
12. Distinguish between herbivores, carnivores, and omnivores.

R17

Unit E Extra Practice

Investigation 3 pages E22–E34

Write the term in each pair that correctly completes each sentence.

13. Animals that hunt other animals for food are called (prey, predators).

14. The path that energy takes as one living thing eats another is called a (food chain, community).

15. A group of plants and animals that live in the same area and depend on one another is called a (community, food web).

Complete the following exercises.

16. Is it possible to have a food chain without a producer? Explain.

17. What is a food web?

18. Explain how DDT affected brown pelicans in California and why this happened.

Investigation 1 pages E38–E45

Use the terms below to solve each riddle.

| camouflage | nutrients | adaptations |

1. I am the behaviors or parts of living things that help them survive in a certain environment.

2. I am the substances that provide materials for growth.

3. I am the ability to blend in with the surroundings.

Complete the following exercises.

4. Give an example of a behavior that helps an animal get food.

5. Give an example of a body part in two different hunting birds that is an adaptation for getting food.

6. Name two adaptations that help a chameleon survive.

R18

Unit E Extra Practice

Investigation 2 pages E46–E56

Write the term in each pair that correctly completes each sentence.

7. Creatures that live on or in other living things are called (predators, parasites).

8. The quills, or spines, of a porcupine are an adaptation for (defense, food-getting).

9. An example of an adaptation for defense in a plant is (thorns, roots).

Complete the following exercises.

10. How can chemicals that a plant produces help protect the plant?

11. Give an example of how animals form relationships that protect against parasites.

12. How could you use camouflage to help you hide in a game of hide-and-seek?

Investigation 1 pages E62–E67

Use the terms below to solve each riddle.

| dam | ecosystem | wetland |

1. I am a place where living and nonliving things interact.
2. I might be a swamp, a marsh, or a bog.
3. I can be built by people or by beavers.

Complete the following exercises.

4. How do the activities of beavers change the environment?

5. What are some ways people have improved their environment?

6. What are some ways people can protect endangered animals?

R19

Unit E Extra Practice

Investigation 2 pages E68–E76

Write the term in each pair that correctly completes each sentence.

7. When animals travel to warmer places, they (migrate, hibernate).

8. Some animals go into a long, deep sleep called (migration, hibernation).

9. The slowing down of a plant's activity in winter is called (dormancy, migration).

Complete the following exercises.

10. Describe some adaptations that cactus plants have for living in the desert.

11. Why do some birds migrate and others do not?

12. How can you tell when a maple tree is in a state of dormancy?